THE
LIBERTY HALL VOLUNTEERS
Stonewall's College Boys

The
LIBERTY HALL
VOLUNTEERS

Stonewall's College Boys

W. G. BEAN

THE UNIVERSITY PRESS OF VIRGINIA

Charlottesville

Library of Congress Catalog Card Number: 64-13721

Printed in the United States of America
by Connecticut Printers, Inc.

To Lucy

PREFACE

O N June 14, 1910, at the unveiling of a tablet to the Liberty Hall Volunteers in the Robert E. Lee Memorial Chapel, Washington and Lee University, the Rev. Dr. Givens B. Strickler, one of the survivors, said:

Time will not suffice to tell in detail the story of the services bravely rendered, and sufferings cheerfully borne in battle, in bivouac, and upon the toilsome march—in summer's heat and dust, in winter's cold, mud and snow. That story must some day be written by some pen inspired by truth and love. When it shall be truly written it will be a story of which any University or any land must be proud, for it will be a story of dauntless courage, of unselfish devotion to duty, of suffering endured without a murmur, and death encountered without a qualm.[1]

This is not a military study of the Civil War; it is the simple story of a group of college boys at war. Unlike most war nar-

[1] "Liberty Hall Volunteers," speech delivered June 14, 1910, at a reunion of the company's survivors, Washington and Lee University. Alderman Library, University of Virginia, William A. Anderson Papers.

ratives, it treats battles and strategy in less detail than it does men—or, in this case, youths—who made that strategy work or fail. It is a story of people. Since these boys were members of the Stonewall Brigade, the brigade furnishes a background for the narrative.

At the outbreak of the Civil War a group of students at Washington College (now Washington and Lee University) formed a military company, which they called the Liberty Hall Volunteers. They entered the service in early June 1861, and the company was assigned to the Fourth Virginia Infantry Regiment in a brigade commanded by General Thomas J. Jackson and later known as the Stonewall Brigade. The company remained intact until May 1864, when it, along with most of the men of the brigade, was captured at the "Bloody Angle" at Spotsylvania Court House. So far as the author can ascertain only one other college company in the Army of Northern Virginia—the University (of Mississippi) Greys— had a comparable record.[2]

Most of the students had been acquainted with Jackson before the war when he was a professor at the Virginia Military Institute. Each morning, at exactly the same time, they had seen him as he strode across the campus of Washington College on his way to his duties at the Institute. He walked "with head erect, chin thrown out, and eyes square to the front." Jackson had known many of the boys and also their fathers. Two of the future captains of the company, James J. and Hugh A. White, were sons of his friend and pastor, the Rev. Dr. W. S. White of the Presbyterian Church; Hugh had been a colaborer in the colored Sunday school which Jackson had organized at Lexington. Another youthful volunteer was the

[2] See Maud Morrow Brown, *The University Greys* . . . , *1861–65* (Richmond, 1940).

son of Jackson's most intimate colleague at the Institute, Colonel J. T. L. Preston.

The college company's devotion to Jackson bordered on idolatry. The boys not only had the utmost confidence in his leadership, but also recognized him as "a Christian man." In the early days of the war Jackson took a fatherly interest in their welfare. When, in November 1861, he was promoted to major general and given a semi-independent command in the Shenandoah Valley, he detailed the company to act as headquarters guard. It performed this duty until the fall of 1862, when it was forced by depletions in its ranks to relinquish the position.

Since most of the members of the company were from either Rockbridge County, Virginia, a stronghold of Presbyterianism, or the Valley, they had been reared in a Calvinistic environment. Several were candidates for the ministry, and in camp they generally held an evening prayer meeting, which Jackson, while a brigade commander, would occasionally attend. The boys often wondered which he admired more, "their praying or fighting qualities." But piety was not their only characteristic. They also loved fun and had an eye for a pretty girl; and there were some "rascals" in the company, as one of the members later wrote.

Many individuals have been helpful by giving encouragement or criticism during the preparation of this narrative. Among these were Edward Aull of Birmingham, Alabama, A. W. Bollingback of Lexington, Virginia, and my colleagues at Washington and Lee University, Frank A. Parsons, Assistant to the President and Director of Information Services, and Professors Cecil D. Eby, Allen W. Moger, and J. Paxton Davis. Some read parts of the manuscript; others all of it; and I am most grateful for their constructive criticism and helpful suggestions. I wish to express my appreciation also to Miss Martha Rebecca Cullipher, Reference Librarian, McCormick Library, Washington and Lee University, who answered some difficult questions in regard to the bibliography, and to Mrs. Robert Stewart and Mrs. Stanley Walton for their patience and excellent service in typing the manuscript.

For the use of the A. T. Barclay Letters, I am indebted to Houston Barclay of Lexington, Virginia. For placing at my disposal the diary of Captain Henry Ruffner Morrison, I owe a debt of gratitude to the late Henry B. Jones of Brownsburg, Virginia, son of Lieutenant J. H. B. Jones, last commander of the Liberty Hall Volunteers. To Dr. James Morrison Hutcheson of Richmond, Virginia, a native of Rockbridge County, an alumnus of Washington and Lee University, and Rector of its Board of Trustees, I am grateful for his unfailing encouragement in the preparation of the manuscript from its inception to its completion. I wish to acknowledge my indebtedness to Washington and Lee University for financial assistance in the preparation of the manuscript for publication.

W. G. BEAN

Lexington, Virginia
June 1962

CONTENTS

	Preface	vii
I.	"Its White Columns Gleaming"	3
II.	"An Awful Sunday"	36
III.	Headquarters Guard	69
IV.	The Valley Campaign	97
V.	"He Fell . . . Sword in Hand"	120
VI.	"Dirty, Ragged and Barefooted"	145
VII.	Capture at the Bloody Angle	170
	Appendix and Selected Bibliography	199
	Index	217

THE
LIBERTY HALL VOLUNTEERS
Stonewall's College Boys

One

"ITS WHITE COLUMNS GLEAMING"

SPRING came early to the Valley of Virginia in 1861; and one of the youthful members of the Liberty Hall Volunteers, Alexander Tedford Barclay, remembered in his old age that "in those piping days of peace nature never looked more lovely, the blue mountains and green fields of old Rockbridge never more beautiful; all nature seemed to be at peace."[1]

While nature was at peace, the serenity of mind of the people of the Valley of Virginia was disturbed by the political controversy raging throughout the land over the issue of secession. By that time the Union had been severed, and the new nation of the Southern Confederacy, composed of the former states of the lower South, had emerged as a consequence of Abraham Lincoln's election as President of the

[1] "Liberty Hall Volunteers," in Washington and Lee University, *Historical Papers, 1890–1904*, no. 6 (Lynchburg, Va., 1904), p. 124 (hereafter cited as Barclay, "Volunteers").

3

United States. Virginia's efforts at the Washington Peace Conference to restore the Union had failed, Lincoln had been inaugurated, and ominous war clouds hovered over the country.

In the meantime Virginia had placed its destiny in the hands of a convention which had been in session at Richmond since February 13, 1861. Although the Old Dominion had recognized secession as a legitimate weapon, it had refused to take its place in the secession movement despite much urging. The ground for Virginia's final action was what Virginians considered to be Lincoln's aggressive policy toward the seceded states. On April 15, 1861, three days after the firing on Fort Sumter, Lincoln called upon Virginia for troops to coerce the lower South. Rather than obey the call for troops and acquiesce in the use of force, the state on April 17 withdrew from the Union and joined the Southern Confederacy.

The excitement prevailing in Virginia in the spring of 1861 was reflected on the campus of Washington College. Its president was the Pennsylvania-born Rev. Dr. George Junkin, a slaveowner, a stanch Unionist, and "a man of strong convictions and passionate utterances." To him, the agitation over the question of slavery in the territories was useless and mischievous. The Southern contention that slaveholders possessed the constitutional right to take slaves into the territories was "an abstraction of no practical value"; likewise he believed the Northern rejection of this claim to be "equally futile as a practical question" since there was no existing territory suitable by either climate or crops for the use of slave labor. It was then a folly, Dr. Junkin asserted, for the South "to assert a right that it never could use, and [for the North] to dread an evil that never could in the nature of things become a reality." This had been the language of Daniel Webster in the great debate of 1850, and Dr. Junkin, a Whig of the Webster persuasion, contended that the acceptance by both North and South, in the crisis of 1860–61, of Webster's reasoning would prevent the disruption of the Union.

Although he had voted for the moderate Bell–Everett ticket in the presidential contest of 1860, as did most Virginians, Dr. Junkin did not regard Lincoln's election as a menace to Southern interests. He urged Virginia to accept the decision of the electorate, declaring that it had nothing to fear from Lincoln, who would administer the government in the constitutional manner. When Virginia cast her lot with the Confederacy, Junkin stigmatized her action as "a rebellion without cause." The unfavorable reaction of the students to Dr. Junkin's unyielding nationalism was first manifested in his presence in the oratorical exercises held every Friday afternoon. The students often selected for their orations recent speeches of Southern Congressmen in defense of secession. The views exhibited by these declamations were characterized by Dr. Junkin as treasonable "with a capital T," and each youthful orator was stridently ordered "to sit down, sir."[2]

During the controversy in Virginia over the issue of secession, Dr. Junkin became intensely wrought up. In the Old Testament he found justification for his denunciation of secession, and likewise in the Book of Revelation he "discovered" a prophecy of the role which the United States was destined to play in "the work of evangelizing the world." Therefore he warned "his blue stocking brethern" of the Lexington Presbyterian Church that "God Almighty can't do without the United States Government [in this mission] and He won't let you break it up." To Junkin the eloquent William

[2] "Exodus of Dr. Junkin," *Presbyterian Standard* (Philadelphia, May 17, 1861), in David X. Junkin, *The Reverend George Junkin, D.D., L.L.D., A Historical Biography* (Philadelphia, Pa., 1871), pp. 518–26 (hereafter cited as Junkin, *Junkin*); Barclay, "Volunteers," p. 124.

L. Yancey of Alabama, ardent advocate of secession, was nothing less than an anarchist, and his name was as "a red flag to a bull." At chapel service one morning, as Dr. Junkin was reading in the Book of Kings about some "turbulent fellow—Jehu or Ziami—" who by his treasonable utterance had stirred up trouble in Israel, he suddenly exclaimed: "That's Yancey!" The growing resentment of the college boys at Dr. Junkin's dogmatic opinions was indicated by their dubbing him "a Pennsylvania abolitionist" and by their scrawling on the columns of the college building opposite his classroom the words, "Lincoln Junkin."[3]

Sometime after the inauguration of Lincoln in early March 1861, students twice ran up Palmetto flags to the top of the wooden statue of George Washington on the main college building, and this brought to a climax the antagonism between them and Dr. Junkin. On both occasions the flags were removed, on the first instance by a student, Willie C. Preston of Lexington. On the second, as the flag was being lowered by the colored janitors, Dr. Junkin seized it and set fire to it, shouting, "So perish all efforts to dissolve the glorious Union."

On the morning of April 17, 1861, the day Virginia seceded, another Southern flag was seen flying over Dr. Junkin's classroom. Summoning the faculty to a special meeting after morning prayers, he declared that the student action was an insult to him and insisted that the faculty order the removal of the flag. At that moment a member of the faculty presented a student petition requesting that the flag not be removed. The flag had been erected, so ran the petition, as an expres-

[3] John Newton Lyle, "Stonewall Jackson's Guard, The Washington College Company," (MS in the McCormick Library, Washington and Lee University), p. 27 (hereafter cited as Lyle, "Jackson's Guard"). A native of Montgomery County, Va., Lyle was a senior at Washington College at the outbreak of war. At the organization of the Liberty Hall Volunteers, he was elected first lieutenant. The manuscript was written about 1890.

sion of their unanimous approval of the action of the State Convention and also of their willingness to sustain Virginia in "the trying scenes" that might follow; therefore they would regard anyone who removed the flag as an enemy of the Commonwealth. The faculty, endeavoring to assuage Dr. Junkin's feelings, assured him that the erection of the flag had no reference to him personally. Dr. Junkin, however, was adamant in his attitude, vowing he would neither give another lecture nor hear another recitation under "a rebel" flag. If the flag were not taken down, he would call a meeting of the trustees and resign instantly. Having delivered the ultimatum, Dr. Junkin retired in order to give the faculty time to deliberate. Alexander L. Nelson, professor of mathematics, took the chair, and the faculty then adjourned to meet their classes and reassemble in the afternoon.

At the afternoon session the faculty unanimously adopted a resolution reassuring Dr. Junkin that the students had no intention of affronting him. Instead the students were only presenting, the professors said, "an open declaration of their sentiments in the present unhappy condition of our national affairs, meaning unflinching hostility to the coercive policies of Mr. Lincoln and a firm adhesion to the South for 'weal or woe!'" After denying Dr. Junkin's right to impose the alternative of resignation which they could not allow to influence their decision, the faculty members unanimously rejected the ultimatum and the flag remained.

The next day, at a special meeting of the Board of Trustees, some of whom lived in Lexington, Dr. Junkin resigned the presidency of Washington College and announced his decision to leave Virginia. Hastily departing for Philadelphia on April 19 with a widowed daughter and his niece, he crossed the Potomac at Williamsport, Maryland, on May 9, having driven the last thirty-five miles from Winchester "without

stopping to feed [his] horses." Once across the river, tradition has it that Dr. Junkin alighted from his carriage and
shook the dust of Virginia from his shoes. But he left behind
two sons and also a son-in-law—"still dear as a son"—destined
to be famous, Thomas J. ("Stonewall") Jackson. Another son-
in-law, J. T. L. Preston, husband of his gifted daughter, Margaret, and a nephew, George G. Junkin, were to serve as
members of General Jackson's staff in the early days of the
war.[4]

In late March the reaction of the students to the mounting
war spirit was manifested in ways other than the erection of
flags. A group petitioned the faculty for permission to form "a
military class," to be drilled by a cadet from the Virginia Military Institute. While the faculty did not prohibit its forma-
tion, they advised the students "to forego" such a plan because it would not prove useful and would bring a rabble to
the campus, an occurrence which all wished to avoid. A week
later the students again asked permission to organize a company. This request was granted with certain conditions stipu-
lated—no firearms were to be allowed on the college grounds,
no drilling was to take place during study hours, no one was

[4] Junkin, *Junkin*, pp. 520–26; Minutes of the Faculty, Washington College, April 17, 1861, McCormick Library, Washington and Lee University;
Harvey Gerald Shields, "Rockbridge County Virginia and the Civil War"
(Senior Honors Thesis, Washington and Lee University, 1960, ch. 1). Willie Preston was the son of Colonel J. T. L. Preston of V.M.I. Although Dr.
Junkin had a pass from Governor Letcher, he had no occasion to use it, for
he was unmolested on the journey northward. Dr. Junkin never forfeited the
admiration of his students. One of them subsequently declared that "his interest in the spiritual welfare of those under him was unflagging. He went to
his reward years ago [1868] and many of his old students still live [1890s]
to praise him" (Lyle, "Jackson's Guard," p. 31). Shortly after Dr. Junkin
reached Philadelphia in May 1861, in a conversation with his brother, Rev.
D. X. Junkin, he predicted that "Jackson will perish in this war" (Junkin,
Junkin, p. 551).

to be employed to command the company without the faculty's approval, and at any time the faculty could prohibit the drilling whenever it interfered with "the proper discharge of the [students'] college duties."[5]

Finally the company was formed in early April under the captaincy of Professor Alexander L. Nelson. It took the name "The Liberty Hall Volunteers" from a similar organization which had been formed at the Liberty Hall Academy, one of Washington College's antecedents, during the American Revolution and which had marched under William Graham, rector of the institution, to Rockfish Gap to repel a threatened invasion by the British General Banastre Tarleton. For several weeks after the beginning of the war on April 17, the company "played military." But in early June, when the faculty declared the session at an end and awarded degrees to the seniors, the campus was turned into a military camp, the drilling took on serious intent, and recruits who had no connection with Washington College were accepted. The West Point-trained rector of Grace Episcopal Church of Lexington, William Nelson Pendleton, drilled the company until he assumed command of the Rockbridge Artillery. Then Cadet W. H. Morgan of V.M.I. took over and soon had the company in a high state of proficiency.[6]

To supply the needs of the volunteers the ladies of the county formed a sewing society, using one of the public halls

[5] Minutes of the Faculty, Washington College, March 26, April 1, 1861 (MS in McCormick Library, Washington and Lee University).

[6] Ibid., May 14, 21, 26, 1861; Lyle, "Jackson's Guard," p. 35. On May 30, 1861, the Lexington Gazette announced that the college company was accepting recruits outside the college. In the session of 1860–61 approximately one hundred students were enrolled at Washington College. Many of the students who were not members of the Liberty Hall Volunteers joined other Confederate units. W. N. Pendleton was later chief of artillery in the Army of Northern Virginia.

of the town as a workshop. Soon linen gaiters to cover the ankles and calves and havelocks to protect the necks were hurriedly turned out; for making blouses and pants, gray cloth was secured from a woolen factory on Whistle Creek, west of Lexington. Muskets and caps on which the initials of the company, "L.H.V.," were emblazoned in brass letters were secured from V.M.I. Each member of the company was furnished a needlebook, thread, and buttons. Reminiscing thirty years later, John Newton Lyle, one of the volunteers, wrote:

Thus tricked out with his white waist belt and cross belts fastened with a big brass buckle, his ankles and calves gleaming in white gaiters and his head adorned with a snowy havelock, [each volunteer] was a nobby soldier calculated to smash a maiden's heart. . . .

Those were good times we were having in old Lexington, with no studies and plenty of leisure from military duties to gallant the girls. The only thing to mar the pleasure was the fear the war would be over and the boys who had gone ahead would be soon returning before we got off.[7]

After repeated application during the month of May for active service, the company received orders on June 2 from Governor John Letcher to report to Harper's Ferry, the mobilization center for the Valley troops. Several days were spent in preparation for the departure, and they were "days of anxious thoughts," as Lyle wrote afterward: "The tested field from a distance had been alluring, but we approached the day of leaving with the trepidation of a bridegroom marching to the altar. Nor was the prospect of leaving friends, loved ones, and the comfortable surrounding assuring, [for it] brought instead heart-sickness and a panicky feeling about the pit of the stomach." Yet for some time, the editor of the

[7] Lyle, "Jackson's Guard," p. 37.

Lexington *Gazette* wrote, the Liberty Hall Volunteers had been spoiling for a fight.[8]

On the morning of June 8 the company was mustered on the college campus under its commissioned and noncommissioned officers: Captain James J. White, professor of Latin, Washington College, and son of the Rev. Dr. W. S. White, pastor of the Lexington Presbyterian Church; First Lieutenant John N. Lyle; Second Lieutenant Joseph R. Sherrard; First Sergeant William A. Anderson; and First Corporal Givens B. Strickler. There were also four additional sergeants (second, third, fourth, fifth), three additional corporals (second, third, fourth), and sixty-one privates. The total membership of the original company was seventy-three. A majority of its members were professed Christians, and several were candidates for the ministry.[9]

Conspicuous among the latter was Hugh Augustus White, another son of Dr. W. S. White and brother of Captain James J. White. A graduate of Washington College, Hugh was a student at the Union Theological Seminary (Presbyterian) at Farmville, Virginia, from 1859 to 1861. As his second year at the Seminary drew to a close in the early spring of 1861, this lad, caught up in the maelstrom of war, was much troubled, not knowing whether he should complete his theological training or shoulder a musket. After much consideration and the observance of a day of prayer and fasting at the Seminary, he told his father "Our decision is formed . . . and since the war is begun, I must help finish it." It would have been more "delightful," he added, to have been able to enter

[8] *Ibid.,* p. 45; Lexington *Gazette,* June 13, 1861.
[9] Lyle, "Jackson's Guard," p. 45; Givens B. Strickler, "Liberty Hall Volunteers," in Washington and Lee University, *Historical Papers,* no. 6 (Lynchburg, Va., 1904) pp. 111–12; (hereafter cited as Strickler, "Volunteers"). For the company's roster see the Appendix. On the eve of the departure of the volunteers, Captain Alexander L. Nelson was stricken with erysipelas and at the advice of his physician resigned as unfit for army life.

upon the work of "saving men's souls" rather than destroying their bodies. Yet he hoped his life would be spared long enough for him still to do "some little good in my Master's vineyard."[10]

Having remained at the Seminary until the end of the session, the twenty-year-old Hugh reached home in the middle of May 1861. His father endeavored to convince him that, "considering his age, his acquisitions, his tastes, and habits," he should complete the work at the Seminary and then enter the service as a chaplain. To his father's entreaty, this patriotic youth replied:

What you say has much force. But this is to be no ordinary war, and for young men like me to hold back will have a very bad moral effect. The superior numbers and resources of the North will make it necessary for every man in the South, not disabled by age or infirmity, to take part in the work of resistance. I have thought and prayed much over this question for two months . . . and the result is as firm a conviction that I ought at once to take part in the defense of my native State, and especially of you and mother, as I ever felt that I ought to preach the Gospel.

Impressed by his son's strong conviction, the father said, "Go, my son, and the blessing of God go with you." Hugh immediately enrolled in the Liberty Hall Volunteers, many of whom he had known in his student days at Washington College.[11]

[10] Hugh to father, Seminary, April 22, 1861; quoted from *Sketches of the Life of Captain Hugh White of the Stonewall Brigade by His Father* (Columbia, S.C., 1864), p. 42. (Hereafter the volume is cited as White, *White*.)

[11] *Ibid.*, p. 46; no date is given, but probably the letter was written in the latter part of April 1861. Before leaving home for the front, Hugh wrote a letter setting forth his views of the nature of the war and its probable results: "If we are conquered, farewell forever to the bright vision of philanthropists and Christians as to civil and religious freedom America was to maintain at home and abroad. But if we conquer, as I think we shall eventually, these visions and hopes may again be cherished" (Hugh to sister, n.d., *ibid.*, p. 49).

From the campus the company proceeded to the court-house on Main Street and halted opposite it, where a large concourse of people had assembled. A beautiful flag, made by the ladies of the Falling Springs (Presbyterian) Church and bearing the inscription, *Pro aris et focis* ("for altar and home"), was presented to the volunteers in an "eloquent" speech by the Rev. John Miller, pastor of this church; it was received by Captain J. J. White in "touching and appropriate" remarks. After a short address and fervent prayer by the Rev. Dr. W. S. White, the college boys then departed by stagecoaches for Staunton.[12] They were accompanied to the North [Maury] River by a large number of parents, friends, and "black mammies" in carriages, on horseback, and on foot. Lieutenant Lyle later recalled that

you could almost hear the heart-strings of mothers and sisters snap as they pressed sons and brothers in farewell embraces. In surrendering their boys to the services of Virginia, they were making sacrifices, such as their heroic ancestors were accustomed to make on the hills and among the mosshags of Scotland, for God and Presbytery. It was a willing sacrifice. And no less, yet more demonstrative than theirs, was the grief of the black mammies, who came to say good-by to their "chillum," now grown to be young masters, and press them to their warm hearts.

Returning to the town, the crowd entered the Presbyterian Church, where prayers were offered for the safety of the volunteers. Commenting upon the Liberty Hall Volunteers, the Lexington *Gazette* declared they were

one of the finest looking bodies of young soldiers that have been sent from this portion of the state. They were well equipped, admirably uniformed and went off in fine spirits, determined to give

[12] Barclay, "Volunteers," p. 114.

the Yankees particular fits whenever and wherever they have the pleasure of an introduction to them. The patriotic fire which animated the breasts of the boys of Liberty Hall in the days of our Revolutionary struggle is still alive in the hearts of their worthy descendants.[13]

En route to the river, the volunteers traveled the Valley Turnpike, which took them past the front of Washington College. "I looked it a loving farewell," Lyle fondly recalled a third of a century later, "its tall white columns gleaming in the sunshine of that bright June morning."[14]

At Fairfield the volunteers stopped at noon to devour the baskets of food which had been showered upon them by people at every crossroad on the way. As a consequence the boys were more lively on their afternoon journey to Staunton because the "belly timber" which had been stored away at noon had made them feel better. Moreover, the sadness of parting had worn off. The girls who swarmed out of every house along the roadside, beaming with smiles and with their handkerchiefs fluttering in the breeze, drew responsive cheers and tossing of hats from the volunteers. To while away the time as they rode along the dusty pike, they engaged in much banter, the good-natured Private Charles Williams who was facetiously promoted to a "colonel" being the butt of their teasing. A red clay embankment resembling a redoubt which loomed upon the face of the Blue Ridge was dubbed "Fort Williams" in honor of the "colonel," a title which clung to Williams for a long time. On another occasion, the company passed a militia company drilling near the turnpike. The college boys teased the militia captain unmercifully for his gorgeous uniform and cocked hat with a gold band and star, calling upon him "to come out of that hat."[15]

[13] Lyle, "Jackson's Guard," p. 45; *Gazette*, June 13, 1861.
[14] "Jackson's Guard," p. 46.
[15] *Ibid.*, pp. 54 f.

Arriving at Staunton about ten o'clock in the evening, the college company was quartered in the freight depot of the Virginia Central Railroad, while Captain J. J. White put up at the Virginia House. The volunteers, forced to sleep on the hard floor of the depot, had their first taste of the hardships of war that night. For breakfast next morning, Private Ted Barclay of Lexington wrote that he had two quarts of strong coffee and chunks of bread about a yard square. The bread, Lieutenant Lyle remembered, would "have thrown our black mammies into spasms"; it was pan-fried, "in consistency resembling india rubber. It could be stretched into ropes and pressed into balls. One bait of it would have raised enough nightmares [for one] to ride a regiment of horses for a week."[16]

Upon their arrival at Staunton the volunteers were ordered by Major M. G. Harman, Post Commander, to join the Confederate forces in western Virginia, under the command of General Robert Selden Garnett; but since Captain White had left Lexington with orders from the Governor to proceed to Harper's Ferry, he refused to obey Harman's orders unless directed by the Governor to do so. In communication with Governor John Letcher, he was told to report to the original destination. On June 10 the college company was mustered into the service of the Provisional Army of Virginia. From Staunton, Ted Barclay wrote his sister on June 11:

We had battalion drill here yesterday reviewed by Ex-Gov. Wise, Gen. [W. H.] Harman, Col. Campbell and Mr. Hall of Wetzel, all of whom made speeches. I was invited to tea last night at Mr. Keizer's and as I was coming back was invited to Mr. Cockran's to breakfast. We have had strawberries three times at camp, and the people of the town send in all sorts of things to us.

[16] Ted Barclay to sister, Camp Terrible, June 10, 1861, A. T. Barclay Letters (hereafter cited as Barclay Letters); Lyle, "Jackson's Guard," p. 57. The Barclay Letters are in the possession of Mr. William Houston Barclay, A. T. Barclay's son.

Our regular eating consists of wheat bread, beef, and coffee, all very good except the bread. We are considered the best company down here. Yesterday whilst on drill we marched through the streets amidst showers of bouquets.

There are some of the best looking girls down here that I ever saw.[17]

As the volunteers awaited orders at Staunton, Hugh White wrote his father:

You will be glad to hear that our destination is Harper's Ferry. We leave tomorrow, and all are in good spirits. The people have been very kind, and made our conditions really pleasant. Many of our men have enjoyed their hospitality at their homes, and others have enjoyed it at camp. Some hearts, it may be, are now swelling with the desire for military distinction, and some heads becoming dizzy with anticipation of early glory. But I confess I am either too cowardly or too stupid to belong to either class. They may win the laurels, provided only that our cause triumphs. And of our final success you would not doubt, had you seen the men who left town this morning to repel the enemy from our north-western border. They appear to be good soldiers and in good spirits.

I am sure it will relieve your mind of much anxiety to know that we are going to Harper's Ferry, to meet open enemies, and not the traitors of the north-west. The boys are packing their knapsacks, laughing, talking, whistling, and singing.[18]

[17] Barclay Letters. Henry A. Wise was governor of Virginia from 1856 to 1860; he was also a general in the Confederate Army. General W. H. Harman, one of five brothers who served the Confederacy, was in command of the Thirteenth Brigade, Virginia Militia, at the beginning of the war. Later he was demoted by General Jackson to colonel of the Fifth Virginia Infantry. Resigning this commission in 1862, he was reappointed a general of cavalry and was killed near Waynesboro, Va., in the last days of the war. Mr. Cockran was a prominent citizen of Augusta County, Va.

[18] Staunton, June 11, 1861, White, *White*, p. 48. Among the troops passing through Staunton en route to western Virginia was a company of Hampden-Sydney students, some of whom Hugh knew. This company was later captured, and when it was exchanged the company disbanded, and the boys joined other units.

"L.H.V.," in a letter to the Lexington *Gazette,* described the reception given to the college company at Staunton:

We fared better than the [other] soldiers generally did, and we owe many thanks to ladies for their kindness to our company in sending us pies, cakes, and other "nice fixings," not found in the soldier's bill of fare. We were not long in coming to the conclusion that the kindness, the bright eyes, and the sweet smiles of those fair damsels could gain a far easier victory over our boys than the swords of the Yankees.[19]

In fine spirit the college boys boarded the train on June 12 for Gordonsville, where they waited for several hours for the train from Richmond which would take them to Manassas Junction. The smiles and chatter of the bevy of girls who were at the depot to welcome the soldiers passing to the front helped the college company to pass the time. One of them pinned a rosebud on the gauntlet of Lieutenant Lyle, and the "vain cockscomb" crowed over the other boys during the remainder of the trip.

At Gordonsville the college boys entered into the line of travel between Richmond and Manassas—troops were then being rushed to the latter town. In Rockbridge County they had seen no soldiers except the V.M.I. cadets and a few companies of volunteers who had left Lexington in the months of April and May. Now all kinds of troops came under their observation. Lieutenant Lyle distinctly remembered "a big warrior with a fierce mustache waxed into rat-tails" and of a military bearing distinctly French. He was arrayed in a gorgeous uniform that made the boys' eyes blink, and his presence was overpowering. Thinking that he was an officer of high rank,

[19] "Correspondent" of the Lexington *Gazette,* June 27, 1861 (hereafter cited as "L.H.V."). The author is convinced that "L.H.V." was Lieutenant Lyle. Apparently in writing his manuscript, "Stonewall Guards," Lyle used the articles which appeared in the *Gazette,* and in many instances the accounts of the same events described by "L.H.V." and Lyle are almost identical.

"doubtless commander-in-chief of all the Confederate armies," the Liberty Hall Volunteers disgustedly learned later that he was only the drum major of the First Virginia Infantry, which was composed of Richmond "swells."[20]

When the train arrived at Manassas Junction in the late afternoon of June 12, the college boys did not tarry long, for the cars which were to carry them to Strasburg were already awaiting them, and soon they were on board, hastening toward the Blue Ridge. Since it was a night's run, the company got only snatches of sleep. Detraining the next morning at Strasburg, after having breakfasted on the cold rations left over from the day before, the college boys were so glum and morose that "[their] own Valley and Blue Ridge had to smile their sweetest to restore [their] good humor." As the college company passed through Strasburg in the morning of June 13, "perfect in drill and discipline," they were the admiration of all who saw them, reported the "Correspondent" of the Lexington *Gazette*. It made the onlookers sad, he added, to see a company of "such superior material going to camp, to contend with the low, debased minions of a miserable, degraded, and almost fallen tyrant and usurper [Lincoln]."[21]

From Strasburg to Winchester, since there was no railroad, the college boys were sent in wagons which the post quartermaster had requisitioned from the neighboring farmers. This was a comedown from stage and railroad transportation, Lieutenant Lyle admitted, but it was better than walking in the hot sun on a dusty, hard pike. In the caravan was the Third Tennessee Infantry Regiment on its way to join General Joseph E. Johnston's army near Winchester. With the Tennesseans in the lead the column was soon on the road, transported northward like "pigs to market."

[20] Lyle, "Jackson's Guard," pp. 62 f.
[21] *Ibid.*, pp. 64 f.; *Gazette*, June 27, 1861.

The first of the war's rude alarms occurred at Newtown (now Stephens City), midway between Strasburg and Winchester. A grapevine dispatch had come in to the effect that the enemy was advancing on the town in strong force from the direction of Romney, and the panic-stricken citizens, hailing the troops as deliverers, appealed to them for protection. The colonel of the Tennessee regiment promptly formed his men in line of battle and, notifying the college company, asked for their support. "Now it is true we were for war," Lieutenant Lyle amusingly said later, "but this was springing it on us with too much suddenness. It was too previous, and besides that was not the place we expected to do our fighting. The news shocked us, sent our hearts to our throats and gave us a cold feeling about the pit of our stomach. The first impulse was to decline the Colonel's invitation with thanks, but as that would have been discourteous we swallowed our hearts, jumped from the wagons, formed in line, and rammed home our cartridges."

Then it was discovered that there were no percussion caps in the company—"a pretty kettle of fish," Lyle confessed. The boys, unable to fire their guns, realized that "to bayonet the foe without first firing on them was rather cold-blooded work for raw troops." To relieve the situation, Captain White had the happy thought of borrowing some caps from the Tennesseeans. Hastening to the front, he ordered Lieutenant Lyle to follow with the company. "And away we went in column of two's, in great hurry to get there [Lyle wrote]. It would have made a dog laugh to see the movement of the company. The long legged boys of the front files were so eager for the fray that their strides kept their comrades in the rear in a trot. It didn't look soldierly, and all were becoming winded," when the news filtered back that it was a false alarm. They then returned to their wagons and, to judge from the bragging after the excitement was over, the Yankees were "lucky" they had not showed up, for they would have been exterminated, said Lyle. The battle of Newtown was later a subject of much jesting around the camp fires of the Liberty Hall Volunteers.[22]

In the late afternoon of June 13 the volunteers entered Winchester. Abandoning the wagons, they marched down the main street, responding to the word of command with promptness and executing their evolutions perfectly amid the cheers of the crowd which lined the streets. It seemed as if the whole town, Lieutenant Lyle thought, was on the sidewalks to welcome them, especially the girls who looked so "fetching" in their white muslin dresses and big hoop skirts.

An amusing incident occurred while the company was marching into Winchester. A small boy who had witnessed its fancy evolutions was so dazed that he appeared to be speechless. He had seen much marching before, but not such "cutting capers" as those performed by the volunteers. He gazed for a time in silence at the passing volunteers and then asked the name of the company. Receiving no reply, he followed in the rear, begging for information. At last, taking his cue from the white havelocks which the volunteers were wearing, the lad shouted, "Hurrah for the Whiteheads." Although the havelocks were worn over the caps and hung over the back of the neck like "the tail of a sunbonnet," they were very comfortable; they were, however, too feminine for men. The volunteers soon discarded them, preferring to risk sunstroke rather than submit to the "gibes of the profane."[23]

During the entire journey from Lexington to Winchester, wrote "L.H.V.", the college company was cheered from every village and cottage by the wayside, and even the slaves paused from their labors "to bid us 'go and kill dem Yan-

[22] "Jackson's Guards," pp. 81 f.
[23] Ibid.

kees.'" The nearer they came to Winchester the more enthusi-
astic was the cheering. As "L.H.V." observed the waving ban-
ners and bouquets which were thrown to the college boys by
"fair hands as they bade us go and fight the battles of liberty,"
he vowed that the volunteers would never be "recreant to the
dictates of patriotism, of humanity, and of love." They would
"shed the last drop of [their] blood ere [the ladies] should
be exposed to insult and shame by the vandal horde of Northern fanatics and cut-throats."[24]

When the Liberty Hall Volunteers arrived at Winchester,
the Confederate force in the lower Valley was being organized into the Army of the Shenandoah. Its commanding officer was General Joseph E. Johnston, one of the senior Virginia officers of the Confederacy, who had recently super-
ceded Colonel Thomas J. Jackson, former professor at the
Virginia Military Institute, as commander of the area. Jackson was assigned to the First Brigade of the Army of the
Shenandoah, and it was eventually composed of five sturdy
infantry regiments of Virginians—the Second, Fourth, Fifth,
Twenty-seventh, and Thirty-third—and the Rockbridge Artillery.

The brigade included in its ranks descendants of "those
patriots to whom Washington in the darkest days of the American Revolution had fondly looked as his forlorn hope," and
it was destined to share proudly with its first commander the
sobriquet of "Stonewall." All social classes of the Valley of
Virginia and the contiguous mountainous regions were represented in its personnel; they were described as "the heirs of
the oldest families and the humblest of the sons of toil. . . .
Youths who had been reared in luxury and rough hunters
from lonely cabins. Some were mountain people, and all had
been nurtured in a wholesome climate, bred to many sports,
and hardened by a free life of the field and forest." They had

[24] Lexington *Gazette*, June 27, 1861.

taken up arms in defense of Virginia and not to perpetuate slavery, since there were relatively few slaves in the Valley.[25]

The brigade remained intact until the battle of Spotsylvania Court House in May 1864, though five of its leaders— Thomas J. Jackson, Richard B. Garnett, Charles S. Winder, W. S. H. Baylor, and Elisha Franklin Paxton—were later to die on the battlefield or from wounds received in battle. Under Jackson's rigid training the brigade soon developed into a fine compact group of fighting men with a spirit of initiative and confidence that made it famous in the annals of the Army of Northern Virginia. One should not think, however, that the brigade was composed wholly of chivalrous lads; it contained its quota of rogues and shirkers. Nevertheless, it is doubtful that any brigade began with a larger percentage of educated men than the Stonewall Brigade. Captain James J. White was amazed at the number of college men in its ranks, observing that "too large a proportion of men of this sort is in our brigade."[26]

To the boys the composition of Jackson's brigade must have appeared like a "cousinwealth"; in its ranks were former classmates of Washington College and friends from the Valley. Hugh White told his sister of the pleasure of meeting

[25] G. F. R. Henderson, *Stonewall Jackosn and the American Civil War* (New York, 1937), p. 93. Washington is reported to have said at Valley Forge, "Give me but a standard and the means of planting it upon the hills of West Augusta [Va.] and I will rally around it a band of patriots who will yet lift my bleeding country from the dust" (Lexington *Gazette*, April 17, 1861).

[26] John O. Casler, *Four Years in the Stonewall Brigade* (Guthrie, Okla., 1893), p. 128; James J. White to wife, June 14, 1861, James J. White Letters, Southern Historical Collection, University of North Carolina (hereafter cited as White Letters). Lyle later observed that there were privates in the ranks of the Stonewall Brigade, who could "while away their leisure hours with Homer's Epics or the love songs of Horace, read fluently in the dead tongues in which they were written" (Lyle, "Jackson's Guard," p. 7).

with old acquaintances, especially some of his fellow graduates of Washington College, in

the largest and happiest reunion we have enjoyed since parting. Almost every day brings some new enjoyment of this sort, awakening memories of the past, and recalling joys which seemed to be gone forever. Do not suppose therefore that mine is a sad condition, calling for sympathy. We have our sources of sadness, like other people. But we also have our peculiar joys. Indeed, one thought of the cause in which we are engaged is enough to scatter all gloom and fill us with gladness.[27]

Earlier Ted Barclay had related to his mother the news of other Rockbridge County companies, saying, "All were glad to see us. As soon as they heard that the company was here our quarters were full of their men, everyone asking a thousand questions and giving no time for answers." After assuring his mother that the fare was good, he then told her about a misfortune which had happened to a member of the college company, Thomas S. Rollins, who had received a box of food from home. Having invited all his friends to share its contents and with all standing around expecting "something good," Rollins took off the lid. "It would have done you good," Ted said, "to see them scatter—such a scent as arose from the box." A chicken which was in the box had spoiled and the other edibles such as cakes, biscuits, and strawberries were in like condition.[28]

At Winchester, Captain J. J. White was invited by an old college friend, Ned Brent, son of the cashier of the Valley

[27] Camp Stephens, June 24, 1861, White, *White*, p. 50. Camp Stephens, was near Martinsburg, Va. (now West Va.), and was named after a Revolutionary leader of the lower Valley.

[28] Camp Stephens, June 25, 1861, Barclay Letters. In the same letter Ted said, "I never saw so many persons I knew in my life, every third person speaks to me."

Bank of Winchester, to share the hospitality of his father's home and, although loath to leave his company, Captain White accepted the invitation. He was graciously welcomed by the father, given a large room to himself, and told to invite any of his friends to occupy it with him. "Certainly so far," he told his wife, "I have had everything to be thankful for and my company considering its experience has fared very well." Captain White had met several of his old Lexington friends, among them S. H. Letcher, Elisha Franklin Paxton, and James K. Edmondson, all officers of the Twenty-seventh Virginia, and they were anxious for the college company to join their regiment. So was Major W. S. H. Baylor of Staunton of the Fifth Virginia.[29]

A few days later Captain White and his brother Hugh were invited to tea at the home of Mrs. Annie Tucker Magill, sister of John Randolph Tucker, wartime Attorney-General of Virginia, and mother of Mrs. James R. Graham. "She is the same lovely, hospitable person & a perfect Florence Nightingale, doing nothing but nursing the sick," the captain told his wife. "Nothing could exceed the kindness of the people here. They have at least 1000 sick soldiers, chiefly with measles & mumps, quartered upon them & the private homes have been thrown

[29] J. J. White to wife, Winchester, June 14, 1861, White Letters. A native of Nottaway County, Captain J. J. White was graduated from the University of Virginia in 1846. Following graduation he taught for several years at the Charlottesville Classical School at Charlottesville, then returned to the University for a year of graduate work, and in 1852 was elected professor of Greek at Washington College. In 1858 he married Mary Reid, daughter of Samuel McDowell Reid, prominent citizen of Lexington. S. H. Letcher was Governor Letcher's brother. E. F. Paxton (known as Frank Paxton) later commanded the Stonewall Brigade, and J. H. Edmondson was later colonel of the Twenty-seventh Virginia Infantry. Lieutenant Colonel Baylor, a native of Augusta County, was a graduate of Washington College and the University of Virginia Law School. When the war broke out, he was Commonwealth Attorney of Staunton.

open to them." He then passed on to his wife a rumor that some of the citizens of Winchester were making ready to flee from the town, perhaps some to Lexington, and he hoped they would receive all the attention they deserved for their kindness to the Confederates. He cited as another example Mrs. David Barton, who had recently prepared breakfast for 180 hungry soldiers.[30]

At Winchester the company of Liberty Hall Volunteers was soon incorporated into the Army of the Shenandoah as Company "I," Fourth Virginia Regiment, First Brigade, under Colonel Thomas J. Jackson's command. Captain White, highly pleased with both the regiment and its officers—Colonel James F. Preston, Lieutenant Colonel Lewis T. Moore, and Major Kent—characterized the assignment as the most desirable in the brigade. The regimental and company officers, all "sociable and affable" gentlemen, cordially welcomed the new company, Lieutenant Lyle declared. Some were men of considerable ability, well posted upon the issues of the day. In subsequent discussions with them, Lyle found that some were of the opinion there would be no war. Captain Charles A. Ronald of Blacksburg, Virginia, known for his eloquence as "the Patrick Henry of the Southwest," upheld this contention so forcefully as to convince Lieutenant Sherrard of the college company that the United States Congress, called to meet in early July, would ask for a peaceful settlement of the issues which had caused the war. Sherrard went to bed that night so happy that he dreamed of "a joyful reunion with the folks at home," only to awaken the next morning to find that the war in the Valley had actually commenced. General Rob-

[30] June 16, 1861, *ibid*. Mrs. Graham was the wife of the Rev. Dr. James R. Graham, pastor of the Presbyterian Church of Winchester (Lenoir Chambers, *Stonewall Jackson* [New York, 1959], I, 414; hereafter cited as Chambers, *Jackson*).

ert Patterson, Federal commander in this region, crossed the Potomac on July 2, 1861.[31]

At the Fair Ground where the college boys joined the Fourth Virginia, they were jestingly greeted by the other companies with "Boys, do your mothers know you are out?" "Go to Jericho and let your beards grow," and other allusions to their youthful appearances such as "smooth red cheeks, with boyish dimples, without the vestige of beards; not a mustache in the whole company." They were assigned quarters near the "Grayson Dare Devils," rough mountain boys from Grayson County, Virginia, who were armed with hickory sticks and had entered the service boasting they would whip the Yankees with them.[32]

The company had scarcely stacked arms before the brigade moved north on the hard and dusty turnpike, and after a march of fifteen miles the brigade bivouacked at midnight in a clover field near Martinsburg. "What a tramp for sappy legs," Lieutenant Lyle later commented on the company's first long march. Captain White said it was "very rough work." (Four of his boys had fallen out during the night but they had come up the next morning.) Although he had a slight cold and headache at the beginning of the march, he felt perfectly well the next morning. Anyone who thought fighting was "the chief business" in a soldier's life was mistaken, he assured his wife. The marching and countermarch-

[31] Barclay, "Volunteers," p. 127; J. J. White to wife, June 14, 1861, White Letters; Lyle, "Jackson's Guard," p. 85. Colonel James F. Preston, a native of Montgomery County, and a graduate of Washington College, was a veteran of the Mexican War. A scion of an ancient Valley family, his father had been governor of Virginia; his brother, William Ballard Preston, had been a Whig Congressman and Secretary of the Navy in President Zachary Taylor's administration, a member of the Virginia Secession Convention of 1861, and later a Confederate senator until his death in 1862.

[32] Barclay, "Volunteers," p. 128.

ing, the fatigue, hunger, thirst, all incident to a moving column, were "the rough parts" of the service. He was glad,
however, to say he had not heard any complaints in his company, the boys behaving admirably and cheerfully. "Do not
allow yourself," the thirty-three-year-old captain urged his
wife, "to imagine any great suffering, for I stand it well. The
last two nights I have slept out in the open air & never felt
better in my life than I do this morning—a little foot-sore and
leg-weary. . . . It is very fine schooling for us all—we will
know how to appreciate *home, family & friends* now, in the
way we never did before."[33]

For two weeks the brigade remained at this bivouac,
Camp Stephens, busily engaged in drilling. Its morale was
high despite the intense training and rigid discipline to which
it was subjected by General Jackson. At that time, before he
had acquired the sobriquet of "Stonewall," he was sometimes
referred to by his soldiers as "Old Hickory," doubtless because his toughness and stern discipline reminded them of
Andrew Jackson. On one occasion Captain White, in commenting on Jackson as a disciplinarian, said: "Jackson is considered rigid, to border on tyranny by the men here, and
some of them have been greatly surprised to get an insight
into his character as a Christian man." But he proudly added
that Jackson "enjoys the confidence of his command."[34]

The carefree Ted Barclay recorded that the brigade drilled
six times daily—once before breakfast, directly after breakfast, then from eleven to twelve, and three times in the afternoon. The troops had no complaint "in the feeding line"; the

[33] Lyle, "Jackson's Guard," p. 86; J. J. White to wife, Camp Stephens,
June 21, 1861, White Letters.

[34] J. J. White to wife, Camp Stephens, June 29, 1861, White Letters. As
late as April 17, 1862, the Lexington *Gazette* referred to Jackson as "Hickory
the Second."

menu on one occasion consisted of stewed chicken, beef, bread, molasses, rice, all of which was good except the bread, which had been baked too long. However it was good enough for an appetite sharpened by a three-hour drill. In a romantic mood the youthful Ted added it was a beautiful sight to see the camp at night, a "thousand lights twinkling here and there through the woods, the merry laugh of the soldiers, the roll of drums, the rattle of arms; all combine to make it a novel sight." Ted then related an accident which had happened to Captain White:

Our captain is the biggest man on the ground . . . and if you could see him strutting along as proud as a peacock you would think he was Jeff Davis, Gen. Johnston, or some other big bug. Today whilst out drilling, he was walking so big and his head so high that when he came across a ledge of rocks, he could not see them and fell head over heels and great was the fall thereof. He hurt his leg a good deal and limps slightly. I reckon he wont walk so big hereafter.[35]

Writing to his wife about the same time, Captain White made no mention of his mishap but he registered a grievance about the mail service. In the first place there was too much delay in sending and receiving letters. Again he thought the regulation requiring the soldiers to pay for their own postage, and in coin which was hard to come by, was unfair to a man fighting for his country; soldiers should get free postage. The captain's great trial, however, was the separation from his loved ones. Turning to a more pleasant subject, Captain White thanked his wife for the box of ham, beef, and pickles which had just come. Although he was living well, the box came at a very good time. Other members of the college com-

[35] Ted to sister, Camp Stephens, June 25, 1861, Barclay Letters.

pany had also received boxes and there was "one universal and wide-spread grin" among the boys.[36]

Captain White's serious-minded ministerial brother Hugh was not thinking of mundane affairs. Instead he was disturbed about the lack of observance of the Sabbath in camp:

Yesterday [Sunday] we heard two sermons and attended a prayer meeting. This gave the appearance, at least, of holiness to the day, but still if you had looked into our camp you would have thought it the busiest day of the week. Some were cooking, others cutting wood, and others were pitching their tents. [I realize, however, that it is] painful but necessary to spend the Sabbath in this way [in the army]. Our religious privations are what we feel most keenly. We seek to remedy this by a brief prayer meeting held every night after roll call. Nearly all of our company attend with becoming seriousness. May the trials of our company work in it a great reformation. If so, we may hope for true and lasting prosperity when peace shall again come.[37]

To cocky little First Lieutenant John N. Lyle, the various groups of men in camp presented an interesting and contrasting study. A man's peculiar characteristic, Lyle contended, cropped out in camp when off duty, and each followed his own peculiar bent. Curious to see what the soldiers did as the guns were stacked and the ranks broken, he found that "the studious went to reading, the greedy to cooking and eating, the sleepy heads to sleeping, the tidy to repairing their garments, the neat to washing their persons and clothes, the idle to idling, the wags to guying their comrades, the politicians to discussing, and the musical to singing . . . there came to the ear a jumble of songs, sacred and profane." The "sportive" spread their blankets and were soon absorbed in "seven-up,"

[36] Camp Stephens, June 29, 1861, White Letters.
[37] Hugh to sister, Camp Stephens, June 24, 1861; White, *White*, p. 50.

a favorite game in Virginia at that time. But at the prospect of battle the gamblers became very pious and discarded their cards. Lyle declared that a regiment approaching the firing line could be traced by the cards thrown away. This reformation, however, was short-lived, for when the battle was over the men got new cards and were at it again.[38]

There was little distinction in the college company between the officers and the college boys. The respect and deference, however, which had been previously shown Captain White as a professor, was continued. His attitude toward the boys was a fatherly one, not that of military commander. In later years Ted Barclay wrote of him:

Stately and dignified, yet urbane and approachable, no one ever felt awed by his commanding presence, such was his affability and genuine sympathy. As a professor he despised the so-called discipline which watched and spied for opportunity to exercise authority over the conduct and habits of students. There was nothing little or indirect in his character, and he thus exercised an influence and control which bound with links of steel the hearts of young men to him. If this was true of him as a professor, how much more so as a soldier, where self-abnegation, tenderness, sympathy, endurance and courage had wider field for the exercise of those grand and noble qualities.[39]

When there were shortages in goods which neither the quartermaster nor commissary could supply, Captain White quietly bought them with his own funds. One morning when there was no coffee available, he made a trip to Martinsburg,

[38] "Jackson's Guard," p. 93 f.

[39] *Ibid.;* Barclay, "Volunteers," p. 133. In a letter Ted wrote: "We have the best captain [J. J. White] and Col [Preston], both are so kind that I do not know which is the kindest, but I suppose the captain. Colonel comes to our camp almost daily [to inquire] of our health, food, etc." (*Ibid.,* July 1, 1861).

returning soon with "the stimulating berry." While the college boys always cheerfully and willingly obeyed the legitimate orders of their fellow students, Lieutenants Lyle and Sherrard, they would have "dirtied our jackets," Lyle said, "if we had dared put on airs with the boys when off duty."[40]

Camp Stephens was located in a grove of forest trees on the north side of the turnpike. The weather was so balmy that no tents were used. The trees gave ample shelter from the sun's rays, and to provide shelter from the summer showers, the college boys stretched their blankets on rails laid in forked sticks which were driven in the ground or spread them over large rocks (as Hugh White did on one occasion) and fitted themselves in the hollow between. So protected was Hugh that when it began to rain he fell asleep with perfect indifference. Hugh learned to prefer "the canopy of heaven for [his] roof, and the stars as [his] light by night."[41] The college boys, according to Lyle, took to camp life like "ducks to water," and this was especially true of Ted Barclay, who enthusiastically told his mother on July 1, 1861:

I have not had sore feet since I left home nor been sick one minute, never was so well in my life, not even a headache. The captain says I stand army life better than any one in the company but I don't know what better is in this company as all are so well. I was on guard last night eight hours and was not the least tired when I came off. We get up every morning at half past four. I have gotten so used to it that I jump up before the drum beats. A drill of six hours a day in the sun makes such a black set of fellows you never saw. If I was to come home you would think I was some Colonel's black waiting boy.[42]

[40] Lyle, "Jackson's Guard," p. 111.
[41] Ibid.; Hugh to sister, Camp Stephens, June 24, 1861, White, *White*, p. 50.
[42] Lyle, "Jackson's Guard," p. 112; Ted to mother, Camp Stephens, July 1, 1861, Barclay Letters.

Jackson's headquarters at Camp Stephens were located in a house on the turnpike, not far from the encampment of the Fourth Virginia, the college boys' regiment. Spurning the idea of sleeping indoors, Jackson spread his blankets on the ground in the yard. To Captain White's suggestion that the exposure to the night air might be injurious to his health, the General replied that he liked to sleep with the wind blowing over him, as he believed it was good for him.[43]

As a student at Washington College, John Newton Lyle had often seen Jackson on the streets of Lexington, at public gatherings, and in the Presbyterian Church endeavoring to resist sleep during the Sunday services. But he would never forget how Jackson looked at Camp Stephens as he poked around the camp on a poorly caparisoned "plug," unpretentiously dressed in a faded blue-cloth coat, with a V.M.I. cadet cap on his head, and with no insignia to indicate his rank. Lyle commented on his appearance: "With the vizor of his cap pulled down over his eyes, leaving no part of his face visible but that covered by a full, brown beard, and his huge feet thrust to the ankles into his stirrup, he rode alone and had a far away look in his face, as if oblivious of his surroundings." No stranger, Lyle continued, would have divined in him a "Stonewall" Jackson. Yet, while his "get-up" was not dazzling, he inspired confidence in his troops, and there was "a granite-like solidity" in his appearance that indicated "he would do to tie to."[44]

Captain White was not only burdened with military duties at Camp Stephens, but he was worried about the condition of his pregnant wife. Apparently she had been complaining of the separation from her husband at a time when she most needed him, for he understandingly wrote: "It gives me un-

[43] J. J. White to wife, Camp Stephens, June 30, 1861, White Letters.
[44] "Jackson's Guard," p. 96.

usual sorrow to hear of your indisposition at such a time as this when it is not in my power to minister to your comfort in any way." Realizing that it was a trying period for her, he encouraged her "to bear her ills" with Christian fortitude and resignation; he tenderly wrote: "I wish it was my privilege to sit quietly by you this Sabbath evening, out of the rattle and clatter of camp; it would be so sweet & refreshing, but I may only anticipate the joy in the early future, for I can't think the present separation is to be long-continued. I never could be a soldier on the condition of a very protracted separation from those I love. In a short time I hope we will be in enjoyment of each others society, never to be disturbed again."[45]

The encampment at Camp Stephens which Lieutenant Lyle called "a prolonged picnic," barring the constant drills, was nearing an end. On the early morning of July 2 General Robert Patterson's Federal army crossed the Potomac and advanced toward Martinsburg. Notified by General J. E. B. Stuart of this movement, Jackson, who had previously been instructed by General Johnston to fall back from his position at Camp Stephens if attacked by a superior Federal force, immediately moved forward with the Fifth Virginia and the Rockbridge Artillery to meet the enemy. On the same day the first clash occurred at Falling Waters, a small village on the south side of the Potomac, between an advanced guard of Federals and the Fifth Virginia of Jackson's brigade. After a brisk encounter Jackson, realizing he was outnumbered, withdrew eventually to Camp Stephens, south of Martinsburg, where other brigades of Johnston's army were posted. When Patterson occupied Martinsburg on July 3, Johnston, after

[45] Bunker Hill, July 1, 1861, White Letters. Previously he had urged his wife "to keep in good heart & trust in the God of truth & justice & right & [let us] do our duty & then all will be well" (Camp Stephens, June 21, 1861, *ibid.*).

waiting at Camp Stephens for him to attack, pulled back his troops to Winchester on July 7. Although the college company, acting in support of the Fifth Virginia, did not participate in the skirmish at Falling Waters, the boys were as "cool as you please," Captain White said, as shells burst around them and bullets whistled by their ears.[46]

Enraged at the enemy's pillaging in that region, the Captain hoped that General Johnston would drive the "pillagers" out of Virginia. They had seized loyal Southern men, destroyed property, and "most shamefully even to conceive" committed outrages upon women. "Will a righteous God smile upon such enormities?" he asked his wife in a rare flight of anger. "I think not & one thing I am assured, the spirit of this army is fully up"; he was certain that the Southerners would fight with "terrible courage," and that the "Hessians" would not fight, having already fallen back in the face of the "little band" at Falling Waters. They had been saved from defeat there only by "an amazing providential intervention," the failure of Jackson's entire brigade to arrive in time.[47] The next day, Captain White reflected upon some of the strange features of army life: "This is certainly the strangest life when one allows himself to reflect a moment. Here we have thousands of men not knowing where they are to be next hour & all subject to the orders of one man. Such is life in an active campaign. I am sometimes amazed at my standing it so well, considering our irregular habits and exposure."[48]

Hugh White also was perfectly well, and Captain White attributed it wholly to his systematic habits and capacity to adjust himself to any situation. In fact, most of the college

[46] Lyle, "Jackson's Guard," p. 112; Chambers, *Jackson*, chs. xiv, xv; White to wife, Bunker Hill, July 4, 1861, White Letters.

[47] White to wife, *ibid*.

[48] *Ibid.*, July 5, 1861.

boys were learning to take care of themselves; army life was excellent training and should eventually be most useful to them. And there was less danger in battle than one could imagine, for the "rascals" (Yankees) had shown at Falling Waters they could not shoot, one prisoner having said he had never fired a gun before in his life. On the contrary, almost every man in the brigade was more or less a marksman. "Don't worry about me," the Captain concluded as befitted a predestinarian, "Providence will take care of me, you & our little Sally & all we love."[49]

[49] *Ibid.*

Two

"AN AWFUL SUNDAY"

RETURNING to Winchester, Jackson's brigade went into camp on the hills northeast of the town, and life there was the most monotonous they had so far experienced. An order had been issued restricting the soldiers to camp, and they did not like it because they were eager to see their lady friends. Furthermore, the site of the camp of the college boys had obviously been the "rendezvous" of hogs, judging by the number of fleas there, and this was another complaint, Captain White told his wife. But it was not the fleas that worried him, as they did not "devote themselves" much to him, but the frequent dreams he had of being at home with his loved ones. It "sickened" him upon awakening to find out they were dreams and saddened him for a few hours until he forgot them in the multiplicity of his military duties.[1]

The night of July 17 would be the last the boys would spend near Winchester for several months, but they did not

[1] Near Winchester, July 7, 1861, White Letters. Captain White asked his wife to send him some sugar and coffee, which were scarce and which would help him to endure the hardships of army life.

know it at that time. On the early morning of the next day General Johnston received a telegram from President Davis urging him to move his army from the Valley to Manassas Junction, east of Blue Ridge, to the aid of General P. G. T. Beauregard, who was confronted by a Federal army under the command of General Irvin McDowell. Johnston put his army in motion in the early afternoon of the same day in the direction of Millwood with Jackson's brigade in front. As the college boys, ignorant of their destination, passed through the streets of Winchester, they encountered the gaze of the girls whom they were seemingly abandoning to the mercy of the enemy, and they had a feeling of guilt and shame that they were letting their fair friends down. "Where are you going?" the girls asked. "Don't know, good bye," the boys answered. "Are you running off to leave us in the power of the Yankees?" "Don't you bother about the Yankees getting to Winchester, Uncle Joe [Joseph E. Johnston] is going to flank Patterson and wipe his army off the face of the earth," the boys hopefully replied.

As the Fourth Virginia swung along the road with the college company in its rear, there was much conjecture among the boys as to their destination. "It looks like a retreat to me," said one; "it's no retreat, for Jackson's Brigade is in front," another replied. In the midst of the speculations cheers were soon heard in front, and the reason for the cheering was soon known. As the head of each company of the regiment came up to the regimental adjutant, Captain James M. Wade, who was sitting on a horse by the roadside and holding a paper in his hands, he read an order from General Johnston: "Our gallant army under General Beauregard is now attacked by overwhelming numbers. The commanding general hopes that his troops will step out like men, and make a forced march to save the country." To this appeal, Lyle remembered, the college boys "not only made the welkin ring, but they tried to split it"; and as for stepping out like men, they hit the road at a pace which, if they had kept it up, would have landed them at Manassas Junction that night.[2]

At Millwood, ten miles from Winchester, the brigade was met by the ladies of the surrounding countryside with toothsome edibles such as fried chicken, ham, cake, pies, and even lemonade, which they served the soldiers. En route from Millwood to the Shenandoah River, the column passed "Greenway Court," the old colonial home of Thomas Lord Fairfax. In the dusk of the lovely July evening the brigade crossed the Shenandoah River, and the soldiers, removing their socks and shoes before plunging into the stream and on the east bank hurriedly pulling them on, started to climb the slopes of the Blue Ridge at Ashby's Gap. Although Captain White was still suffering from an injured leg, he walked from Winchester with his company. To the entreaties of the boys that he ride in the company wagon, he retorted that he had accepted the captaincy at the insistence of their parents and, having promised to care for them, he intended to stay with them.

Shortly after midnight the brigade was halted at a small hamlet with the pretentious name of Paris, on the eastern slope of the Blue Ridge, and the troops, exhausted after the twenty-mile hike, sank prostrate on the ground. In the darkness the college company bivouacked in the village cemetery, and Lieutenant Lyle, finding a depression which fitted him "like a glove," tumbled into it and was soon asleep. Upon awakening at daybreak, he found he had slept in a sunken grave of "a mortal long dead and buried," and the thought of it gave him the "creeps," as he later wrote.[3]

The brigade was up and on the road by dawn the next

[2] Lyle, "Jackson's Guard," p. 77.
[3] *Ibid.*, p. 181.

morning, expecting to "foot" it to Manassas Junction, but to their surprise the leg-wearied soldiers found at Piedmont Station, cars for their conveyance to Manassas Junction; the cavalry, artillery, and wagons went overland. With the cars full of soldiers, piled inside and on top, Jackson's brigade was soon under way, whirling along the beautiful countryside of Piedmont Virginia, with the boys shouting, laughing, and singing. Along both sides of the track, as the train thundered by, were groups of people, some doubtless refugees from the Valley, greeting the soldiers with cheers and the waving of hands. One old woman, dressed in a calico dress and wearing a simple sunbonnet, was kneeling not far from the track with her eyes and hands devoutly raised to the sky. Her moving lips and reverent attitude indicated she was invoking God's blessing upon the soldiers, and "it comforted us," Lyle wrote. So far, war had been to the Liberty Hall Volunteers a romantic adventure, but they were soon to find it was not always rosy.[4]

The brigade, reaching Manassas Junction in the late afternoon of July 19, detrained and bivouacked that night in a thicket of pines near Blackburn's Ford on Bull Run. The following day, Saturday, was given over almost entirely to rest, although some of the college boys visited Blackburn's Ford, the scene of an encounter the previous day between General James Longstreet's brigade and a Federal force.

General Jackson had established his bivouac in a cluster of trees near the front of the Fourth Virginia, and early on Saturday morning when General Beauregard came by on a round of inspection, he found Jackson lying on the "mother earth . . . and sleeping quietly as an infant." He paused a moment and then, refusing to allow the soldiers to arouse him, Beauregard rode away, leaving Jackson to his slumbers.[5]

[4] *Ibid.*, p. 182.
[5] *Ibid.*

On Sunday morning of July 21, 1861—the day of the battle of First Manassas—the sun rose brightly in a clear sky, and the day promised to be clear and warm. Lieutenant Lyle lyrically remembered that,

The birds were singing their morning hymn from the trees along the banks of Bull Run—the catbird and the thrush leading the choir—as sweetly as if no hostile armies were near. It was Sunday and the thoughts of the College Boys naturally turned to home and the village church and its sacred services, and to the home-folks who would spend the hours of the holy day in prayer for the loved ones in the army.[6]

The battle opened about daylight with a Federal feint against the Stone Bridge on the Warrenton Pike which spanned Bull Run and behind which was posted General N. G. Evans' brigade of South Carolinians. Soon, however, General McDowell's real plan—turning the extreme left flank of the Confederate line of battle which extended southeastward from the Stone Bridge along Bull Run to Manassas Junction—was revealed when a large Federal force was observed crossing Bull Run at Sudley's Springs farther up the stream. Suspecting the attack on the bridge was not the main one, Evans moved with a portion of his command and took up a position on high ground about one mile north of the pike. Repeated Federal attacks were forcing him back when Generals Bernard E. Bee and Francis Bartow came to his assistance. Fresh troops were thrown against the weak Confederate lines, which soon broke, requiring the men to retreat across the pike to the plateau on which the Henry House was located. It was at this climactic phase of the battle that Jackson made his appearance.

[6] *Ibid.*, p. 184.

Up to this time—about ten o'clock—Jackson's brigade had not fired a gun, but had marched and countermarched up and down Bull Run. Hearing the roar of guns to the left, Jackson put himself at the head of his brigade, marched to the sound of the firing, and formed a line of battle on the plateau, south of the Warrenton Pike, placing his artillery just behind the crest of the plateau. The brigade was then ordered to lie down behind the artillery, and for several hours it lay there under the well-directed and terrific fire of the Federal batteries. The shot and shell, coming over the crest of the hill, fell in the ranks of the brigade, mangling many of the men. About two o'clock Federal infantry advanced to carry the crest in Jackson's front. At this time General Bee, whose troops had been pushed back by overpowering numbers of the enemy across the pike, rode up to Jackson and said, "General, they are beating us back." Jackson coldly replied, "We will give them the bayonet." Galloping back to his men, Bee cried out, "There is Jackson standing like a stonewall," thus baptizing him with the name which was to make him immortal.

Jackson's opportunity had come. The brigade charged, and for several hours the battle swayed back and forth on the plateau, with additional troops arriving and taking position on the flanks of Jackson's command. Late in the afternoon, as the Federals were forming a new line of battle on the Confederate position, General E. Kirby Smith arrived on the field with his brigade and, outflanking the Federals' extended right, drove them back across the pike. The defeat soon turned into a rout, and the enemy fled to the fortifications at Washington.[7]

The Liberty Hall Volunteers, under fire for the first time,

---

[7] For excellent accounts of the battle, see Chambers, *Jackson*, I, ch. xvi, and Frank Vandiver, *Mighty Stonewall* (New York, 1957), pp. 147–64 (hereafter cited as Vandiver, *Stonewall*).

had proved their mettle. During the terrific artillery fire of the enemy which preceded the charge, Captain White, "the towering and beloved Zeus," walked back and forth in front of his boys, seemingly unconscious of the deadly missiles flying past him, allaying their fears with encouraging words and inspiring them by his example.[8] Two days after the battle, Captain White told his wife:

Sunday the 21st witnessed the most terrific battle ever fought on the continent. I lost five of my boys & have seven wounded, two of whom I fear mortally. They behaved with admirable gallantry. Our regiment [Fourth Virginia] was ordered to support a battery. For three hours we were required to occupy a position about 20 steps in the rear of our batteries & of course to receive the fire of that of the enemy. Here two of my boys fell dead & two were wounded. We were then ordered to charge the enemy's battery— we did it in the face of a terrible fire of musketry, the balls falling thick as hailstones. . . . I fought through with my sword in hand, having cut away the scabbard to avoid falling & why I was not killed is a mystery, but God in his good Providence spared me. We routed the enemy & drove them from the field with old [General Winfield] Scott at their head. When we came out [of the charge] I had four of my boys around me, Hugh [White] and Sam Moore [Dr. Moore's son] among them; they fought like heroes. Hugh's face was black as suet; he fired twenty rounds [in the battle]. With a fraction of the regiment, about twenty, with Col. [James F.] Preston at the head, we led the pursuing column. . . .

My dear Mary, I feel that God will surely take care of me here in the midst of danger as anywhere & I pray I may always have faith in him & be able to do my duty. . . .

[8] J. H. B. Jones, "The Liberty Hall Volunteers at First Manassas," Rockbridge *County News*, Feb. 2, 1911 (hereafter cited as Jones, "First Manassas"). As a professor of classics at Washington College, Capt. J. J. White was known as "Old Zeus."

The Captain expressed the wish that his "eyes shall never behold another such Sabbath day." He was disturbed that the battle had been fought on a Sabbath, but after all, it was "a gratifying reflection" to know that the enemy had purposely begun the battle. After the victory, he was sustained with the hope that the war would soon be over, exulting: "How I would drop with joy to turn my face homeward, but I must keep back such feelings."[9]

The next morning in a driving rain, Captain White and Lieutenant Lyle, accompanied by a detail, returned to the battlefield to perform "the holy duty" of burying the company's dead. A spot was selected near the place where the company had fought; since no coffins were available and the relatives were soon to remove the remains home, the bodies were laid side by side in one grave, each wrapped in a blanket. As the Captain offered prayer, tears streamed down the cheeks of all, swelling "the tide of rain drops that the raging storm beat upon [them]."

Although Captain White was heavy-hearted over the casualties in his company, on the day following the battle a piece of cheerful news came. His wife had presented him with an-

[9] To his wife, near Manassas, July 23, 1861, White Letters. Gen. Winfield Scott, commander-in-chief of the U.S. Army, was not present at this battle. The casualties of the college company were seven killed and six wounded (Strickler, "Volunteers," p. 120). Among the latter was First Sergeant William A. Anderson of Lexington, Va., who was shot three times, the third bullet shattering one of his kneecaps and leaving him permanently lame. Anderson later studied law at the University of Virginia and in the post-war period had a successful career as a lawyer in both Lexington and Richmond, serving at one time as attorney general of Virginia. He was for many years a member of the Board of Trustees of Washington and Lee, his alma mater, and its Rector for a period. The last surviving member of the Liberty Hall Volunteers, he died in 1930 (Ellen Glasgow Anderson, "Wounding and Hospital Care of William A. Anderson," *Virginia Magazine of History and Biography*, LXII [1954], 204–5).

other child, "another pledge of a dear wife's affection"; affectionately he wrote, using the religious language of the day, "God be praised for all his goodness to us & may his comforting grace be with you in the hour of suffering." Yearning to be with her, he could not understand why "a most strange & unnatural Providence" prevented their being together; the only thing left for them to do was "to trust in a gracious God and do [their] duty."[10]

"Where are [the] souls" of my dead comrades? was the question which perplexed and saddened Hugh White, who vowed thereafter to be more zealous in bringing sinners "to Christ, that if they die, they may sleep in him." Then, turning to some of the events of the battle, he said:

Every one was in imminent danger. Balls flew fast around and over us. . . . But brother James and I, though separated for a while during the first charge, soon met, and side by side, we passed through the remaining scenes of the day. We were unhurt. The killed on either side . . . will number hundreds. . . . But when we remember that in [the enemy's] attack on us, they were prepared in every way for advancing to Richmond, with having haversacks filled with provisions, preparations for rebuilding bridges, confidently expecting to march over us here, and pass on [triumphantly] to our capital—when we remember this, we may hope that their defeat will so dishearten them materially to check their progress. It was a full trial of their strength. They fought bravely . . . but they could not stand the charge of bayonets. . . . But who would not praise God for thus overthrowing those who, on this holy day, fought to execute their wicked purpose to crush those who sought to defend their liberties and homes. It was an awful Sabbath. . . . The scenes in which I am now engaged are very sad; yet the taste of victory, though bought with precious blood, is sweet. But to preach would be far better.[11]

[10] Near Manassas, July 23, 1861, White Letters.
[11] Hugh to father, Manassas, July 23, 1861, White, *White*, p. 51.

Writing to his young brother a week later, after describing the battle, Hugh concluded: "It was a great victory, but may I never pass through such a scene again. Death and hell may rejoice on the battlefield, but let man be silent. May God, who has won this victory for us, now give us peace."[12]

Reminiscing after the war, Lieutenant Lyle said the crash of the shells in the pines to the rear of the college company was "appalling." Although the boys lay flat as pancakes, they could hear the shells grazing their backs. The shrieking of the shells and the thunder of the guns would have filled "a warrior's soul with delight," but not being a warrior, the Lieutenant saw nothing especially entertaining in the performance. He admitted he was scared, had resorted to uttering all the prayers he knew, including "Now I lay me down to sleep," and had thrown in some of "the shorter catechism and scripture for good measure."[13] General Jackson, Lyle later recalled, sat "erect, as he rode in the charge. His head was uncovered as in reverence for the God of Battle. His only demonstration was to wave his hand forward as if urging his troops forward. His face was aflame with the light of battle. He looked the King of War. Homer would have named him 'the God-like one.' "[14]

In the charge of the brigade, the college company had tangled with the gaudy New York Zouaves. One member, Bronson Gwynn, had met in a hand-to-hand struggle with one of "those red-breeches fellows," who had jumped from behind a pine bush and made a lunge at Gwynn with his bay-

---

[12] Aug. 5, 1861, *ibid.*, p. 53.

[13] "Jackson's Guard," p. 186. "L.H.V." wrote that he believed the battle would "hasten the downfall of the usurper and tyrant [Lincoln] and inaugurate the bright era of Southern Independence, when peace and prosperity will reign over the land of the Sunny South" (Lexington *Gazette*, Aug. 4, 1861).

[14] Lyle, "Jackson's Guard," p. 189.

onet. The thrust was inaccurate, the bayonet only passing through his uniform between his arm and side. Extracting the bayonet from his clothes, "poor, little, stammering, stuttering" Gwynn cried out, "Now d-damn you, take that," and turned loose the contents of his musket on the Zouave's fez-covered head. Having seen that his shot was effective, he hastened to join in the charge.[15]

"You should see the battlefield," Ted Barclay, less concerned with sacred matters than the White brothers, wrote to his mother: "One side is dotted here and there with graves of our men, the other side you see covered with dead Yankees, horses, etc. . . . The cowardly dogs Yankees left their wounded and dead to be taken care of by our troops, but I would let them rot on the field before I would bury them. Ellsworth's pet lambs [New York Zouaves] were literally cut to pieces. There is no doubt that they are brave men and one of them said, 'they could fight men but not devils.' "[16]

[15] Jones, "First Manassas," Rockbridge *County News,* Feb. 2, 1911. The New York Zouaves was a company of New York firemen who were organized by Col. Elmer Ellsworth in the spring of 1861. One of Lincoln's youthful friends, Ellsworth had previously studied law in Lincoln's law office in Springfield, Ill., and had accompanied him on his inauguration trip to Washington. His regiment was one of the first to march into Virginia on May 24, 1861, and after having cut down a Confederate flag atop the hotel in Alexandria, Ellsworth was instantly killed by the irate proprietor, who in turn was shot to death by one of Ellsworth's soldiers. Ellsworth's body was taken to Washington and lay in state in the White House.

[16] Manassas, July 27, 1861, Barclay Letters. In the early days of the war, Mrs. Lizzie Redwood Goode and her mother and sister were detained in Washington en route to their home in Georgia. As they stayed on Pennsylvania Avenue, they witnessed the daily arrival of troops in the capital. Among the troops which attracted their attention was the New York Zouave Regiment with its gaudy uniforms. A few days after the battle of First Manassas, they were aroused one morning by a great commotion on the avenue, and, raising the window, Mrs. Goode saw the avenue filled with troops, artillery, wagons—all in great confusion. Recognizing some of the Zouaves, she opened the front door and asked one of them the cause of the confusion.

The battlefield also presented a sad sight to Lieutenant Lyle. From the pine ridge, where the Confederate batteries had stood, to the Henry House, the plateau was so thickly covered with dead Federals that one could walk the entire distance without touching the ground. One handsome young Yankee soldier who had fallen near the guns seemed to gaze with his eyes into the sky, and his appearance touched all who saw him. One satisfaction, at least, which Lyle derived from viewing this scene of carnage was the hope that the "Abolition oligarchy [at Washington]" which had sent the soldier to his death would answer "for a crime in a court from which there was no appeal."[17]

After the battle the victorious Confederates pursued the retreating enemy to the Potomac, and active campaigning ceased for several months in this theater of the war. General George B. McClellan, who had been summoned to Washington, superseded General McDowell and, devoting his time and energy to the reorganization and training of the Federal army, stood on the defensive until February 1862. Meanwhile General Joseph E. Johnston assumed command of the Confederate force in the vicinity of Centreville and, erecting fortifications, also took up a defensive position. For several months the two armies faced each other, confining their activities to drilling and occasional brushes between cavalry outposts.

Jackson's brigade, which was thereafter known as the Stonewall Brigade, temporarily established camp a short distance from the battlefield. This was called by the soldiers

---

After telling her of the Federal rout at Manassas, he exclaimed: "They told us those rebels wouldn't fight, but they fought like h---" (Lizzie Redwood Goode, "Wartime Scenes on Pennsylvania Avenue," *Confederate Veteran,* XXXI [1925], 378).

[17] Lyle, "Jackson's Guard," p. 203.

Camp Maggot for the impurity of the water and the stench
from the battle area. Ted Barclay complained that the drinking water came from puddles, a mixture of rain and branch
water. The most pleasant incident remembered about the
camp by Lieutenant Lyle was a religious service conducted
by the regimental chaplain, the Rev. Charles Miller of Christiansburg. It was very impressive to the Calvinist Lieutenant
to see men worshiping in a forest without "every fringe and
furbelow" tacked on God's ritual to detract from its spiritual-
ity. Although the chaplain was a fine Christian and a zealous
servant of his Master, he was not an eloquent speaker. In addition to his spiritual qualities, he was somewhat of an anti-
quarian with a mind stored with "curious rather than useful"
information. Another member of the congregation, Ted Barclay, comparing the sermon and surroundings with what he
had been accustomed to at Lexington, mused how different
the situation was in camp. While they worshiped the same
God, he still wished he could have been sitting in the Presbyterian Church at home, "hear [ing] old Dr. White."[18]

The brigade remained at Camp Maggot until early August, when it moved to Camp Harman, east of Centreville.
Finally, after being shifted to two other camp sites in that
area, the brigade went into winter quarters near Centreville,
where it stayed until its return to the Shenandoah Valley in
December 1861.[19]

To Captain White the change from Camp Maggot to
Camp Harman was like going "from Hell to Heaven." One of
his worries at Camp Harman was his wife's insistence that he
get a furlough home. Seeing no possibility of securing one at

[18] Casler, *Stonewall Brigade,* p. 40; "Jackson's Guard," p. 220; Ted to sister,
Aug. 6, 1861, Barclay Letters. Jackson's old brigade was not officially designated the "Stonewall Brigade" until May 30, 1863 (Chambers, *Jackson,* II,
450 n.).

[19] Casler, *Stonewall Brigade,* pp. 56–57.

the time, he feared an application would prejudice him with his superiors. Their friends at home, he informed his wife, had no idea of the rigor of military regulations. Applications for leave of absence, even for a day or two, had to be approved by all superiors, even by General Johnston. Furthermore, since the college boys' parents had entrusted their sons to him, he felt a deep sense of responsibility. Several members of the company were either sick or convalescing from wounds, and all required his attention. He was conscious of his duty to his family, yet he believed it could best be fulfilled "by standing up for his country. . . . My dear," he urged, "let us put on a cheerful courage and place our trust in the Lord God of Hosts who has the destinies of all of us in His hands."[20]

Later Captain White managed somehow to obtain a furlough home and, on his return to camp, he brought with him boxes of food for the boys from their parents, which he left, along with his baggage, at Manassas Junction. When he returned next morning to the Junction, "that rendezvous of roguery," he discovered that "some kind friend" had taken the baggage. In a subsequent letter, commenting on the boredom of camp life as he occasionally did, he told his wife that the most insignificant events in camp were often the most interesting, citing as an example the pleasure he got from listening to "the mellow music" of a fox race, which, conducted by a solitary hound, took place one morning at daybreak near the camp. In fact, he had such a dull existence that he begged his wife to write him about all the most trivial happenings at home.[21]

During this period of relative inactivity, Jackson did not

[20] Camp Harman, July 25, 1861, White Letters. Camp Harman was named in honor of Maj. John A. Harman, brigade quartermaster, who had selected the site.

[21] Same, Aug. 14, 1861, *ibid.*

permit the Stonewall Brigade to fall into lazy and slovenly habits. He discontinued the Saturday afternoon drill; otherwise he refused to relax discipline and constantly drilled the troops until they could move like a machine. Although Jackson was "rigid in his requirements but not more so than security required," Captain White said, his men would follow him anywhere; such was their confidence in his courage and ability. In fact, his reputation in the army ranked next to that of Generals Johnston and Beauregard.

The regimentation of army life was still irksome to the scholarly Captain White. "This life is constantly attended," he complained, "with as little cultivation as can be imagined, with nothing to read, for we cannot transport anything of the kind, and nothing to do but drill, drill, & obey orders. There is nothing of a man's individuality left." He pined to live once more "subject to nobody's orders in the full enjoyment of the society" of his family and friends. Realizing that he should not indulge in such feelings, as they would unfit him for his arduous duties, the Captain nevertheless found great satisfaction in airing his views to his wife. "How strange a thing is life!" the former professor of the classics philosophized. "How utterly worthless when considered in itself! Men desire life and cling to it, but what is it worth if devoid of its charms? Mere living is not worth a rush." He had even noticed that the morale of the boys, when oppressed by despondency, began to wilt, and he had to bring them up to their mark again. Despite these reflections, however, he asserted that his place of duty was with the defenders of Virginia; neither he nor his wife would be easy in conscience if he were at home.

Turning to the wholesome aspects of army experience, Captain White expressed the hope that the parents of the college boys were not excessively anxious about the morals of their sons. They had formed no habits of a vicious nature, such as profanity, drunkenness, and gambling—vices generally associated with military life. On the contrary, they read their Bibles more and behaved better than ever before. "If this life," Captain White observed, "makes Christian men of them, it will be a great blessing to their friends and country that they entered upon it." The routine drudgery and chores of camp life were beneficial to some of the members of the company, especially to young men like Watson Woods, "with all his fastidious notions of life." The Captain added that if his wife could see this lad "churning away over a pan of flour or making a march of 15 miles," she would realize "the infinite advantages" to him.[22]

In this respect Hugh White agreed with his brother. Having abandoned hopes of returning to the Seminary for the fall session, this earnest young man, though disappointed at his misfortune, uncomplainingly accepted it. He consoled himself with the thought that,

if my life is spared, I may derive benefit. Service in the army may give me the hardihood and experience which will help me in the ministry. You may smile at this and say it is easy to extract sweet from the bitter when misfortune is inevitable. So it is, and that is just what I am trying to do. It is no use to fret and destroy your peace and that of others, and do no one any good. So, if the winter is before me, I must contend with frost, and snow, and ice, instead of grappling with Hebrew roots and knotty points of theology.

With a warm fire in the daytime and blankets at night he would get along comfortably. Moreover, he stated that the

[22] Aug. 18, 1861, *ibid.* Watson Woods, a native of Buckingham County, was a student at Washington College in 1860–61. Captain White asked his wife to send him some newspapers as he had not seen any for over a month, and he added, "The whole company had a scramble over one of Harper's Magazines, dated 1855, a few days ago" (*ibid.*).

hardships of a soldier's life might fit him "the better, if need be, for being a missionary in the Arctic."[23]

But Ted Barclay, unlike his comrade Hugh White, was not concerned at that time about the effect of army life upon his future; instead he was writing about material things—food and clothes. The countryside around Centreville where the Stonewall Brigade was encamped, Ted acidly remarked, was so destitute of food that the rabbits and foxes carried haversacks; a poorer place in all Christendom could never have been found for a camp site. Yet he apparently was faring well, for he had just received two boxes of food from home, and they came in time to supplement army rations which were pretty slim, consisting mainly of "sea cracker," of scarcely any substance. He was doing well in the cooking line, for he boasted to his mother that since he had entered the service he had learned to make the "best coffee, bread, etc. etc."; but his proudest achievement in the culinary art was baking a blackberry pie, and "it does very well," he admitted. In fact he was so proficient that when he came home from the war he wanted his mother to appoint him "the chief cook in the cooking department." While his clothes were in fair condition, except for a hole in a pair of pants which he could mend, he reported his need of a pair of shoes, as those which his mother had recently sent had been "kindly" taken by "some gentleman without leave or license."[24]

Although the college boys, like all soldiers, grumbled about

[23] To his father, near Centreville, Aug. 31, 1861, White, *White*, pp. 56–57.

[24] Camp Harman, Aug. 8, 1861, Barclay Letters. Captain White wrote his wife some days later that Ted was not feeling well, and although he did not have any fever neither did he have any appetite. The captain had persuaded Ted to eat some of "the nice beef tongue and crackers" which she had sent him. Yet Ted was still low in spirit imagining himself suffering from brain fever, an ailment which had caused the recent death of his close friend, Edward Mitchell (Camp Harman, Aug. 27, 1861, White Letters).

rations which at times were "tough and trying," as Lieutenant Lyle said, they got along very well, especially with
the boxes which came from their parents. One morning when
the commissary issued some "rotten" beef which had been left
out in the rain all night, the boys kicked up such a row that
General Jackson appointed a board to investigate, and it declared the beef "worthless, being infested with maggots and
fit only to be burned."[25]

Jackson's interest in the welfare of his troops was shown
in other ways. In the regions around Camp Harman the
"honest" farmers in their greed for gain were practicing extortion in the sale of their products to the soldiers. As soon as
this came to the General's attention, he appointed a committee of regimental officers, Colonels James F. Preston, James
W. Allen, and Kenton F. Harper, to fix "a tariff of prices"
for articles brought into camp by the hucksters. The prices
for a few items were: butter, twenty-five cents a pound; eggs,
twenty cents a dozen; green corn, one and one-half cents an
ear; potatoes, twenty-five cents a peck; cabbage, two to five
cents a head; beans, twenty-five cents a peck; chickens,
eighteen to twenty-five cents each; ducks, twenty-five cents
each; lamb, eight cents a pound; skimmed milk and butter-
milk, three cents a pint; and peaches, eight to ten cents a
pound. The administration of this effort at price control was
placed upon the brigade officer of the day, who was stationed at the brigade guardhouse where the hucksters were
required to bring their wagons. The control was effective,
Lieutenant Lyle declared.[26]

[25] "Jackson's Guard," p. 223.
[26] Ibid., pp. 228–29. The cook of the officers' mess of the college company
was Black Pete, a free Negro, whom Captain White had brought along
from Lexington. He was an excellent forager and cook, and although he was
provided money by the mess to purchase provisions Lieutenant Lyle said he
would not "swear" he got them by purchase (ibid., p. 249).

Price control apparently did not apply to goods sold by the sutlers, who generally did not deal in agricultural products. The sutler who served the college company at Camp Harman was known as "Old Short-Grass." One morning he initiated the boys into the "mysteries" of green tomato pie. They had been reared on all kinds of pies, cobblers, and tarts, but never before had they heard of this "plebian pastry," and when it was offered for sale their comment was, "well, 'Old Short-Grass' must be hard put to for pie-stuff."[27]

At Camp Harman the Stonewall Brigade enforced the most rigid sanitary regulations. The tents were struck several times weekly to permit the sun to reach the floor, and the camp was policed daily by an officer who saw that all refuse matter was burned. Consequently, Lyle asserted, the brigade suffered less mortality from diseases in the summer and fall of 1861 than did other brigades whose commanders were not as strict in this respect as Jackson.[28]

On September 6, 1861, Captain J. J. White resigned his commission and returned to civilian life. He had been considering this action for some time because of military hardships which had impaired his health and also because of the insistence of some of his friends that he resume his teaching at Washington College, the trustees having announced in the late summer that the college would reopen in the fall. Closely interwoven with the latter reason was the agitation in certain quarters of Virginia that all college students in the service who had not completed their education be discharged and permitted to continue their studies until graduation.

Captain White had first intimated the possibility of his retirement on August 10, 1861, writing, "My opinion now is that I will have to throw up my commission sooner or later,

[27] *Ibid.*, p. 229.
[28] *Ibid.*, p. 231.

as the effect of such an evening and day [when he spent a miserable afternoon and night suffering from a severe cold] is eventually pernicious." A few days later, he told his wife he had been suffering "a great deal," though his general health was pretty good. On August 26 he was sick again and he attributed his indisposition to "wholesale" exposure. When other regimental company officers were "asleep & comfortable" at nighttime in their tents, he constantly went the rounds of his company to see that all was right. He then related to his wife his experience during the night following the battle of First Manassas. On this occasion, since there were not enough tents to afford shelter for the college boys from the rain, the Captain spent the entire night sitting up in the rain. When one of the company's junior officers discovered the Captain's exposed condition, he crawled out of his tent and insisted that Captain White take his place. He did not allude to this incident, the Captain assured his wife, to parade his sense of duty, much less to broadcast it, but only to let her know that he had done what appeared to be his duty.[29]

Although Captain White approved of the trustees' action in reopening the college, it placed him in a quandary—whether to resign his commission and return to the college or continue in the service. Had it not been for his responsibility to the college company in the present crisis, he would gladly have left the army. While he did not "wish to be *in the way* by being *out of the way* in his relationship to the college," yet he was reluctant to resign the professorship. Instead he preferred that the trustees declare it vacant, and he suggested that Professor Carter J. Harris could then doubtless perform his own and Captain White's college duties; in all probability there would not be much to do anyhow. But after all, the college authorities must consider what was best

[29] Camp Harman, Aug. 10, 14, 26, 1861, White Letters.

for the institution and leave him out of the question for the present.[30]

In the meantime, on August 20, 1861, the Board of Trustees of Washington College, in a letter to the "proper authorities" at Richmond, requested "the discharge of the students of Washington College who had not completed their course of study at college and who are now in the military service of the Confederacy, from further service until their education is completed."[31] This request was eventually rejected, and Captain White confessed he was not surprised, because there were so many other young college men like the Liberty Hall Volunteers in the service. After all, their war experience was not a total waste; it had some beneficial features, as Providence appeared to be giving them "a salutary training by this life."[32]

Active in the cause of keeping the doors of Southern institutions of higher learning open were the Rev. Dr. Robert L. Dabney, former professor of theology at the Union Theological Seminary and chaplain in one of the Virginia regiments, and Professor W. H. McGuffey of the University of Virginia. In a lengthy article in the *Central Presbyterian,* published at Richmond, the learned professors insisted it was of utmost importance for the South to maintain its colleges, universities, and seminaries during the war. Otherwise, where would it get its future teachers, doctors, ministers of the gospel, jurists, and other professional men? Hence

[30] Same, Aug. 21, 1861, *ibid.*

[31] Minutes of the Board of Trustees, Washington College, Aug. 20, 1861, (MS in the McCormick Library, Washington and Lee University). It was not until July 3, 1863, that the rejection of the application was recorded in the board minutes. Apparently no board meeting was held between the two dates. Captain White approved of the application for deferment of the students until graduation (J. J. White to wife, Camp Harman, Aug. 21, 1861, White Letters).

[32] To his wife, Camp Harman, Aug. 23, 1861, *ibid.*

it was vital to the "honor and safety" of the Southern Confederacy that during the war it should raise up a supply of educated men.

Professors Dabney and McGuffey were especially concerned about the wartime closing of the seminaries in Virginia; it would be a fatal blow to the cause of religion. There was already a dearth of ministers, they asserted, pointing out that in the Southern Presbyterian Church one-half of the "ministerial laborers" had been "borrowed" from the North. Furthermore, the war situation, they contended, was not so dire at that time as to justify the enrollment of youth at the expense of education; the prowess of the enemy did not warrant such a tribute. And they were confident that the Confederacy had the resources and ability both to hurl back "the insolent assailants" without the use of its "precious youth" and at the same time to carry on "with undisturbed equanimity all the high functions of civilized society." The students could best demonstrate their patriotism and courage by putting aside their guns and coming back to the classrooms, wherever they could honestly do it.[33]

[33] R. L. Dabney and W. H. McGuffey, "The Interest of Education," *Central Presbyterian*, Aug. 31, 1861. Professor McGuffey, a native of Ohio and an ordained Presbyterian minister, came to the University of Virginia in 1845 as a professor of philosophy—the first minister to be given professorial rank at Jefferson's university. He is best known as the author of a series of readers. As a matter of fact, neither Washington College, the University of Virginia, nor the Theological Seminary closed their doors during the war, but after the passage of the Conscription Act of 1862 they had only a few students, the seminary having only two (Thomas C. Johnson, *Life and Letters of Dr. Robert Lewis Dabney* [Richmond, 1903], p. 273). Although Captain White agreed in general with Dabney's and McGuffey's views, he recognized that "war [was] an imperious business and [acknowledged] no conditions" (J. J. White to wife, Camp Harman, Aug. 22, 1861, White Letters). Lieutenant Lyle stated that the college boys regretted "this move [to have them sent back to college]. The other companies in the brigade were disposed to make fun of us, as if we were sick of the service" (Lyle, "Jackson's Guard," p. 216).

In addition to Dr. Dabney, Captain White had other friends who were anxious for him to return to the classroom: Doctors J. Staige Davis and James L. Cabell of the medical faculty of the University of Virginia and Major Elisha Franklin Paxton of the Stonewall Brigade. Dr. Dabney, a firm believer in divine intervention in human affairs, remarked to Captain White, in a conversation at Camp Harman, that his "ill-health" was God's "judgment" for his desertion of the classroom, which had resulted in the "breaking up" of Washington College. In relating this conversation to his wife, Captain White wrote that Dr. Dabney's remark was in character, because he "could not have said anything else; he thinks I should go home & get to my books." While the Captain was undecided about hastening back to the college, he felt he might find it difficult to remain at home, notwithstanding the ties binding him there. Moreover, it would be "dreadfully hard" to leave the company at a time when it was trained and had made a name for itself in the regiment and brigade; his leaving might affect its morale.[34]

Several days previous to the conversation with Dr. Dabney, Major Frank Paxton had called upon Captain White and insisted upon his "packing up & going home," arguing that he owed it to himself. Paxton then mentioned another matter which was doubtless embarrassing to the captain; he reported that there was a rumor of "uneasiness" among the parents of the college boys about the casualties suffered at First Manassas. Captain White, aware of the rumor, was worried about it, and he told his wife he knew he should not feel that way about the matter. He had always tried to do

[34] To his wife, Camp Harman, Aug. 26, 1861, White Letters. Dabney's remark that Captain White was responsible for the closing of Washington College in early June 1861 is unfair. The wholesale desertion of the students was the cause. Later Dabney resigned his chaplaincy and returned to Farmville.

his duty according to his ability, leaving the consequences to God. Yet he found himself sighing to be relieved of the responsible trust of the company. This rumor was another argument used by Paxton in endeavoring to convince Captain White to tender his resignation as "a necessary step towards accomplishing [the parents'] wishes."

In the meantime, a letter came from Dr. Staige Davis who wrote: "I can hardly think that patriotism requires you to continue in a position which your duty to yourself should have prevented your assuming. I feel sure that Dr. Cabell's opinion on the subject would coincide with mine, but he is so overwhelmed with our hospital labors that I am reluctant to trouble him with a conference." "How distressing my situation," agonized Captain White after relating the pressures to which he had been subjected. "I must come to a painful conclusion it appears—namely to resign & let things take their course."[35]

On August 27, 1861, after much reflection, Captain White informed his wife that he had made up his mind to resign but that he would remain at his post until the resignation was approved. While his duty now seemed clear, he could not repress his regrets at parting with his boys, and he was gratified at both the confidence which they had shown him and their appreciation of his exertions in their behalf. But he warned his wife that, after resting at home, she should not be surprised to see him again in some branch of the service.

One matter which still engaged Captain White's attention before his retirement was the question of his successor, and he wrote Professor A. L. Nelson that he thought First Sergeant Henry Ruffner Morrison would make an excellent captain and that First Corporal Givens B. Strickler merited promo-

[35] *Ibid.* A large Confederate hospital was located at the University of Virginia during the war.

tion to the position to be vacated by Ruffner's promotion. He had discussed, he told his wife, his proposal with General Jackson, who was pleased with so propitious a solution. Jackson also expressed his willingness to give the company a testimonial of "gallantry & good conduct" should the request of the Board of Trustees of Washington College be approved by the authorities at Richmond.[36]

Captain White next consulted First Lieutenant Lyle and Second Lieutenant Sherrard about the proposed changes in the company command, and, though they normally would have been promoted—Lyle to the captaincy and Sherrard to the first lieutenancy—they willingly acquiesced in the proposal. Just how this came about Lieutenant Lyle later explained:

An old bladder trouble [which had plagued Captain White] returned and forced him out of the service. He was loathe to leave the boys whom their mothers had committed to his care. His resignation would leave matters in the fix they were in before we left Lexington, their children in the care of [beardless] boys [Lyle and Sherrard]. To relieve [Captain White's] embarrassment Lieutenant Sherrard and I consented to waive our right of promotion and let H. R. Morrison, an alumnus of [Washington] College, and a Rockbridge County man with beard on his face, in whose steadiness the good women had ever confidence, be elected captain.

The other regimental officers thought it strange that Lyle and Sherrard had submitted to the promotion of a sergeant over them, and their friends at home, who did not understand the delicate situation, were critical of the treatment they had received. Lyle and Sherrard were willing, however, to sacrifice their personal ambition in order to allow Captain White to

[36] Camp Harman, Aug. 27, 1863, *ibid.*

leave the army happily and to pacify "those anxious mothers back home, whose heartstrings [they] had heard when they gave their sons to the service."[37]

Captain White's resignation, which was not accepted until early September 1861, was deeply regretted by the college boys, and by none more than his young brother Hugh. Between the two brothers there had always been mutual affection and respect, and it had been strengthened by their common war experience. It so happened that Captain White left Camp Harman a few days before the Stonewall Brigade was shifted from this camp to another site near Fairfax Court House. Hugh found the new encampment a very pleasant place, although he had come to look upon Camp Harman as a home. After his brother departed, the old camp had become lonesome to Hugh. Every tree in the grove, every pebble, in fact everything about the camp, was associated with his brother, and for that reason he was glad to leave Camp Harman, certain that the change of scenery would make him happier.[38]

The tenor of Hugh White's letters did not generally reflect much discontent with the daily trials of war; on the contrary,

[37] Lyle, "Jackson's Guard," p. 225. Hugh White was promoted to second corporal, the position vacated by Givens B. Strickler.

[38] Hugh to father, near Fairfax Station, Sept. 16, 1861, White, *White*, p. 57. At Camp Harman, resolutions were adopted by the Liberty Hall Volunteers in September 1861, expressing regret that "physical affliction had rendered it necessary for our late highly esteemed and beloved Captain to resign" (Lexington *Gazette*, Sept. 26, 1861). In a letter to his brother written a week after he had left the company, Hugh lamented his "absence much. I have not the pleasure of sitting now in your tent and enjoying your company. I feel lonesome. But this will wear off in a few days." He was happy his brother was out of the service both on account of the status of his health and of his responsibility to his young family (near Centreville, Sept. 12, 1861, White, *White*, pp. 54–55. After his resignation Captain White returned to Washington College, where he resumed his teaching. He continued as a member of the faculty until his death on April 23, 1893.

he accepted them with Christian resignation. But on one occasion he did complain about the harsh discipline of military life. At sunrise on September 6, 1861, when Hugh arose from his hard bed, he remembered that the day was his twenty-first birthday, that he was legally a "freeman." Yet in reality he was not as free as he had been before he entered the service, for he was fettered by military regulations on all sides and unable to move freely about without a pass from someone. And this was only one instance in which his freedom was restricted. Under parental discipline he had been free to roam the woods and fields at will with no one to prevent his full enjoyment of their delights. Hugh wryly observed: "If that was servitude and this freedom, let me always live like a slave." Doubtless gladdening his father's heart, this devoted son then declared that, instead of desiring freedom from paternal control, he was more disposed than ever to do its bidding and to follow in the path which his father had marked out for him. Hugh stated that he would always be grateful to his father for having inculcated in his children a spirit of independence by encouraging them to make their own decisions in many matters. To Hugh, his father was the exemplar, and he never wished to be free either from his control or advice.[39]

So interested was Hugh in the religious welfare of his comrades that he acted unofficially as company chaplain, conducting a daily prayer meeting. One pleasure which Hugh and the college boys eagerly anticipated was a visit from Hugh's father, Dr. W. S. White. "How refreshing to us it would be. . . . I am certain you would be gratified, and we benefitted," Hugh joyfully told him. He wished his father to come particularly for the sake of the company's members who, though they faithfully read the Bible and constantly attended the prayer meetings, were not affiliated with any

[39] Near Centreville, Sept. 6, 1861, White, *White*, p. 60.

church. "For their sakes as well as my own," Hugh implored him to come.[40]

To his sister, Mrs. Wade of Christiansburg, Virginia, who was visiting in Lexington in the fall of 1861, Hugh urged that she not let his absence detract from the pleasure she was deriving from seeing their parents. He insisted that she ease "her heart of the burden of anxiety" she felt for him. Apparently, he said, his loved ones thought he was "homeless, friendless—pinched with cold and hunger—cast forth as food for the invading enemy." While he admitted he was often deprived of many comforts and subjected to many hardships, yet he insisted that he also had many joys with all his sorrows. Assuring his sister that exposure had not injured his health, he added that he often awakened from his bed of earth and pillow of rocks feeling more refreshed than if he had slept in a feather bed.[41]

In the new encampment in the vicinity of Fairfax Court House there was no relaxation from drilling in the Stonewall Brigade. Instead Jackson insisted that it was the duty of both officers and men to prepare themselves for future battles, and he held his brigade to a strict performance. As the boys grew tired of the repeated executions of the company evolutions, Lieutenant Lyle, in an attempt to vary their exercises, got hold of a Zouave drill manual and trained the company with it. Some of the boys who had crossed bayonets with the New York Zouave Regiment at First Manassas had been impressed by their expertness with the bayonet; therefore they eagerly took to the new drill and were soon proficient in its execu-

[40] Near Fairfax Court House, Sept. 16, 1861, *ibid.*, p. 58. Dr. White later visited the Stonewall Brigade, staying at General Jackson's headquarters. He and the general attended the daily prayer meeting held by the college boys, both participating in it (*ibid.*; Lyle, "Jackson's Guard," p. 285).

[41] Centreville, Sept. 1861(?), White, *White*, p. 59.

tion. One day when the boys were making the bayonets "fairly hum," General Jackson rode by. Reining up his horse, he sat looking for some minutes at the drill, seemingly pleased with the performance. As his headquarters were located on a knoll overlooking the drill ground, often after that he would sit in his tent door and watch the boys in their Zouave drill.[42]

While the brigade was quartered near Fairfax Court House, the Liberty Hall Volunteers were assigned to guard duty at General Gustavus W. Smith's headquarters, an assignment which relieved them from daily drill. The company, Lyle later boasted, was in "mighty high military society and no ordinary every-day soldiers." Since only a few men and a noncommissioned officer were at any one time on guard duty, the rest either assisted the adjutant general of Smith's division in his clerical chores or lounged around headquarters. Recalling this scene, Lyle remarked, "You would have thought that [the General] was the father of a large family of boys."[43] Writing to his sister about the duties of the headquarters guard, Sergeant Joseph T. Chester said:

Your ideas about a General's body guard certainly are original. Did you suppose that everywhere he goes he has a great crowd of men following around him to keep the "boogers" off? If so you are certainly mistaken. On the contrary unless you are acquainted, you can only distinguish a general from any private citizen by his uniform. They generally have their headquarters at some house where there is a good deal of property to be protected from thieving soldiers—*a sentinel is necessary to watch it*. There are always a great many couriers & dispatch bearers constantly arriving. A

[42] Lyle, "Jackson's Guard," p. 272.

[43] *Ibid.*, p. 272; Serg. Joseph T. Chester to sister, near Winchester, Nov. 13, 1861 (letter in the possession of Judge Harry J. Lemley, Hope, Ark., who graciously gave the author a copy). G. W. Smith, a West Point-trained Kentuckian and a veteran of the Mexican War, was one of Gen. Joseph E. Johnston's divisional commanders.

sentinel is necessary to direct them where to carry them. Prisoners are constantly being brought in. A guard is necessary to watch them until they can be otherwise disposed of. This is the kind of duty the *body guard* has to attend to. They have no roll calls or drills or picket duty or anything of the kind to do, and can be detailed to no regimental *extra* duty, such as *digging ditches, throwing up breastworks* and divers other duties worth shirking when there is an opportunity. There are generally eight or nine posts to guard at once, and the sentinels are divided into three reliefs. Each relief has to stand guard two hours. It is the Corporal's duty to take charge of the guard—to march each relief around promptly at the right hour and instruct them in regard to their duty and see that they perform it. There are other privileges and exemptions pertaining to the honorable office which I have not time to give now.[44]

Shortly after the boys had gone on duty at Smith's headquarters, the Confederate army was pulled back from Fairfax Court House to Centreville, where it remained until February 1862. Here it fell to the lot of the company to act as provost guard on the first night. It was a night never to be forgotten; the company was busily occupied keeping Wheat's Battalion of Louisiana Tigers and the First Kentucky Regiment from scrapping continuously. It developed that they had been feuding before, and to prevent this they had been kept several miles apart. This precaution, however, had been overlooked when the army took up quarters at Centreville, and the two units found themselves neighbors in the new encampment. During the night groups from the two commands, fortified with whiskey, encountered each other in the street which paralleled the pike and engaged in a rock battle. The stones striking the frame houses on the street resounded with noises sounding like horses kicking the side of a barn. The college

[44] Chester to sister, *ibid*.

company, hurrying to the scene of the fray in double-quick time, soon scattered the combatants with the exception of a few who were either too drunk or injured to get away.[45]

General Smith immediately ordered the college company to confiscate and destroy the supply of liquor, and the next day several barrels were located in the cellar of a house occupied by a sutler. He vowed he did not have "a drop" and was not selling "the ardent." Searching the premises, the boys discovered several barrels and, although they looked as if they contained flour, they were filled with bottled whiskey. The boys seized the barrels and rolled them down to a small stream, where they broke the bottles and emptied their "inspiring contents." The town was full of soldiers, and they lined the banks of the stream, "kneeling and drinking inspiration from its tide of grog." A few of the members of the company who had "a nose for whiskey" managed to salvage some bottles, which they stowed in their tents. Black Pete, the officers' mess boy, had not overlooked their interest, for he put away a large supply—"quite a lot"—in their tent. When the news got around in the brigade camp, the tent was overrun with visitors "variously afflicted." There was an epidemic, Lieutenant Lyle remembered, of "belly-ache and our remedy was sought after more than any medicine in the camp. The surgeons thought their occupation gone, and if our supply had lasted they might have resigned."[46]

[45] *Ibid.*, pp. 272–73. Wheat's Battalion of Louisiana Tigers was organized by Maj. Roberdeau Wheat, a native of Virginia, in New Orleans at the beginning of the war. A group of daredevils, rakish-looking in gaudy uniforms and much feared by the civilian population, they were ferocious in battle and disorderly in camp. When passing through Lynchburg to the front in 1861, they took over the city and only a posse of citizens was able to subdue them (Charles L. Dufour, *Gentle Tiger: The Gallant Life of Robert Roberdeau Wheat,* Baton Rouge, 1957).

[46] "Jackson's Guard," p. 273.

At Centreville, while the boys missed the companionship of their friends in the Fourth Virginia, their duties at headquarters were less exacting and more pleasant than the "beastly" drill and picket duty. As only a few men were needed as sentinels and the orderly sergeant looked after them, the captain and the lieutenants had nothing to do but "play the gentlemen" with staff officers. Since most of the families had gone to other areas in Virginia, there were not many girls left. One family, however, had not fled—the Utterbacks; their home was frequented by the college boys because of the presence of Miss Penelope Utterback, "a great toast" among them.[47]

The camp was overrun, during this period of relative cessation from military operations, by the wives of both officers and privates. It was the season of dinner parties, especially at officers' messes. Lieutenant Lyle later said he could never forget the delicious odor of browned turkey which came on one occasion from the outdoor table of his mess and which made the passing soldiers sniff hungrily as they gazed upon the seasonal bird.[48]

Hugh White, unlike Lieutenant Lyle, was not concerned with the delicacies of the table. He deplored the lack of a house of worship, which deprived him of "the delights of a Sanctuary." One day of sacred rest in a church, he told his mother, would be "a feast of fat things for [his] soul. We are entirely cut off from the reviving influence of social worship," its only substitute being a nightly prayer meeting. He implored his mother, in her anxiety for his bodily comforts, not to forget his soul. The atmosphere of military life, he lamented, was not conducive to soul saving, being as hostile to religion as the weather was wintry. Though cast down, Hugh

[47] *Ibid.*, p. 284.
[48] *Ibid.*, p. 293.

assured his mother that he would not despair, that he was
"still trust [ing] in God."

Among the distinguished visitors to General Johnston's
army at this time was Virginia's Governor John Letcher, who
was honored by a review of the Virginia troops. After the review the Virginia regiments were massed in front of a redoubt, and Letcher, standing on the embankment, addressed
them and then presented to the colonels of each regiment a
Virginia flag. Describing the scene as exciting, Hugh White
said that the faces of the soldiers, who were dressed in their
new uniforms, showed their hearts were both brave and
cheerful.[49]

[49] Hugh to father, Centreville, Nov. 1, 1861, White, *White*, p. 64.

Three

HEADQUARTERS GUARD

O N October 7, 1861, General Jackson was promoted to the rank of major general and was soon ordered to Winchester to take command of the Valley district, which embraced the section of Virginia between the Blue Ridge and the Allegheny Mountains. Before he departed from Centreville the Stonewall Brigade was drawn up in line near its encampment, and Jackson and his staff rode into its midst. He gazed into the eyes of the men and, after a few moments of silence, bade them farewell. His parting words were:

In the army of the Shenandoah you were the First Brigade; in the army of the Potomac you were the First Brigade; in the second corps of this army you are the First Brigade; you are the First Brigade in the affections of your General; and I hope by your future deeds and bearing you will be handed down to posterity as the First Brigade in our second War of Independence. Farewell.[1]

[1] Chambers, *Jackson*, I, 404. Jackson's immediate successor as commander of the Stonewall Brigade was Gen. Richard Brooke Garnett. A Virginian and a graduate of West Point, Garnett had served in the U.S. Army after his

This separation from his brigade was, however, to be of short duration. Accompanied by a portion of his staff, Jackson departed on November 4, 1861, for Winchester, and upon his arrival at the new post found the Valley district defenseless except for a small and ineffective force of militia. Informed that a Federal advance upon Winchester was imminent, Jackson dispatched Lieutenant Colonel J. T. L. Preston to Richmond with a request for reinforcements. The War Department, anticipating the need for veteran troops in this important area, had already ordered the Stonewall Brigade and General W. W. Loring's force of six thousand men to the Valley district. Never again until Jackson's death was the Stonewall Brigade separated from him. He had been its first commander; now it was a part of his newly created division; and later when his command was enlarged to include a corps, the Stonewall Brigade would still look to him for leadership.[2]

The Liberty Hall Volunteers, on detached service at General Smith's headquarters, did not muster with the brigade to hear Jackson's farewell address. They were dismayed at the thought of being separated from him, and their reaction was reflected by Hugh White, who wrote that no man could replace Jackson in the confidence and love of the college boys. Hugh had learned to trust him implicitly and had found that he could approach General Jackson in perfect freedom, knowing he would receive a kind and attentive hearing.[3] The boys welcomed, however, the prospect of leaving the barren

---

graduation to the outbreak of the war. Lieut. Col. J. T. L. Preston called him "a good soldier and a pleasant man. It was my office to take him out and introduce him to brigade. . . . Nevertheless the brigade ought to be commanded by one of its own colonels; they have made their own glory, and a stranger should not have been made to share it" (Elizabeth Preston Allan, *Life and Letters of Margaret Junkin Preston* [New York, 1903], p. 125; hereafter cited as Allan, *Preston*).

[2] Chambers, *Jackson*, I, 403–17.

[3] Hugh to father, Centreville, Oct. 1861, White, *White*, p. 61. This letter

fields and piney woods around Manassas Junction and setting foot again on the beautiful and fruitful Valley—"a glorious country to fight for." At the same time they were reluctant to leave General Smith's headquarters and its pleasant life, and neither did they like the idea of resuming the unpleasant regimental duties such as drill, picketing, and guard duty.[4]

When General Smith was informed that the Stonewall Brigade had been ordered by the Secretary of War to report to General Jackson in the Valley, he intervened, Sergeant Chester reported, and endeavored to get Colonel James F. Preston, temporary commander of the brigade,

to remain until he could write to the Secretary of War and have us permanently detailed; but as we were in Col. Preston's regiment, and he did not wish to lose us, he pretended that he did not feel at liberty to do so. When General Smith found that he could not retain us he sent for Captain [H. R.] Morrison, and told him that we had attended to our duty as well as it could have been done, that he had placed the most implicit confidence in us & had given himself *no* uneasiness about anything which we had been appointed to do, that he had found us every one to be *perfect gentlemen,* that now perhaps a company would be sent him that he could not trust, and a great many things very complimentary to us. He then wrote a letter to Gen. Jackson and gave it to Captain Morrison to deliver, complimenting us very highly & recommending us to him as a body guard.[5]

Marching from Centreville to Manassas Junction, the Stonewall Brigade bivouacked without shelter at the Junction in a cold November rain. The college boys, missing the com-

must have been written in late October because the order assigning Jackson to the Valley district was issued Oct. 28, 1861. Jackson left for Winchester on Nov. 4, 1861.

[4] Same, Winchester, Nov. 1861, *ibid.,* p. 67; Lyle, "Jackson's Guard," p. 295.

[5] Serg. Joseph T. Chester to sister, near Winchester, Nov. 13, 1861.

fortable accommodations at General Smith's headquarters, kept dry by the roaring fires made from worm-fence rails, notwithstanding orders against burning them. Their food consisted of scraps which they had brought along or had begged from the inhabitants along the wayside. These discomforts, however, were soon forgotten the next morning, a clear and bright Sunday, when they entrained in freight cars for Strasburg.

The journey from the Junction to Strasburg was not as exciting, according to Lyle, as the one the brigade had made the previous July 19 when it had raced to the assistance of General Beauregard. The countryside was now quiet, and there were no "bevies of beauties" to wave and cheer the soldiers. A cold chilly wind was blowing, and the beautiful green landscape of July was now brown and seared.[6] The brigade arrived at Strasburg about sunset, and after devouring their scanty rations the men bedded down in the cars and were soon asleep, most of them having forgotten it was the Sabbath. But not Hugh White, whose mind that day dwelt on sacred subjects, especially on the services which he had previously enjoyed at home and in which he longed again to participate. When the train pulled into Strasburg, the first sound Hugh had heard was the ringing of a church bell, and though he wished to obey its summons he knew he could not.[7]

The next morning the brigade left Strasburg and reached Winchester at sundown, the first long march—fifteen miles— the college boys had taken for some time. The night was bleak and cold when the brigade made camp in a forest of oaks two miles south of the town. The company's wagon was far in the rear, and until it came up the bivouac was cheerless.[8]

[6] "Jackson's Guard," p. 302.

[7] To his father, near Winchester, Nov. 1861, White, *White*, p. 67.

[8] *Ibid.;* Lyle, "Jackson's Guard," p. 302. Sergeant Chester also described the return journey from Manassas Junction to Winchester: "When we re-

During the months of November and December 1861, when the fields were too muddy for drill, the college boys devised many expedients to entertain themselves. One of the popular amusements was the old cakewalk with many variations such as "fling a backstep," "cut the pigeon-wing," and the "double-shuffle." This form of entertainment was confined strictly to the soldiers.

Some of the boys also sought amusement in the houses of the neighboring farmers, who were generally of German de-

---

turned [from General Smith's headquarters] to the regiment we immediately took up our line of march to Manassas Junction. The road in some places was almost impassably muddy, and to make it worse we had not gone more than five miles (half way) before it commenced raining. When we arrived at the Junction we were perfectly saturated. While a cold northeast wind commenced blowing, you can guess how unpleasant a situation we [were] placed in, when I tell you that no cars were in readiness for us, and there we had to wait in that condition, all night, in an old field, with not even a tree within a mile for protection, without a mouthful of supper or breakfast next morning. I did not sleep a wink, but sat up all night by a fire, made of a widow's fence, trying to dry as fast as the rain would wet me. The cars came down from Strasburg about 9 o'clock the next day, such as they were—old baggage cars with nothing but a nasty floor to sit on. We were packed in as thick as we *could stand* and such a trip as we had to Strasburg, where we arrived at 6 o'clock I leave to your imagination to describe. Such a hungry set of boys as we had there, I hope never to see again. We had not had a bite to eat since breakfast the day before, with two days march on top of that. We dispatched our cook up town who spoke for supper for our mess at a hotel for a dollar apiece and had to slip off like runaways to eat that. Next morning at 8 o'clock we took up a line of march for Winchester 18 miles distant and arrived at our present encampment about dark. *Strange to say* I have survived it all, with nothing more serious resulting than *extreme fatigue* & very sore feet. I would have suffered for something to eat on the march to Winchester if it had not been for my cook who would run ahead and have something to eat at every little town on the road (Joseph T. Chester to sister, near Winchester, Nov. 13, 1861). The men of the Stonewall Brigade were anxious after reaching Winchester to go immediately into winter quarters; that is, to erect huts. "Our General Jackson doubtless thinks it unhealthy," wrote "L.H.V.," "for us to proceed thither now, but first [we must] try the virtues of tents, wind, and rain" (Lexington *Gazette*, Nov. 28, 1861).

scent. It was the season of making apple butter, which the
farmers called "black-spread" to distinguish it from "white-
spread," or ordinary butter. The soldiers were expected to
assist in stirring the apple butter while it cooked, as well as to
frolic. The stirring was done with a paddle held by a soldier
and a daughter of the house; the two faced each other and
as they gripped the paddle, it was not considered "disorderly"
for the soldier to kiss the maiden under her sunbonnet as
compensation for his assistance.[9] The apple butter, generally
eaten on bread, was highly prized by the soldiers. When a
soldier sauntered up to a farm house, Lieutenant Lyle wrote,
and asked for a snack with "the oft-told lie of having nothing
to eat for three days," the good house "frau" would ask if he
wished "white-spread" or "black-spread" on his bread. He
generally took both, Lyle said, adding that the Confederate
was a genius in asking for a cup of water, for something to eat,
and for a night's lodging all in one breath: "Madam, can I get
a drink of water, I'm so hungry I don't know where I'll sleep
tonight."[10]

Much hilarity was evoked by such games as "blind man,"
"pussy in the corner," and "Sister Phoebe"—the favorite of
the young people. In the last, the boys, marching around
young ladies seated in a circle, sang:

> Sister Phoebe, how merry were we,
> When we sat under yon juniper tree;
> Yon juniper tree, hi-oh!
> Put the hat on her head, and keep her warm,
> And take a sweet kiss, it will do her no harm,
> Do her no harm, I know.[11]

Shortly after the Stonewall Brigade returned to the Valley,
Ted Barclay went home on a furlough. When he returned to

[9] Lyle, "Jackson's Guard," p. 305.
[10] *Ibid.*, p. 310.
[11] *Ibid.*

camp, he brought back a box of food, and he arrived just as the company was drawing its pay for the past two months. Feeling rich, Ted filled his canteen with rye whiskey, and he and his messmates proceeded to devour the contents of the box of food, finishing off the turkey in one sitting. The contents of the canteen were also very acceptable and, judging from the way his friends were consuming it, Ted said he would soon have to refill the canteen, this time with medicinal whiskey.

Commenting on the weather, Ted remarked that "it was as cold as charity in a big city," but he added that they were prepared for this as the tents had fireplaces and were as warm as a room. While chatting with his tentmates, Ted stuck one of his legs too near the fire and burned his pants. The other boys teasingly told him he should be put on double guard duty for his carelessness and "I suppose you agree with them," Ted twitted his mother. Reminding her of a promise to send him a Christmas box, he then asked her to include some "white pudding."[12] Ted sent up a distress message to his mother a few days later. The mess's cook, Jim Holly, a free Negro, had left them, feeling he had been insulted, and the mess was badly off as none wanted to try his hand again at cooking. In fact, not a member could cook "worth a cent," Ted said, and he added that one cause of sickness in camp was the lack of good cooks. He requested either his mother or Uncle James Paxton to get another cook, and he stated that although they had paid Jim twenty dollars per month, they would pay more rather than do without one.[13]

Jackson, as usual, was not inactive at this time, despite the lull in military operations in the lower Valley. In the middle of December 1861, he partially destroyed an important dam on the Potomac River, temporarily impairing the use of the

[12] Near Winchester, Dec. 1, 1861, Barclay Letters.
[13] Near Winchester, Dec. 6, 1861, *ibid.*

Chesapeake and Ohio Canal, which was an artery of communication between the West and Washington. While the entire brigade took part in the operation, the Fourth Virginia, the college company's regiment, was not actively engaged; nevertheless, one of its members was killed by an enemy shell. After describing the difficulties which confronted the detail assigned to destroy the dam, Hugh White stated, "It equals, in thrilling interest, anything I ever read or heard of in Indian Warfare." But he was more concerned about his dead comrade, hoping that he had been prepared to die. Since he had died in defense of his native soil, Hugh considered it an act "full of glory." On this expedition Hugh had satisfactory talks with several of the college boys who were not church members and, finding that there was a dearth of Bibles in the company, he wrote his father that they were needed more than either "guns or powder."[14]

On the other hand, Ted Barclay's account of the expedition revealed, among other things, Jackson's secretiveness in regard to the plan. At two o'clock in the morning of December 15 the college boys were aroused, ordered to strike tents, pack baggage, eat as "much beef and bread as you could stuff in yourself," and be prepared to move at four o'clock "to what place it was a mystery to us all." The company thought it was to Romney, some thirty miles northwest of Winchester. When, however, it found it was headed in a different direction, the company was puzzled to know its destination. Finally the brigade came to Martinsburg, "that abolition hole, which ought to be burned as close to the ground as fire can get it." After marching and countermarching, the brigade came to the Potomac, where crowbars, axes, picks, and shovels were piled up on its bank, along with "a barrel of whiskey. Old Jackson gave each man [engaged in the operation] a tin

[14] Winchester, Dec. 24, 1861, White, White, p. 69.

cup full and took some for himself and told them to pitch into the dam and tear it down. So for the first time we found what the expedition meant." Ted apparently did not think much of the expedition, questioning if "there was any glory in it." After the brigade returned to Winchester, he wrote, "Well, here I am at the old camp near Winchester, broken down, halt, lame, blind, crippled, and whatever else you can think of—but I am still kicking."[15]

Back in Winchester, the brigade made preparations for its permanent quarters. By putting two tents together, the officers of the college company made a double house, the outer room for dining and the inner for sleeping quarters. This arrangement protected the door of the bedchamber from the cold wind, and a log fire in the fireplace made it warm and comfortable. When the sleet and hail beat on their canvas house and the officers lay between the blankets as snug as "a bug in a rug," they often thought of their mothers at home who were doubtless moaning: "Oh! how the poor boys are suffering this dreadful night in the army!"[16]

There was much visiting back and forth by the officers of

[15] To his sister, Dec. 23, 1861, Barclay Letters. About Martinsburg "L.H.V." had previously written: "We do not meet with such a hearty welcome as we did in Winchester, but were rather received with an air of cold indifference. . . . The atmosphere around the place is still somewhat infected with the odor of Unionism. Yes, some of the traitors to the welfare of the Old Dominion still desire to be united with the people of the blood-thirsty North; a people among whom sprung first the germ of Mormonism and all other isms which now curse our land, by whom treachery and all kinds of evil doings are cherished, where virtue has almost ceased to be held sacred, where the moral tone of the great mass of the people is corrupted and degraded, amongst whom the religion of the Cross is accustomed to be spurned and instead the poisonous germ of infidelity planted" (Lexington Gazette, July 4, 1861). It should be said, however, that both Martinsburg and Berkeley County, furnished many brave soldiers and women to the Confederacy, among them being Belle Boyd, famous Confederate spy.

[16] Lyle, "Jackson's Guard," p. 313.

the Fourth Virginia Regiment during this period. One night, while Captain Charles A. Ronald was chatting with the officers of the college company, he gravely asserted that he believed the war would soon end. Whereupon Lieutenant Sherrard jumped from his campstool and thundered: "Hush, Captain Ronald, the Yankee'll chase us out these comfortable quarters before morning. You made just such an assertion at Camp Stephens one night, and the next morning [General] Patterson had us on the jump."[17]

At this camp Captain Albert G. Pendleton of the Smyth Blues, Fourth Virginia, who had received a Christmas box containing both solid and liquid "refreshments," invited some of his fellow officers to his tent to partake of the liquid contents of the box. Under the "inspiration" of the occasion some of the officers became very affectionate, calling the Captain "Cousin Al"; Lieutenant Lyle recalled that some maneuvers were executed in the afternoon company drill which were not to be found in the military manual.[18]

The college company did not, however, stay in its winter quarters long. On December 23, 1861, an order came for the college boys to report to General Jackson's headquarters for guard duty, and it was joyfully obeyed without a murmur. They were, however, informed by the General that when an engagement with the enemy was imminent, they would take their place on the firing line with their comrades of the Fourth Virginia.[19]

General Jackson's quarters were located in the northern part of Winchester in a house surrounded by extensive

[17] *Ibid.* Charles Ronald, it is to be remembered, was captain of Company "E," Fourth Virginia.

[18] *Ibid.*

[19] *Ibid.*, p. 314. Jackson is reported to have said to Capt. Henry Ruffner Morrison, "You will be expected to join your regiment when an engagement takes place, for I cannot spare such soldiers from the field of action" (Barclay, "Volunteers," p. 133).

grounds, the property of Lieutenant Colonel Lewis T. Moore of the Fourth Virginia. The company's tents were placed in the west corner of the lawn, and the boys proceeded to prepare for the winter. The situation, Lyle later remembered, was preferable to General Smith's headquarters in one respect— they were at "Glorious old Winchester." The General's office was conveniently located, being the front room on the left as one entered the building, and the adjutant general's was opposite and across the hall, one sentinel guarding the doors of both offices. Since only one noncommissioned officer and three privates were needed at headquarters for guard duty, the commissioned officers were left with "elegant leisure to devote to the fair tyrants" of the town.[20]

Another factor which added much to the pleasure of the college boys was the fact that four members of Jackson's staff were alumni of Washington College: Lieutenant Colonel W. S. H. Baylor, brigade inspector-general, Captain A. H. Jackson, brigade assistant adjutant general, and Lieutenants Sandie Pendleton and George G. Junkin. The boys were free to enter their offices at any time; the "gay and genial" Alf Jackson especially welcomed them, and in turn they assisted him in his clerical duties. But they did not dare to idle around the General's office door. "Not that he was cross," Lieutenant Lyle declared, "but anywhere in his neighborhood was a proper place to put on your dignity."[21]

During this time Mrs. Jackson arrived at Winchester to be with her husband, and they occupied for a short time the

[20] Lyle, "Jackson's Guard," p. 314.

[21] Ibid., p. 315. Lieut. Col. Baylor of Staunton soon resigned from the staff, accepting a similar rank in the Fifth Virginia Infantry. After the battle of Kernstown, March 23, 1862, he became its colonel. Capt. Alf Jackson was the general's cousin. Resigning his commission in the spring of 1862, he rejoined his old regiment, the Thirty-first Virginia, and was mortally wounded at Cedar Mountain in August 1862, dying at Lexington in 1863. A graduate of Washington College, he and Sandie Pendleton were classmates. For San-

Moore house and took their meals at the home of the Rev.
Dr. James R. Graham, pastor of the Presbyterian church at
Winchester; later they took up their residence at the Graham
home.[22] Though the enemy was closing in on Winchester,
these were happy days, Lieutenant Lyle recalled. The college
boys welcomed the presence of Mrs. Jackson, for she was
known to many of them for the "amiable qualities" she had
displayed in Lexington before the war. "The sight of the little
woman was refreshing," Lyle later wrote. The officers of the
company were often visitors at the Graham home, and both
music and games such as chess, backgammon, and battledore,
in which the young ladies were skilled, afforded much amusement. Another center of the social circles to which the officers
gravitated was the home of the Millers, relatives of Lieutenant
Sherrard, and the charming young ladies of the household
saw that his fellow officers had a royal time during the holiday season. Such was the Christmas of 1861, the last "old
time, be-fo'-de wa' " Christmas in which they frolicked.[23]

die Pendleton's career, see W. G. Bean, *Stonewall's Man: Sandie Pendleton*
(Chapel Hill, 1959); hereafter cited as Bean, *Pendleton*. Lieut. George
Junkin, nephew of Dr. George Junkin and cousin of General Jackson's first
wife, was a native of Pennsylvania.

[22] Chambers, *Jackson*, I, 414.

[23] Lyle, "Jackson's Guard," pp. 319–20. Conditions were not so rosy at
Winchester, according to "O.P.H.," another soldier of the Fourth Virginia:
"Most of the merchants in this place are selling their goods almost as high
as the seventh heaven." There were exceptions, however. A Mr. Gelwicher
was still charging the old prices, as was C. B. Rouss, who was called one of
"the most active, energetic, and liberal-minded men in Winchester." An instance of his liberality was cited. When the Stonewall Brigade returned to
Winchester in November 1861, as it passed in front of his store it was
showered by his clerks with "bushel baskets full of plugs of good tobacco
and cakes. . . . Thus by his generosity and fair dealing he has drawn around
himself a host of customers, thereby honestly and honorably making a fortune, and at the same time gaining the confidence and esteem of the people.
Rouss' name will live while that of the money sharks and speculators will be
consigned to oblivion" (Rockingham *Register*, Dec. 27, 1861).

At the end of 1861 the military situation in the Valley district was briefly as follows: Jackson's army of ten thousand men, consisting mainly of the Stonewall Brigade under the command of General Richard B. Garnett and General W. W. Loring's three brigades, was encamped near Winchester. The Federal troops in this region were under the command of General N. P. Banks, and his headquarters were at Frederick, Maryland; his thirteen thousand troops were stationed nearby. General B. F. Kelley with five thousand soldiers was garrisoned at Romney, thirty-five miles northwest of Winchester. Jackson's first test as an independent commander of the Valley army was the Romney expedition, and his primary objective was to capture or rout the Federal army at Romney, thereby upsetting Banks's campaign against Winchester and throwing him on the defensive.[24]

On January 1, 1862, when Jackson's army left Winchester, the day was bright and unusually mild for the season of the year. The roads were in good condition and the air so balmy that the soldiers left their blankets and tents behind in the regimental wagon trains. The college company was ordered to take charge of the headquarters wagons, which contained the General's and staff officers' blankets, overcoats, and army records, and to follow in the rear of the long column of soldiers and the other wagon trains. On the first day it did not get far because the weather suddenly turned cold, and a fierce storm of snow and sleet followed during the night, making the roads almost impassable. In fact, for the next three weeks bad weather interfered seriously with the expedition.

Not much progress was made on the second day, January 2, because the roads were steep in places and cut up by the wagons ahead of the company. The boys spent most of the

[24] William Allan, *A History of the Campaign of General T. J. (Stonewall) Jackson in the Shenandoah Valley* (Philadelphia, 1880), ch. i.

day and night either standing in the rain, listening to the drivers cursing their stalled teams, or assisting in extricating the wagons from the mudholes. The shouting of the wagon train leaders and the oaths of the drivers were a revelation to Lieutenant Lyle as "to variety, point, and eloquence that men of that calling can give to their profanity. The peaks and gorges echoed and multiplied the cursing and swearing into a blasphemous roar which doubtless shocked the mountainous vermins."[25]

Since the headquarters wagons contained General Jackson's camping equipment, the boys were anxious to reach his bivouac before nightfall of January 2 in order that he might be comfortable; but with nightfall approaching and with the stalled teams ahead, they abandoned all hopes of overtaking him. So Lieutenant Lyle went on foot to report the situation to the General. After floundering all night in the mud, he found at daybreak the General's bivouac in a log cabin on the roadside. His only shelter from the cold, in the absence of his blankets, had been the cabin roof and a fire in the chimney.

After Lyle's report General Jackson directed the college company to rejoin its regiment, leaving only a small guard with the headquarters wagons. In the late afternoon of January 3 the boys caught up with the regiment in camp and, after warming themselves around the camp fires, they sought shelter for the night under the bushes—their tents being in the regimental wagons. During the night the snow spread "a white counterpane" over the bodies of the boys, making them resemble white mounds and giving the camp the appearance of scattered graves. When the boys popped out of the snow the next morning, it looked to Lieutenant Lyle as if "a resurrection was going on."[26]

---

[25] "Jackson's Guard," pp. 323–24.
[26] Ibid.; Hugh to father, Bath, Morgan County, Jan. 4, 1862, White, White, p. 71.

The worst experience of the march from Winchester to Bath, Hugh White wrote his father, was when the company marched to rejoin its regiment: "We had eaten nothing since morning, our wagon was several miles before us, we had no shelter for the [previous] night, not even a blanket to protect us from the snow and the cold. We have seen some hard times, but this was the worst of all." However, after reaching Bath (a prewar health resort) and settling down in a warm cottage at the Springs, and doubtless after a refreshing bath, Hugh was more cheerful: "This is a happy close to a most dreary march. So now let the memory of the past only stimulate [us] to warmer gratitude for our safe deliverance from danger and hardship, and give us stronger confidence for the future. God's hand that has helped will continue to help; and now, with a happy good-night to you all, I close my letter to enjoy a good night's rest in a house by a fire."[27]

After entering Bath and finding no enemy there, Jackson pushed on in the direction of Hancock, Maryland, which was across the Potomac from Bath. The college company, however, was left behind to act as a provost guard, and its principal duty was to round up stragglers and send them on to the army. It was an unpleasant duty, and it infuriated the stragglers who, swearing at the college boys, called them "Jackson's pet lambs."[28] The chief attraction at Bath was Berkeley Springs, the property of the father of David Hunter Strother, an artist and writer of the antebellum period whose

[27] *Ibid.* J. H. Langhorne of Company "A," Fourth Virginia, wrote his mother of the hardships of the Romney campaign: "I have witnessed and experienced all of a winter's campaign that I desire, the romance of the thing is entirely worn off, not only with myself but with the army. I have endured & seen others endure that if a man had told me 12 months ago that men could stand such hardships I would have called him a fool" (Unger's Store, Jan. 12, 1862, J. H. Langhorne Letters, Virginia Historical Society, Richmond, hereafter cited as Langhorne Letters).

[28] Lyle, "Jackson's Guard," p. 325.

pseudonym was "Porte Crayon." Both father and son were stanch Unionists and the latter was a member at that time of General Banks's staff. Since the boys were quartered in the cottages of the Springs, they visited David Strother's study and read some of the manuscripts of his articles which had previously appeared in periodicals. Finding his fencing masks and foils, they confiscated them as "semi-offensive weapons and contraband of war" with the approval of Lieutenant Colonel Baylor, who declared that Strother, a traitor to Virginia, had forfeited all rights to his property. As "the pressing was general," Ted Barclay also "pressed" several pictures and other items from "Porte's" study.[29]

On January 7, after driving the enemy across the Potomac and destroying a considerable amount of supplies, Jackson evacuated Bath and turned south to Unger's Store. He rested there several days and then pushed on to Romney, entering it without any resistance on January 14, after a most difficult march.[30] That night march from Bath to Unger's Store was described by Lieutenant Lyle:

Such a tramp it was; something like Napoleon's crossing the Alps. The mercury was below zero, and the northwest wind cut like a knife. The snow and the ground under it were frozen hard, and the roads beaten down by the trains and the artillery were smooth as glass.

Neither men nor horses could keep their feet and were falling constantly. There would be a gleam from four bright horseshoes in the moon beams, and then a crash as the saddle on the horse's back hit the earth. Mounted men had to walk like ordinary foot soldiers, or risk getting their necks broken. The brink of the road had to be shunned, to avoid a slide like a toboggan down the side

[29] *Ibid.;* Ted to sister, Winchester, Jan. 25, 1862, Barclay Letters. For a description of Berkeley Springs, see Cecil D. Eby, *Porte Crayon: The Life and Letters of David Hunter Strothers* (Chapel Hill, 1960), pp. 56–58, 120.

[30] Chambers, *Jackson*, I, 423–25.

of the mountain. Men's rumps were continually hitting the road with a thud like that of a pile driver.

To the college boys was assigned the duty of guarding the Yankee prisoners who, though more accustomed to snow and ice, were unable to walk any better than they. One of them, a somewhat elderly man, dislocated a hip by a fall, and Captain Ruffner Morrison of the Company snapped it back with "a pop." Scrambling to his feet, the prisoner thanked the Captain for "his surgical operation." Crossing the swollen creeks was a source of amusement to the boys, according to Lieutenant Lyle. Since wading was impossible and since the rails and poles which had been thrown across the streams were too near the water for "cooning" (crawling on the knees and hands), the boys had to walk across the icy and treacherous improvised footbridges. Those who had never had such an experience fell into the water and were greeted with "a horse-laugh" by the others as they rescued them.[31]

Since the hardships of a march always intensified the soldiers' love of fun and deviltry, they were constantly chaffing and teasing each other; the noncombatants, such as the quartermasters and commissaries, caught it on all sides. Although they were necessary to the army, the fact that their position was one of relative safety made them the butt of sharp and caustic wit. The sight of one of them passing a column was, according to Lyle, the "signal for the fun to begin." One day a Mr. T—, the regimental commissary, was passing the college company. "Who issues rotten beef?" yelled the company wag; "T—" was the answer from a hundred throats. Such a "soothing salutation" greeted him until he disappeared from sight. Although the quartermasters were "honest, patriotic" men, Lyle declared, they were suspected by some to be practicing extortion at the public expense. The regimental

[31] "Jackson's Guard," p. 327.

chaplain was once discoursing on the relationship between Judas Iscariot and the other apostles. "Comrades," he innocently remarked, "you will better grasp the relation Judas bore to the other apostles when I tell you he was the quartermaster of the company [of apostles]." The parson, Lyle said, had no intention of reflecting upon the regimental quartermaster, but the soldiers gave their own interpretation to his remark. When the quartermaster next appeared, from the far end of the column of the regiment a voice was heard: "What was Judas Iscariot?" "Quartermaster," echoed a chorus of voices.

The surgeons were much respected because the men did not know when they might come "under their saws." The assistant surgeons, however, were not spared. "Who drinks the hospital whiskey?" "The assistant surgeon." "Who doesn't know salts from saleratus?" "The assistant surgeon." "Who cuts off a man's leg, just for practice?" "The assistant surgeon." The following conversation took place in the ranks of the Fourth Virginia:

"Our assistant surgeon," said J—, "is a contract surgeon. He hasn't a commission." "Why don't he stand the examination and get one?" asked a comrade. "He 'cussed out the examining board," replied J—, "and is barred." "What did he do that for?" "The first question the president of the examining board asked him was one on obstetrics. Whereupon he flew all to pieces and told the board they could go to Halifax if they thought he was fool enough to attempt the practice of that branch of his art on soldiers, and sailed out of the room ruffling his feathers like a mad hen."[32]

At Unger's Store Lieutenant Lyle came down with yellow jaundice and was immediately sent in an ambulance to Winchester, but the rest of the company continued on to Romney with the army. Learning that the enemy had evacuated Rom-

[32] *Ibid.*, pp. 329–30.

ney on January 10, the college company, at Unger's Store, was ordered by General Jackson on January 13 to proceed to Romney "as fast as possible." Marching ahead of the army, the boys entered Frenchburg, a hamlet seven miles from Romney, in the late afternoon, where they had planned to camp for the night. Since it was snowing and there was not a single house standing, the Yankees having burned every house before leaving, the boys pressed on to within four miles of Romney, where they found a half-burnt house. There they spent the night and the next day entered Romney—the first infantry troops to arrive at the place. Ted proudly boasted to his sister that the Liberty Hall Volunteers had "captured" Romney.[33]

Of the enemy's devastation in the vicinity of Romney, Ted reported that there were

not less than fifty or sixty houses burnt around Romney, and cattle, hogs, and horses shot down and left lying. One man was shot whilst making shoes in his house and the house burned over him, although his wife and children begged the dogs [Federals] to take the body out of the house before they burned it, and a poor old woman who lived at Romney had her house burnt down and when she asked them to allow her to save some of the things they told her to take out whatever she pleased; she took out some bedding and an old clock, and, after the house was burnt, they set fire to the things she had taken and burnt them too. Hampshire County in which Romney is located is just a wilderness; you see only ashes where a few days ago beautiful houses stood.[34]

Although the college company was comfortably housed near Jackson's headquarters, Ted declared that Romney was "one of the dirtiest holes man ever came into." A few days later he informed his sister that the army would soon leave

[33] *Ibid.;* Ted to sister, Jan. 16, 1862, Barclay Letters. For the Yankee devastation at Frenchburg, see Bean, *Pendleton*, p. 53.
[34] To his sister, Jan. 26, 1862, Barclay Letters.

"this hog pen" for Winchester, where he would satisfy her in "the letter line."[35]

Leaving General Loring's brigades at Romney, Jackson returned to Winchester on January 24, 1862, with the Stonewall Brigade. Although he had not been satisfied with Loring's handling of his command in the Romney campaign, Jackson hoped that, once in winter quarters, conditions would improve in this command and that Loring would be able to hold Romney. Disaffection, however, soon appeared in Loring's brigades, and a petition signed by their principal officers was forwarded through military channels to the Secretary of War, Judah P. Benjamin, requesting the withdrawal of the command to Winchester. Without consulting Jackson, Benjamin ordered him to recall Loring's troops to Winchester. Jackson complied with the order but at the same time tentatively resigned. Fortunately both Governor Letcher and General Joseph E. Johnston intervened in the controversy and persuaded Jackson to withdraw his resignation. General Loring was soon transferred to southwestern Virginia, but Jackson retained in his command all of Loring's Virginia regiments and two batteries.[36]

The rumor of General Jackson's resignation stunned the boys of the college company. They were indignant at the thought of losing their general, especially under the circumstances. Hugh White had difficulty in restraining his feeling of indignation:

There is but one feeling with us—that of perfect devotion to Gen. Jackson. With him we are ready to go anywhere, and to endure everything. But if he is to be run down, our spirit is utterly broken, and we can never re-enter the service with cheerful hearts. But I trust his resignation will not be accepted, and if so, all will be

[35] Same, Romney, Jan. 22, 1862, *ibid.*
[36] Chambers, *Jackson,* I, 428–42.

well again, and our noble commander will come forth as triumphantly from the assaults of Southern *friends* as he has done from the bullets of Northern enemies. The Government must know how essential he is to the success of the Southern cause.[37]

Ted Barclay was less restrained in his comments on this affair. While he confessed that he could hardly blame Loring's men for being dissatisfied with being left at Romney, "the most miserable hole in creation," Ted vowed that the veterans of the Stonewall Brigade would never serve under Loring. "What the consequences will be I cannot tell. But if the orders of such a man as Jackson are to be disregarded by such trifling people as Loring and seconded by Benjamin I think the Southern Confederacy is in a bad fix. I never saw a more unsatisfied set of men than the Stonewall Brigade just now. I hear that Loring's men are just as much attached to their general as we are to ours, so I would not be surprised to hear of a bust up soon." After Loring's troops had returned to Winchester from Romney, so abusive were some of them about Jackson that collisions occurred between them and the men of the Stonewall Brigade; to "cuss old Jack" was a privilege reserved to his men, Lieutenant Lyle boasted.[38]

[37] To his father, Winchester, Feb. 5, 1862, White, *White,* p. 73. J. H. Langhorne gloried "in [Jackson's] 'pluck.' It was certainly a grave offense, offered him by the Sec. of War, and any Gen'l who had a high sense of honor & self respect would not have allowed such an indignity to pass unnoticed. . . . We are all deeply grieved at the prospect of losing our brave old Gen'l. We all know in losing him we lose the firmest *stone* in our wall" (to Mrs. Roger Martin, Feb. 1, 1862, Langhorne Letters).

[38] Ted to sister, Winchester, Feb. 1, 1862, Barclay Letters; Lyle, "Jackson's Guard," p. 357. John Apperson noted in his diary of Jan. 24, 1862, that Loring's men seemed insulted in being left at Romney, calling the men of the Stonewall Brigade "Militia [a derogatory term], cowards, and many other names. [They said] Gen. Jackson [was] partial to his Old Brigade" (Apperson, "Civil War Diary, 1861–1865," Jan. 24, 1862, in the possession of the Virginia Historical Society, Richmond, Va.; hereafter cited as Apperson, "Diary.")

When the college boys came back from the Romney expedition, as "chipper as larks," they found Lieutenant Lyle completely recovered from the attack of yellow jaundice. Upon his arrival at Winchester on January 9, he had been taken in by his old friends, the Millers, and they had installed him in the room of one of the daughters who was away at school. The lieutenant improved rapidly under the ministrations of Mrs. Miller and the medical care of Dr. Joseph McClung of Rockbridge County, who was attached to the soldiers' hospital at Winchester. He prescribed hard cider to be "drunk freely," and this prescription—the treatment of that period for yellow jaundice—was faithfully followed by Lieutenant Lyle, who consumed enough "to bleach him as white as a lily." One of the college boys who had been detained at Winchester by sickness during the Romney campaign called upon the Lieutenant and found him stretched out on a sofa in the parlor, with Mrs. Miller sitting by and reading aloud to him from one of Bulwer's volumes. As he grew better, there was a party almost every night for him at one of the homes of the Miller clan, and Lieutenant Lyle, "cutting a wide swath," would appear as "slick as a dandy with pomaded hair and a perfumed handkerchief," which his hostess had lavished upon him.[39]

When Lieutenant Lyle and his comrade had sufficiently recovered, they started to rejoin the company at Romney. At the end of the first day they stopped at a wayside inn with a sign swinging from a high post which informed the traveler that "rest and refreshments for man and beast are to be had within." The landlady was a fascinating "buxom young widow" who was "fatally" smitten by Lieutenant Lyle at first sight and treated them as special guests. She gave them the best room and, before dinner and supper were served, a black

[39] Lyle, "Jackson's Guard," p. 357.

servant in a snow-white apron appeared with a tray of tumblers, a bowl of sugar, and a decanter of applejack. They were seated at the landlady's table. The lieutenant was so well satisfied that his comrade was unable to persuade him to quit the inn until they heard that the brigade was on its way back to Winchester. Then the two immediately set out for the town, arriving there a day or two before the brigade. The lieutenant was still "a fascinating dog," another of the boys remarked upon hearing of this episode.[40]

From January 24 to March 11, 1862, Jackson anxiously and vigilantly remained in Winchester, watching the gradual approach of Banks's army from the north and east. Jackson was busily occupied during the daytime with the inspection of the troops and the strengthening of the fortifications around Winchester. In the evenings he shared the hospitality of the Graham home with Mrs. Jackson, who was still with him.[41]

Both the unmarried officers and men of the Stonewall Brigade enjoyed the society of Winchester. Ted Barclay, always a lady's man as well as a bold warrior, told his sister that "we are enjoying ourselves hugely going to see the ladies ... who think there is nothing equal to the L [iberty] H[all] V[olunteers] or as we are called here Jackson's body guard. ... You want me to see the prettiest girl in the town; well the prettiest one and the belle of the town is the daughter of a gambler; would you advise me to go to see her or the richest one and the ugliest who is a Miss Logan?" But Ted did not confine his attention to any one girl. One night he called upon two young ladies, remaining from eight to eleven.[42] Later he boasted that

[40] *Ibid.*

[41] Mary Anna Jackson, *Memoirs of Stonewall Jackson* (Louisville, 1895), p. 236.

[42] Ted to sister, Winchester, Feb. 5, 1862, Barclay Letters. Miss Logan was the daughter of Lloyd Logan, a wealthy and enterprising merchant of Winchester.

the college boys were "sweeping everything before [them] down here; the ladies don't stand a chance. I don't think Winchester will have any old maids in it after the [boys] leave as every [boy] seems to have a Dulcenia Debosa [*sic*]."[43]

Apparently the condition of Ted's wardrobe did not interfere with his social activities. Describing its depletion to his mother the day after the Stonewall Brigade returned to Winchester from Romney, he said his most urgent need was a coat since the one he was wearing was both burned and worn out, but he could either have one made at Winchester or she could get one at Lexington. The lower part of one pair of pants also had been burned, but by sticking them in his boots he could wear them every day and by using his good pair only on Sunday, he could get along well "in that line." As for shirts, he was well off; at Romney, since he had not changed his clothes for three weeks and had left his baggage at Winchester, he had bought a change of underclothes, some shirts, and socks. Meanwhile he had discovered that his boots, which a cobbler had just half-soled, had a small hole on the side of one of them, but he could have it patched at Winchester. "Ah! I forgot my hat [Ted wailed]; well, you tell cousin John [Woods] that he cheated me," for the hat which he had sent Ted had worn out in less than three weeks, but after all he had a good cap.[44]

The question of a coat and shoes still bothered Ted. On February 1, he urged his sister to try to buy a coat for him, gray if possible but any color except blue or brown. He had been unable to have his boots "footed," simply because he had no money on hand, having loaned it to some of his comrades. Reduced in funds to "one old copper," he had to borrow money to buy a postage stamp, and he added, "the Confederacy must be short of money." Although he had never

[43] Same, Feb. 10, 1862, *ibid.*
[44] Winchester, Jan. 25, 1862, *ibid.*

before asked the homefolk for money, he now requested a loan, promising to repay it as soon as possible and assuring them he was finished with "the loaning business." Ted ended by asking his sister to send him, in addition to the coat, a pair of shoes or boots, not very heavy ones, since he did not expect to "tramp" soon; instead he planned to go into "the courting business," and to succeed in this he must have "some dikes; I still have some of my pride left," he reminded his sister.[45]

A matter of much more concern at this time to the soldiers of Jackson's Valley army than girls and wardrobes was the question of reenlistment, since the twelve months for which they had originally enlisted were approaching an end. To prevent the reduction of the Virginia troops in the Confederate army, the Virginia Secession Convention, still in session, passed an ordinance in the late fall of 1861 which provided for the reorganization of the state militia. Briefly, this act provided that the volunteers whose terms of service expired in May 1862 could either volunteer for one more year or be mustered into the service in the "active class" of the militia for two more years, with exemption thereafter from further service.[46]

For a while, Ted Barclay was undecided about the problem presented by the Militia Act, weighing in his mind whether to reenlist in the infantry or enter another branch of the service. Writing to his sister in early February, he enthusiastically asserted that the entire army was reenlisting by "the hundred every day. . . . Every one thinks here if all the soldiers re-enlist we can put this war through by spring. I never saw such enthusiasm, it beats the first of the war." Ted,

[45] Winchester, Feb. 1, 1862, *ibid.*

[46] "The Militia," in the Richmond *Whig,* copied in the Lexington *Gazette,* Dec. 5, 1861. The militia of "the active class"—all males between the ages of twenty-one and thirty-one—who had not been in the army, would serve for three years. This Militia Act applied only to Virginia troops and had no connection with the Confederate Conscription Act of April 1862.

however, did not wish to continue in the infantry, and he considered waiting until his term had expired, to then join with other members of the college company in forming a cavalry company; however, he would sign up at that time if "they would let him have a horse. . . . This thing of walking don't pay," he insisted. Though too young to be drafted, Ted had no intention of leaving the army or proving recreant "to the call of [his] country, as long as the abominable flag of despotism hovers over a foot of southern soil; rather would I have my bones rot on the hillside than live a slave, for it would be the most degraded slavery" to live under Northern domination. Ted thought "every scoundrel" in Rockbridge County who had been evading the active service by hiding in the militia should also be drafted, writing: "For are not the volunteers fighting for their liberty while the militia are at home enjoying the luxuries and we enjoy none?" He also declared the volunteers were displeased by being subjected to the draft unless they reenlisted; rather than be stigmatized as draftees, however, the men of the Stonewall Brigade were determined to sign up again. "If the cause was not worth fighting for, it was not worth having," Ted affirmed and ended by uncomplainingly remaining in the infantry: "I ain't caring a cent, I reckon one place is as good as another and I suppose that all will have to fight before the thing is over," Ted philosophically admitted.[47]

Hugh White was also faced with the problem of continuing in the service or resuming his studies at the Seminary and, after some anxiety and with prayer for divine guidance, he resolved it by deciding to remain at his post. To him it was a most momentous decision; it meant the temporary abandonment of "the most cherished object of [his] heart"—the resumption of the preparation for the ministry. The military situation of the South during the spring and summer would

[47] To his sister, Winchester, Feb. 10, 1862, Barclay Letters.

either become better or worse, this youth reasoned. If better, General Jackson had assured him he would recommend his discharge from the army; if worse, Hugh would not think of returning to the Seminary. It was needless, Hugh added, to tell his father how important it was for the soldiers "to stand firm in their places, resolved never to give up the cause which they had espoused. . . . [Furthermore] it was the duty of every [Southerner] to die, resisting the Northern invader, [rather] than bow his neck to the cruel yoke he seeks to impose upon us."[48] There were other reasons for Hugh's decision to remain in the army. His experiences so far had been a much-needed schooling, which he could hardly find elsewhere. In addition to his military duties, he had also been performing ministerial work such as distributing religious tracts and Bibles among the company and attending to their spiritual needs, which had been woefully neglected as a result of the lack of chaplains. There was also the chance that he could get permission from the Lexington Presbytery to act unofficially as a chaplain, in which case he could do more than he had previously done.[49]

At Winchester, the college company had abandoned its "huts" and moved into a large house near Jackson's headquarters. The house contained six rooms and a kitchen with a cooking stove and utensils, which were used by the various messes of the company. Ted and his four messmates, however, being without a cook, soon took their meals at an adjacent private home where they could sit down at a table to be waited upon by "a lot of pretty girls." There was plenty of "everything" including real coffee and butter. "Good coffee, too. Bah! Who would drink rye [coffee]," Ted scornfully wrote.[50]

On the eve of Jackson's famous Valley campaign of 1862,

[48] Winchester, March 7, 1862, White, *White*, pp. 75–76.
[49] Same, March 4, 1862, *ibid.*, p. 74.
[50] To his mother, Winchester, March 7, 1862, Barclay Letters.

there was some grumbling in the Fourth Virginia in regard to the selection of the successor to Colonel James F. Preston, its popular commander, who had died in January 1862 at his home in Montgomery County, Virginia. It had been rumored in the camp that Lieutenant Colonel Lewis T. Moore, ailing from a severe wound at First Manassas, would be Preston's successor, Major Kent would be promoted to a lieutenant colonel, and Captain Albert G. Pendleton of Company "D" would be elevated to a majority. When Kent, however, heard that Pendleton was to be his successor, he refused to accept the lieutenant colonelcy and resigned his commission. Upon the retirement of Lieutenant Colonel Moore, Major Pendleton was left temporarily in command of the regiment. Apparently Pendleton, whom Ted Barclay called "the nastiest little squirt" in the regiment, was so unpopular with the men in the Fourth Virginia Regiment that Captain Charles Ronald of Company "E" was promoted to the rank of lieutenant colonel and entrusted with the command of the regiment.[51]

[51] Ted to sister, Winchester, Feb. 5, 1861, *ibid.* Commenting also on the proposed regimental appointments, J. H. Langhorne wrote: "I think old [Governor John] Letcher must have been on the 'same old drunk' when he made these promotions. I used to be proud of the old 4th & proud that I was one of its numbers, when it was commanded by our loved, honored & brave Col. Preston, & would be still if Major Kent had been appointed our Col., but my pride now all dwells in memory, and in the brave hearts of the privates and [company] officers. What a wound it would have been to the heart of our dear lost Col. [Preston] if he had known that such a man as Capt. Pendleton would hold a field office in his [be]loved Reg't. . . . There is uproarious dissatisfaction in the Reg't on account of the appointments. Major Kent [Langhorne's cousin] had written his resignation and was only waiting for the appointments to be made before sending it in. He could no longer with honor to himself hold office in the Reg't [with Captain Pendleton]" (to mother, Feb. 2, 1862, Langhorne Letters). Ted Barclay had also said the soldiers would have preferred Major Kent to Lieut. Col. Moore as regimental commander.

Four

THE VALLEY CAMPAIGN

ON March 4, 1862, Captain Henry Ruffner Morrison of the Liberty Hall Volunteers confided to his diary:

Just one year ago today "King Abe" ascended the throne. During this time what incalculable injury he has done! The whole land which was then smiling with plenty & peace has since become a vast arena of deadly strife. . . . The year that has passed since the accession of tyranny to the reins of government in the Old United States has witnessed the fervor of [Virginia's] devotion to the cause she has thus espoused. Her noblest sons are in the field and many of them have poured out their lives in her defense. The armed hordes which have come to devastate the homes of her people have been driven back & made to feel the power of Virginia's own strong arm defending her rights. The contest is deepening & grows daily more & more serious. Trusting in God as our deliverer, we will go forward, confident of ultimate success.[1]

[1] "Diary, 1862," March 4, 1862 (in the author's possession). The diary was written in an old Latin composition book used by Captain Morrison while a student at Washington College.

The brief pause in the war was soon cut short for the Confederates at Winchester. At the end of February 1862, the Federal armies in northern Virginia were ready to launch their spring offensive. Near Washington, McClellan was poised for a thrust at Richmond, either by way of Fredericksburg or by the Peninsula, and on February 29 the vanguard of Banks's army crossed the Potomac at Harper's Ferry; in a few days 30,000 Federals were south of the river. Believing that McClellan's intention was to move southward to Fredericksburg on his way to Richmond (McClellan actually chose the peninsular route), General Joseph E. Johnston pulled back his army from Centreville to the Rapidan-Rappahannock River line. Faced with the approach of a superior enemy force and isolated from Johnston's army, Jackson with 4,500 men at his disposal reluctantly abandoned Winchester on March 11 and retired up the Valley, first to Strasburg and then to Mt. Jackson.[2]

During the month of February 1862, Winchester was in a state of unrest, for it was believed that Banks was ready to pounce upon Winchester when the roads were passable. Although its citizens had confidence in General Jackson, they were not so sanguine as to hope that he with his small army could resist the Federal horde confronting him across the Potomac. The absorbing question in the town was, would Jackson fight or evacuate Winchester? Since the college boys were stationed at headquarters, it was taken for granted that they knew the General's plan. Everywhere they went the first question thrown at them was, "When is old Jack going to evacuate?" The words became a byword to them, and even the women used them as glibly as the men. One evening, when one of the boys was "eloquently beseeching" one of

[2] Vandiver, *Stonewall,* ch. x.

the belles to surrender "the citadel" of her heart, she whispered, "Darling, I evacuate."[3]

But Jackson had no intention of withdrawing from Winchester without a fight. On the morning of March 11, informed that the enemy was advancing on the Martinsburg road, he marched north to engage them, directing that the wagon trains be sent a short distance south of the town. The college company was ordered to follow the trains, which included headquarters baggage. The boys did not like the idea of moving to the rear while the rest of the brigade was advancing to the front, and they requested permission from General Jackson to rejoin their regiment until the fight was over. The request was granted, but a small guard was left with headquarters wagons. The rest of the company joined its regiment, the Fourth Virginia, which had occupied a hill north of the town where a fort called Fort Alabama had been erected.

Though General Banks came within four miles of Winchester, he did not attack, and Jackson's army held its position there all day waiting. At dusk the Confederates withdrew to Winchester, and about ten o'clock that evening Jackson abandoned Winchester. "I was surprised when the order came for I was not expecting it," Captain Morrison wrote, and he was certain Jackson had had no idea of leaving Winchester:

When we returned from the field, [Jackson] sent for me and asked me to give him all the information I could in reference to the movements of the enemy as observed during my stay at Fort Alabama. He asked very particularly whether I had seen any enemy's forces on the Pughtown Road. I had not seen any such force and reported it to him. But a few minutes later I had evidence from persons who had observed more particularly than I

[3] Lyle, "Jackson's Guard," pp. 362–63.

had that the enemy had certainly moved from the Martinsburg Road in the direction of the Pughtown Road. I immediately returned & reported this to the General.

Jackson then directed Captain Morrison to quarter his company in the same house it had been occupying for some time. "I felt elated at the prospect of seeing the enemy soundly thrashed" the next day, the Captain said. In the meantime, however, Jackson had called a council of the brigade and regimental officers, and since they had disapproved of attacking the enemy the next morning, Jackson decided to abandon Winchester. Captain Morrison was convinced that "to this council alone is due the retreat from Winchester." As soon as the council had dispersed, the college company was ordered to move; it was the last infantry to leave the town.[4] It was with sad hearts that the college boys evacuated "grand old Winchester" and left "its noble citizens" to the mercy of the "Abolition" invaders. They left before daylight, so they missed the reproachful glances of their lady friends. "We felt mean and must have resembled a gang of burglars," Lieutenant Lyle thought, "as we marched silently toward the south. We were bankrupt as to joy, and if laughs had been at a premium, we could not have raised a smile in the whole company."[5]

On the night of March 12 the troops camped about two miles from Strasburg, and the college company was quartered in the academy building in the town. Headquarters were established at an old inn on the pike which had a porch on the front running the full length of the building where the staff and the college company officers lounged and spun yarns. The General, Captain Morrison recorded, was "in good

[4] Morrison, "Diary," March 11, 1862. This was Jackson's first and last council of war with his subordinates.

[5] "Jackson's Guard," p. 369.

spirits."[6] Continuing the retreat, Jackson reached the vicinity of Mt. Jackson on March 15, having been pursued by General James Shields's division of Banks's army. Here Shields was recalled to Winchester by Banks, who, thinking that Jackson was abandoning the Valley, meanwhile was moving from Winchester with his other troops to cover the approaches to Washington after McClellan's forward movement to the Peninsula. Since it rained most of the time on the retreat, a house became a thing much sought after. The General, his staff, and the college company occupied a residence near the pike one night, and it was the only time, Lyle recalled, that he ever saw "the old man" sociable; before retiring he talked and laughed cheerfully despite the gloomy outlook.[7]

At Strasburg on the retreat, the college company under the supervision of Lieutenant Colonel Baylor of the staff was bundled into a boxcar during the night and dispatched on the Manassas Gap Railroad to destroy the rail and turnpike bridges which spanned the Shenandoah River near Front Royal. The old engine wheezed and snorted, seemingly barely able to pull the car at a snaillike pace. After destroying the bridges, the company raced back to Strasburg. Why the work had been assigned to the college boys was never explained, but they felt complimented in being selected and were as proud as if they had won a battle. The boys had destroyed so much property since entering the service that they had become "pretty fair vandals," Lyle observed. The only danger encountered on the foray was the possibility that either the old, shaky car would collapse or the old, windbroken locomotive blow up.[8]

---

[6] *Ibid.;* Morrison, "Diary," March 12, 1862.
[7] "Jackson's Guard," p. 366. Jackson's troops camped at Hawkinstown, two miles north of Mt. Jackson, while his headquarters was at Mt. Jackson.
[8] *Ibid.,* p. 367.

Rumors were floating around Mt. Jackson as to the destination of Jackson's Army, but Captain Morrison was certain
that it would soon move to join General Joseph E. Johnston's
army east of the Blue Ridge, because orders had been issued
to move the ordnance stores farther up the Valley, probably
to Staunton, and also because the militia of both Augusta and
Rockbridge counties was being organized for active service.
Already the Captain was beginning to feel that he was an
exile, and he feared that the Yankees would soon occupy the
entire Valley and cut him off from home and friends.[9] On
March 20 there was a tinge of expectancy throughout the
brigade. In his diary Morrison noted:

Our Brigade which has for several days been encamped near this
point [Hawkinstown] was ordered to be in readiness to move this
morning. The wagons were packed & sent off but up to a late hour
this evening the troops had not moved. It is probable that Genl
Jackson expected a skirmish. The enemy was reported four miles
beyond Woodstock this morning at 4 o'clock. At noon, however, a
courier arrived from Col. Ashby with intelligence of the enemy's
falling back to Strasburg this morning. Genl Jackson contem-
plated a move backward [south], I think. He sent out to-day to
select a place for Headquarters. A house was selected about 7
miles [south] from his present quarters on the Harrisonburg
Road. We shall probably move tomorrow.[10]

His diary entry of the next day revealed the various rumors
concerning the sudden withdrawal of the Federals from Strasburg:

Late in the afternoon I received orders to be ready to move as
soon as possible. At 3½ o'clock we started. To our surprise & delight, we moved in the direction of Strasburg. The Yankees have

[9] "Diary," March 19, 1862.
[10] Ibid., March 20, 1862.

fallen back to Strasburg and are reported to be hastening on to Winchester. Great excitement prevails as to the probable cause of this sudden departure of the Yankees. As usual there are many rumors. Gen. Johnston is said to have thrashed the Yankees at or near the Rappahannock [River]. Others say that a signal victory has crowned our arms at Fredericksburg and that the Yankees are afraid of being flanked. One thing is sure. Something has occurred to frighten them most desperately. Another rumor states that the Marylanders have revolted and are destroying the roads & bridges in the rear of the enemy. Baltimore is reported to be in a condition of revolt. Hope it is all true—Glorious news. Never was a set of boys more cheerful than were my boys this evening. As an evidence of this it is sufficient to note that they made the march from Hawkinstown to Woodstock [a distance of 11 miles] in two hours and twenty minutes. Arrived at Woodstock late in the evening and quartered my men in the same house we had occupied last week during our stay in this town. The General took up his headquarters in the house of a Mr. Bird, a very nice gentleman of strong & established Southern proclivities.[11]

Notified by Colonel Turner Ashby of General Shields's retirement from Strasburg, Jackson retraced his steps on March 21 from Hawkinstown to Woodstock. On Saturday, March 22, Jackson's troops left Woodstock at ten o'clock in the morning and arrived at Strasburg in the early afternoon, having made a forced march of twenty-eight miles. Here the college company bivouacked in a large stone building near the house used as headquarters, and the troops went on to Newtown [now Stephens City], eight miles from Winchester, where they bedded down for the night.

The bitterness of the people of Strasburg at the conduct of the Yankees was described by Captain Morrison:

The citizens here are all down upon the Yankees, who seem to have a very unfortunate way of making unto themselves friends.

[11] *Ibid.*, March 21, 1862.

Their policy of conciliation is very good so far as it goes. But their stealing and plundering proclivities are rather vigorous for the good sense of the good people of this Valley. Hence it is no wonder that when their horses, cattle, money, chickens, etc., were plundered by the Vandals who invade our soil, the hearts of these honest people became filled with loathing for the contemptible Yankees.[12]

At Kernstown Jackson caught up with the rear guard of Shields's division and as he was under instructions to prevent the enemy from leaving the Valley, he made preparations to attack what he mistakenly believed was only four Federal regiments. Another miscalculation was Jackson's belief that Shields had already withdrawn from Winchester with the remainder of his division and was following Banks to Manassas. Jackson planned to force both Banks and Shields to return to the Valley by attacking at Kernstown. In fact, however, Shields was still in Winchester with nine thousand men. Jackson, misinformed, immediately engaged the enemy, and the battle raged indecisively for some time. When General Garnett ordered the Stonewall Brigade to fall back, their retreat necessitated the withdrawal of the rest of Jackson's army.[13]

On the morning of the battle of Kernstown, March 23, 1862, the college company marched leisurely with "merry hearts" to Kernstown, expecting to spend the night at Winchester after a slight skirmish. Remaining behind with the General's wagons until it saw them cross Cedar Creek, the company then went ahead. As it approached Kernstown and heard the roar of the cannons, Captain Morrison, realizing

[12] *Ibid.*, March 22, 1862.

[13] Vandiver, *Stonewall*, p. 204–10. For retreating from the battlefield without being ordered to do so by Jackson, Garnett was deprived of his command. He was later assigned a brigade in Gen. Longstreet's command and was killed at Gettysburg on July 3, 1863. Gen. Charles S. Winder succeeded Garnett as commander of the Stonewall Brigade.

that a battle was in progress, halted the company and ordered it to load its muskets. Since the cannonading had become quite loud by that time, the company quickened its pace to join its regiment and, after wandering about for a short time, found the regiment as it was leaving the pike to cross a field to its left, where the battle was raging.[14]

General Jackson was sitting on his horse nearby, and Lieutenant Lyle got what subsequently proved to be his last look at General Jackson—a picture that never faded from the Lieutenant's mind. "What was remarkable," Lyle wrote, was the fact that "his countenance was pale and showed anxiety. But there was a set about his jaw that boded no good for the foe. He was then commencing one of his daring moves . . . stripping his front almost bare of troops to hurl the bulk of his small force on the right flank of the enemy many times their number. It was time to look pale and anxious."[15]

The regiment (the Fourth Virginia) soon came under terrific artillery fire before it reached a stone wall, and there the battle continued for some time. Finally General Garnett, finding his troops exposed to a Federal flanking movement, withdrew. "We therefore retreated, loading and firing on as we ran. Once, when I looked back," Hugh wrote, "I saw the old 'Stars and Stripes' waving over the ground we had just left, and this vexed me more than anything else during the day." As Hugh was leaving the field, he saw one of the college boys, William J. Bell of Augusta County, Virginia, lying on the ground. Rushing up to him, Hugh discovered that one of his hips had been broken by a musketry ball; being unable to

[14] Hugh White, in Morrison's "Diary," March 23, 1862. As will be later narrated, Captain Morrison was captured in the battle, and Hugh White, who succeeded Morrison, made a notation in the diary on the night following the battle.
[15] "Jackson's Guard," p. 396.

help his wounded friend, however, and fearing either death or capture if he remained with him, Hugh regretfully left his friend. Bell groaned and rolled over. Hugh later wrote sorrowfully:

This is the saddest thing in a battle. To do violence to the feeling of friendship by leaving a wounded comrade to the hands of a cruel enemy is very painful but sometimes must be done. With a sad heart I turned away to make my escape. We had to retreat under the enemy fire for half a mile. I wonder at the escape of any one, but not a ball touched me.[16]

Telling his father that the college boys who had been captured and taken to Winchester would find "warm friends," Hugh commented upon the loyalty of the people of Winchester. "If we leave behind us when forced to retreat, as true and loyal Virginians, as are the people of Winchester, the Yankees may march through the whole land, and yet accomplish no more towards our subjugation, than the arrow which pierces the air and leaves no trace." He assured his father that the soldiers, despite the reverse at Kernstown, were not discouraged in the least. Their confidence in General Jackson was undiminished, and they would follow him anywhere at any time. Another cause for encouragement, Hugh boldly declared, was the fact that "God is on our side, and on this, as an immovable rock, we can rely."[17]

Hugh White was more fortunate than both Captain Morrison and Lieutenant Lyle, who were captured by a squad of Federal cavalry just as they were approaching a forest which they hoped would enable them to escape. A command to stop,

[16] In Morrison's "Diary," March 23, 1862. Bell, however, survived, living to a ripe old age. In 1910 he was present at the reunion of the survivors of the company.

[17] March 29, 1862, White, *White*, pp. 79–80.

accompanied by "very impolite language," had suddenly greeted them from the rear. While trying to break a handsome sword presented to him by Captain William Terry of the Wythe Greys (Fourth Virginia), Lyle heard a gruff voice shout: "If you break that sword, I'll shoot you." Looking up, he found himself gazing into the muzzle of a six-shooter which looked as wide as the mouth of a cannon. The Yankee trooper had his finger on the trigger; he was shaking like "an aspen leaf and I concluded without further argument not to break the sword." The only other incident that Lyle vividly recalled about the retreat from the battlefield was the witness of an old black mammy who was standing near a deserted house, shouting, "Oh, good Lawd, de judgment day am sho'ly come."[18]

As Lieutenant Lyle walked back to Winchester with the trooper riding behind like "a cowboy after a yearling," he felt humiliated and degraded. "I would have swapped places with a galley slave," the Lieutenant reminisced. At a halt near Winchester, a Federal trooper of the First West Virginia Cavalry, who had been skulking in the rear during the battle, dashed by on his way to the front, hurling an insulting oath at Lyle. Whereupon Lyle's captor swore "fearfully" at the trooper and threatened to shoot him for insulting an unarmed prisoner. Continuing on their journey to Winchester, the trooper and Lyle soon became so "sociable" that the former invited his prisoner to ride behind him on his horse. At Winchester, Lieutenant Lyle was taken to the fairground, where other Confederate prisoners were being corralled; soon he, Captain Morrison, and other captives were sent to Fort Delaware, located on an island in Delaware Bay, off the coast not far from Wilmington. There they were confined until they

[18] "Jackson's Guard," pp. 398–99. The losses of the college company in this battle were one killed, four wounded, and two captured.

were exchanged in August 1862. Before their release, however, an election had been held in the college company, and other officers chosen. Captain Morrison and Lieutenant Lyle therefore sought service elsewhere.[19]

After Kernstown, Jackson, followed by Banks, retired up the Valley and reached Harrisonburg in the latter part of April 1862. From here Jackson marched to Swift Run Gap in the Blue Ridge, seventeen miles east of Harrisonburg, and encamped near this gorge. This position afforded him a strong defense if he was attacked by Banks. On the other hand, if Banks continued his advance toward Staunton, Jackson could threaten his line of communication. With new enlistments Jackson's strength was increased to 6,000 men. Close by on the east base of the mountains was the strong division (8,000 men) of General R. S. Ewell which had been posted there by General Johnston upon his retreat toward Richmond; Ewell was to cooperate, if necessary, with Jackson. A smaller force of 3,000 men under General Edward "Allegheny" Johnson was also stationed on the crest of the Alleghenies, guarding the approach to Staunton.

Meanwhile the authorities at Washington feared for the safety of the capital after Jackson's audacious attack at Kernstown. Believing that his army outnumbered that of Banks, they detached troops from McClellan's army and sent them to join the army of General John C. Frémont in West Virginia. A portion of McDowell's corps, earmarked to join McClel-

[19] *Ibid.*, p. 400. Upon being exchanged, Captain Morrison served as adjutant of the Twenty-third Virginia Battalion until the end of the war. His subsequent career can be summarized as follows: professor of Greek at Oakland College, Mississippi, and lawyer in Vicksburg, Miss., and later in Delta, La., where he died in April 1879. Lieutenant Lyle served in the Eleventh Virginia Cavalry, returning after the war to his native county, Montgomery, where he practiced law and served as county judge until he moved to Waco, Texas.

lan's army in its advance upon Richmond, was retained at Fredericksburg. But when Banks reached Harrisonburg, instead of continuing southward and occupying Staunton—a strategic place—as Jackson had anticipated, he made a leisurely return to Strasburg on the Valley Pike, forty-five miles north of Harrisonburg. Informed of this movement, Jackson saw an opportunity to strike both Banks and Frémont before reinforcements arrived. Such was the military situation in late April 1862, when Jackson launched his famous Valley campaign.

On April 30, after ordering General Ewell to cross the Blue Ridge and take up a position at the Valley end of Swift Run Gap, Jackson left Swift Run Gap, crossed the Blue Ridge at Brown's Gap, and marched to Mechum River Station, west of Charlottesville. By this movement he created the impression among both friends and foe that he was abandoning the Valley and joining Johnston's army in the defense of Richmond. Jackson, however, retraced his steps on May 1 across the mountains to Staunton and, uniting his army with that of General Edward Johnson, moved west on the Staunton-Parkersburg Pike to strike a blow at the vanguard of Frémont's army under General Milroy at McDowell. Defeating the enemy on May 8 and pursuing him northward to Franklin, Jackson returned to McDowell on May 12, debouched from the mountains into the Valley Pike at Harrisonburg, and marched down it to New Market. At this village Jackson turned to the right and hastened toward Front Royal. Joined by Ewell's division in the Luray Valley, Jackson drove the Federals from Front Royal on May 23. He then moved rapidly toward Winchester, hoping to intercept the retreat of Banks, who was at Strasburg. Banks escaped to Winchester, however, after losses in both men and supplies. The battle of Winchester followed on May 25 with a complete defeat and rout of the enemy, which scampered back across the Potomac. Within three weeks Jackson had driven the Yankees from the Shenandoah Valley.[20]

In the Valley campaign of 1862 the correspondence of Ted Barclay and Hugh White revealed the spirit which had inspired the youth of Virginia in its determination to drive the invader from its soil. While these lads, along with their comrades of the college company, shared in the glory of the campaign, they also encountered hardships, personal problems, and new responsibilities. At Hawkinstown, on the retreat from Kernstown to Swift Run Gap, Ted Barclay wrote his sister that, although the army had been forced to withdraw from the battlefield at Kernstown, it had given the Yankees more than they had bargained for. News had filtered through from Winchester, Ted added, that the people there had cheered the Confederate prisoners of war as they had marched through the town and also that the good people of Winchester had buried the Confederates killed at Kernstown, marking each grave with the name of the dead.

Ted then told his sister that the militia, in which their cousin John Barclay was a captain, had just come up and would be assigned to the brigade for distribution among its regiments. Ted, who regarded militia members as skulkers, was opposed to filling up the regular companies with them, especially since the college company would have to take fifty. Realizing that the militia, when enrolled in the company, would have a numerical majority and could elect the officers for the vacancies left by the capture of Captain Morrison and Lieutenant Lyle at Kernstown, the boys persuaded the regimental commander, Lieutenant Colonel Ronald, to call an election before the militia was activated in the company, with

[20] Vandiver, *Stonewall*, chs. x–xi.

the result that Hugh White was elected captain and G. B. Strickler, first lieutenant.[21]

Hugh was surprised at his election. He had hoped for a lieutenancy at the most, and was not sure of that. But since he had been chosen, he accepted the position "with much fear." He was thoroughly aware of the "perplexity and toil" inherent in the position, and he did not anticipate any "increase of happiness, only an increase of responsibility." The duties of the office were so appalling to the newly elected young captain that he realized more than ever the need of divine guidance; to this source of help he looked, praying that by example and effort the men of his company might become "good soldiers and good Christians."[22] In a similar vein Hugh wrote his young brother Henry:

Promotion in itself brings neither peace nor happiness, and unless it increases one's usefulness it is a curse. An opportunity is now afforded for exercising a wider influence for good, and if enabled to improve this aright I shall then be happier than before. My life is now given to the army, and will be spent in it, even to the end of the war. But if my life is spread to see the end, and we are successful in our struggle, it will be the delight of my heart to spend the remainder of it in the ministry. I am not fond of the army. Indeed many things in it are hateful to me; but nothing is so much so as the invader of my native soil.

In addition to his official responsibilities, Hugh was further burdened by a personal problem—anxiety about the spiritual welfare of his brother Tom, not a church member, who had recently joined the college company. The thought of his responsibility for his brother's salvation made Hugh tremble:

[21] Ted to sister, Headquarters, March 31, 1862, Barclay Letters.
[22] Hugh to father, undated, White, *White*, p. 87. The probable date of the latter is early June 1862.

"I can only pray that God would visit him with His grace and save him. Let us never forget him in our prayers; for it may be that while you pray he is exposed to all the dangers of the battle, or possibly on the verge of eternity. If unprepared how sad will be [Tom's] end. The thought is dreadful."[23]

Ted Barclay was also wrestling with a personal problem. An unbeliever, Ted confessed to his sister that he still remained

a hardened sinner [in spite of] the voice of a mother and sister, the early death of a brother, and two bloody battlefields [First Manassas and Kernstown], all [of which] warn me of the uncertainty and shortness of life. Sometimes I try to give myself to Christ but the world lures me on and again I am in the old state. I wish I was a Christian, but some profess to be Christians who really are not, which, I think, is mockery. God grant that I soon will be a good Christian.[24]

Two weeks later, after a conversation with Captain Hugh White on the subject of religion, Ted joyfully announced he had "found the way to heaven. . . . I trust I have not deceived myself and pray that I may not fall back." Reminding his sister that May 16 was his eighteenth birthday and also the day appointed by President Davis as one of Thanksgiving, Ted was thankful that he had awakened "from his sins and looked forward to a blessed eternity."[25]

The hardships of the journey from Swift Run Gap to Mechum Station were borne cheerfully by the college boys, as they slugged up the mountainous road through mud and

[23] *Ibid.*, p. 88.
[24] Headquarters, April 15, 1862. Barclay Letters.
[25] Same, Mt. Solon, May 16, 1862, *ibid.* Jefferson Davis had issued a presidential proclamation designating May 16, 1862, as a day of prayer and fasting.

water to their knees. Although they complained, they pushed on, and when they straggled into camp about ten o'clock in the evening, "shouts of laughter echoed through the woods. Everyone had an Iliad of woes to recount, always with something ludicrous, and we all made merry over the toils and mishaps of the way," Hugh said.

While it pained Captain White to leave the Valley and to be cut off from all communication with his homefolk, yet he was glad to tread again the soil of Albemarle County; particularly did he long to spend a week or two at Charlottesville, his birthplace. With Jackson's army apparently abandoning the Valley, the possibility of a Yankee invasion of Rockbridge County weighed on Hugh's mind, but he hoped if their "unholy feet" should ever touch its soil the defenseless people would remain in their homes, calmly but firmly following a policy of passive resistance to "those who thus come to rob and ruin them." The only assistance he could render his loved ones under the circumstances would be his prayers that God would give them courage in that time of trouble. Hugh's fears that Jackson was abandoning the Valley to the enemy were groundless. At Mechum River Station his troops boarded cars which they assumed would take them to Richmond. But to their delight, the train moved westward to Staunton, and from there they marched to McDowell, where on May 8 he defeated the enemy under Milroy.[26]

Although the Stonewall Brigade had been in the rear and not present in this battle, it led the pursuit of the fleeing Federals with the Fourth Virginia in the vanguard. At Frank-

[26] Hugh to father, undated, White, *White*, pp. 82–83. The probable date of the letter was early June 1862. At the time of Hugh's birth his father was chaplain at the University of Virginia (*Rev. William S. White, D.D., and His Times, 1800–1873: An Autobiography*, ed. by his son, Rev. H. M. White, D.D. [Richmond, 1891], ch. ix).

lin, Virginia (now West Virginia), the enemy made a stand, and the college boys, with men of two other companies of the regiment, were deployed as skirmishers. After coming in contact with the enemy, the college company found itself subjected to a devastating fire from Federal artillery in front and a burning mountain which the enemy had set on fire in the rear. "You can imagine our dilemma," Ted Barclay wrote his sister, with "the enemy in front and a burning mountain in the rear." Finally the company managed to get through the fire and rejoin its regiment. The pursuit was abandoned, and Jackson's army fell back to Mt. Solon, where weary with fatigue and sore feet, his men rested a short time.[27]

Ted, rather fastidious about clothes, was hopeful that the army would return by way of Staunton to the Valley (which it did not) so that he might get a new suit of clothes. He had worn his present suit for three weeks. He also needed some underclothes, shirts, and socks. The knapsack in which he carried them had been lost and, although later found, its contents were so wet as to be worthless. With the approaching summer an order had come from headquarters that all overcoats were to be sent back to Staunton, but blankets and clothes were to be carried by the soldiers. Ted, who had experienced trouble with his back, doubted whether he could stand the strain of the load. Still obsessed with the idea of transferring to the cavalry, he thought of appealing to his uncle James Paxton for assistance, confident that he could effect the transfer through his acquaintance "with influential men in Richmond." Ted, however, remained in the infantry.[28]

From Mt. Solon, Jackson moved rapidly down the Valley to Front Royal, where after a skirmish, he succeeded in routing the Federals on May 23, 1862, and capturing many pris-

[27] Ted to sister, Mt. Solon, May 16, 1862, Barclay Letters.
[28] Same, Front Royal, May 23, 1862, *ibid.*

oners and a large quantity of stores. After this victory Jackson relentlessly pushed his columns toward Winchester by two routes during the day and night of May 24, hoping to prevent Banks, who was camped with his main army at Strasburg, from escaping to Winchester. On one of the roads during the night, the Confederates constantly ran into Federal ambushes, which threw them into temporary confusion. But skirmishers were thrown out, the enemy was pushed back, and the pursuit was resumed. Despite the enemy tactics Jackson pressed on until three o'clock in the morning of May 25, when the soldiers, a mile from Winchester, lay down by the road and rested until dawn.

"We rose, shook the dew from our limbs," and the battle was on, wrote Captain Hugh White. The tide soon turned in the Confederate favor, and the enemy fled, pursued through the town by the exultant Confederates amidst the rapturous cheers of the citizens, who left their cellars and appeared on the streets, "frantic with delight." The college boys stopped long enough to shake hands with acquaintances whom they saw as they passed through the town.

Hugh White was enraged by the stories of "insolence and cruelty" which the Yankees, "from the [officers] down to the lowest Dutchman that wallowed in the streets," had inflicted upon the inhabitants during their occupation of Winchester. The crowning infamy was their attempt to burn down the town, including a building filled with medicine, but fortunately the Confederates extinguished the fire. "These are the friends who come to protect us, and to seek a more permanent union with us. Deliver me from such friends," the seething Hugh White sarcastically remarked.[29]

Ted Barclay described the battle of Winchester and commented:

[29] To his father, Winchester, May 27, 1862, White, *White*, p. 85.

It is pronounced here to be the greatest victory of the war. . . .
The rout was general and complete, the enemy throwing away
guns, knapsacks and everything that impeded flight. You have no
idea of the extent of the booty. . . .

We came on through Winchester at double quick time, driving
the enemy four miles beyond the town when we were so tired
we could not pursue farther; here we camped and will stay today
[May 26]. The enemy are now at Martinsburg reported to be
making a stand. I suppose they have been reinforced, as Banks'
columns will not be fit for service for a long time, if ever. Our loss
was very slight. We are in a very critical place, as we have no
army at Manassas, and we are liable to be cut off. . . . Our army
is completely broken down. . . . We have been on the march for
forty-four days with only two days' rest.[30]

During a lull of three days when the Stonewall Brigade
rested at Winchester, Ted Barclay wrote that the brigade was
enjoying the fruits of victory, eating "everything good" and
momentarily unconcerned about the Yankees who were beyond the Potomac. The booty which had been abandoned at
Winchester contained such delicacies as coffee, molasses, or-
anges, lemons, figs, and "every conceivable thing." In fact, so
abundant were the choice edibles that the hungry Confederates scorned eating the beef and bread on which they had
been subsisting. The spoils of war also allowed Ted to equip
himself with a captured Belgian rifle, "a perfect cannon" in its
effectiveness. Always appreciating a pretty maiden's face,
Ted did not hesitate to call upon some of his former fair
friends in Winchester, although he had no clean clothes and
was still "living dirty." Among the stores left by the Yankees
were uniforms which Jackson's troops had taken, and with
which they had outfitted themselves, but as some of them had
been mistaken by their cavalry for Yankees, Jackson had or-

[30] To his sister, Winchester, May 26, 1862, Barclay Letters.

dered the uniforms to be taken off. "So today we see the old Confederate gray, while yesterday every one was in Yankee blue." Ted added, "I do not care to get any clothes anyhow."[31]

Jackson was not to be satisfied as long as the invader remained south of the Potomac. Banks paused briefly at Martinsburg and fell back rapidly to Williamsport, where he crossed over into Maryland. On May 28 Jackson dispatched the Stonewall Brigade toward Harper's Ferry, a movement which threatened an invasion of Maryland and an assault upon Washington.[32] At Winchester, Ted Barclay had expressed to his sister the belief that Jackson should be content with the advantage gained so far, fearing that the General would endanger the safety of his army if he thrust "his neck" farther down the Valley, for Banks could easily be reinforced by troops from Washington. Moreover, Jackson's troops were broken down by hard, continuous marching. But two days later Ted endeavored to allay any fear his sister might have had of the movement of the brigade to the environs of Harper's Ferry by assuring her that Jackson's sole purpose was to gain time to remove the captured stores from Winchester and Martinsburg. Furthermore, he declared, Jackson had no intention of attacking the enemy at Harper's Ferry because he himself had remained at Charlestown, and he never stayed behind when any fighting was to be done.[33]

The Lincoln government, panicky at Banks's defeat at Winchester, reacted to Jackson's diversion as he had expected, and a plan was concocted in Washington to bag his army. Banks was to recross the Potomac and advance up the Valley; Frémont at Moorefield, Virginia (now West Virginia), was ordered to strike toward Strasburg; and McDowell at

[31] *Ibid.*
[32] Vandiver, *Stonewall*, p. 260.
[33] Winchester, May 27, 1862, Barclay Letters.

Fredericksburg was directed to suspend his movement to Richmond and hasten Shields's division to Strasburg. Thus the noose of the trap would be closed at Strasburg and Jackson's army destroyed. Such, at least, was the anticipation of the Washington authorities.

This calculation, however, had not taken into account Jackson's resourcefulness and the marching ability of his "foot cavalry." With 15,000 men to meet the proposed concentration of 50,000 Federals, Jackson, warned by Southern sympathizers of the various movements of the enemy, withdrew all his forces except the Stonewall Brigade from Harper's Ferry and on May 30 retreated up the Valley, entering Strasburg that evening. In the late afternoon of the next day the Stonewall Brigade rejoined the army. The trap was a failure, to be blamed in part on the ineptitude of Banks, Frémont, and Shields. Jackson then continued up the Valley to Harrisonburg, where, changing the line of march, he moved in the direction of Brown's Gap in the Blue Ridge. En route to the Gap, he checked the slow-moving Frémont at Cross Keys on June 8 and, crossing the south fork of the Shenandoah River, routed Shields at Port Republic the following day.[34]

The campaign which had resulted in Frémont's and Shields's defeat was, Captain Hugh White declared, brilliantly conducted:

[General Jackson] not only extricated his whole army from a trap, skillfully set for him, but defeated one portion of their army [Frémont's], holding the other [Shields's] in check at the same

[34] Vandiver, *Stonewall*, pp. 262–83. Commenting upon Jackson's "foot cavalry," Apperson quoted a wag as saying that any woman who married a young man who had served under Jackson would be deceived; she might think that she had "a prize" but would find that he was "nothing but a worn out specimen of a man—no use at all on her hands to nurse and support" ("Diary," Oct. 29, 1862).

time, and on the next day utterly routing the second portion
[Shields's]. . . . Yes, [Frémont and Shields] conspired to catch
and destroy our General and his troops, but it had signally failed.
It is true, at one time, they had surrounded us. In their own favorite language, they had us "in the bag"; but then they had no man
brave or skillful enough to tie the bag and hold us in.[35]

The armies of Frémont and Shields withdrew down the
Valley after their reverses, Frémont to Mt. Jackson, Shields to
Luray. Jackson's army then bivouacked near Brown's Gap.
There it stayed until June 17, when it secretly and swiftly
slipped away for the Chickahominy River to aid General
Lee in his attack upon McClellan.

[35] To his father, Brown's Gap, mid-June, 1862, White, *White*, p. 93. An unusual "casualty" of the Valley campaign of 1862 was the loss of a rooster
which belonged to Pete, cook of the officers' mess of the college company.
Pete had always carried the fighting rooster on the officers' wagon and he
boasted that it had whipped every rooster from Harrisonburg to Winchester.
But in the retreat up the Valley in early June 1862, the gamecock met its
match, and Pete consigned it to the pot, explaining: "No chicken dat kin be
whipped shall go 'long with Gen. Jackson's headquarters [wagon]" (Edward
A. Moore, *The Story of a Cannoneer under Stonewall Jackson* [New York,
1907], p. 66; hereafter cited as Moore, *Cannoneer*).

Five

"HE FELL...
SWORD IN HAND"

AT BROWN'S Gap in early June 1862, after the strenuous campaign of the preceding weeks, the company of Liberty Hall Volunteers enjoyed a respite from marching and fighting. One day a group of them visited Weyer's Cave, near which the company was camped, and it was a delightful recreation for the youthful veterans accustomed to the hardships of soldiering; the sojourn reminded them of the peaceful and happy life that they had enjoyed before the war. After taking a "roll" in the Shenandoah they returned to camp feeling clean and in good spirits.[1]

Since they were camping in the open with "the sky [as their] roof and the earth [as their] bed," the boys were having a delightful time. The weather was beautiful and, they

[1] Hugh to mother, near Weyer's Cave, about June 11, 1862, White, *White*, p. 93.

were near enough to their homes to receive boxes of food. In fact, never before had conditions been better, and they lived and felt "like princes."[2] Their present encampment was too pleasant to last long, Captain Hugh White said, and he confidently expected an order to move; when and where, no one could tell. The brigade, however, was willing to go wherever General Jackson ordered, so implicit was their confidence not only in his integrity and fearless courage, but also in his generalship.[3]

During this period Captain White's company still served as headquarters guard for General Jackson and was relieved of all drills and the numerous annoying details common to camp life. Consequently there was leisure for reading and time for enjoying the society of friends. The situation was so enjoyable that Hugh feared he might become contented with this way of life. In his youthful meditations he had often wondered why one would choose the profession of soldiering with its dangers and privations; but now, despite them, he sometimes felt that a return to civilian life would be dull, at least for a time. Indeed, but for the fact that "the most blessed work" of the ministry, to which he had formerly dedicated his life, occupied the supreme place in his heart, he could easily become a soldier for life. Lest his parents should think his previous desire to preach had been weakened by his army experience, however, Hugh hastened to reassure them that he was "exceedingly anxious to close this army life, and enter upon that of the ministry."[4]

As an earnest of his determination to follow in the footsteps of his father as a minister of the gospel, Hugh urged him to make "a visit of Christian love" to the tents of the college

[2] Hugh to sister, near Weyer's Cave, mid-June 1862, *ibid.*, p. 95.
[3] To his mother, near Weyer's Cave, June 11, 1862, *ibid.*, p. 92.
[4] To his father, near Weyer's Cave, mid-June 1862, *ibid.*, p. 93.

boys, bringing with him religious tracts and Bibles. His presence would be appreciated by them, and they would listen to him and thank him for "any manifestation of love for their souls." To Hugh personally, seeing and talking with his father not only would be "a rich treat," but would gratify the "longings" of his heart.[5] Hugh was confident that his father would find the atmosphere very congenial at headquarters with General Jackson and his assistant adjutant-general, Major (Rev.) Robert L. Dabney. Though the latter was busy with official duties, he never neglected an opportunity to conduct religious services. Hugh termed an account of a service in which the college boys and other soldiers were administered the sacraments by Major Dabney "a spiritual feast indeed." Turning then to the subject of religion in the college company, a subject which weighed heavily upon his mind, Hugh added:

The religious element in our company is very strong; sufficient, I hope, to control all other elements and give tone to the whole body. We hold a brief meeting every night, just after roll call. The man whose turn it is stands up, while the rest stand around him. He reads a chapter, sometimes sings a hymn, then leads in prayer. There is some profanity in the company, but this is lessening. Why should not the army be a school for reformation of the wicked? Such it had proved to J[ames] W[ilson] and J[oseph] R[aymond]. They are now perfectly sober men and good soldiers.[6]

While Jackson's troops were encamped near Weyer's Cave, Hugh described to his sister the difficulty of finding time, whether the army was on the go or in camp, for "connected,

[5] *Ibid.*

[6] Hugh to sister, near Weyer's Cave, mid-June 1862, *ibid.*, p. 96. Apparently the father did not visit the army at this time.

sober thought. As for instance, today, I have been soldier, cook and *washerwoman*. Around me, as I write, some are cleaning their guns, others putting away the remnant of dinner, some are washing plates, and some are trying to sleep. I am sitting on a knapsack, with a tin pan as my writing desk. I write a sentence and have to stop to do something or talk to some one." Yet amid all this commotion Hugh was thinking of home. Although his thoughts, like the needle of a magnet, might be diverted somewhat from his loved ones by an object near him, they always turned again toward "the home circle and hover[ed] around the much loved places."[7] Hugh had previously told his father that "only a clear and strong conviction of duty, with an approving conscience," had kept him contented with the painful separation from his parents. But since the Christian soldier was always faced with the presence of death, he often thought more about God and heaven than of his earthly home and friends. While he cherished the memories of both the parental threshold and the family altar, yet this consecrated son reminded his father, "our true home is in heaven."[8]

The college company did not remain long at its delightful encampment at Weyer's Cave. On June 17 Jackson hastened to join Lee to take part in the battles that were to drive McClellan from Richmond. By June 25 Jackson's troops had advanced to Ashland, a point about twelve miles from the capital city of the Confederacy. From this point they marched toward Gaines' Mill where they joined Lee in his turning maneuver which ended with the retreat of McClellan to Harrison's Landing on the James River. In the fighting around Richmond in the summer of 1862, known as the

[7] *Ibid.*

[8] Near Weyer's Cave, mid-June 1862, *ibid.*, p. 93.

Seven Days' Battle, the Stonewall Brigade participated only in the battles of Gaines' Mill and Malvern Hill.[9]

At Charlottesville, en route to Richmond, Captain White was granted a sick leave and spent several days at home; during his absence the college company was commanded by Lieutenant G. B. Strickler. From Lexington, Hugh wrote his aunt, Mrs. Hutchinson of Monroe County, Virginia: "It is really painful to be absent, to be lying at ease here, in the lap of luxury, while . . . my comrades are bearing the burden of the service, perhaps struggling with our enemies. I would not remain at home [permanently] now, for any consideration. Our army seems to be making its way to Richmond. The great struggle must come off soon."[10] During the same visit Hugh also wrote his brother Henry, a Presbyterian minister, that he could not be happy with all the delights of home while a battle was imminent which might be decisive. He could only hope and pray that General Jackson would be as "richly blessed" as he had been in the Valley; and Hugh, an earnest Calvinist, had no doubts of the outcome: "I do believe that God has [Jackson] in His special favor, and guides him in all his course. Otherwise he could not run such risks in safety, and gain the most brilliant successes, when circumstances make defeat and ruin seem so inevitable."[11]

While Hugh yearned for peace with all its happiness, he was willing to fight in such "a glorious cause" as that in which "our young Confederacy" was engaged, he wrote the same brother on another occasion. Continuing the letter, he said, "If we give up, everything is lost. If we struggle on, endure

[9] Vandiver, Stonewall, ch. xiii; George F. Maynard, III, "The Stonewall Brigade" (MS, Senior Honors Thesis, McCormick Library, Washington and Lee University, 1953), ch. v.

[10] Lexington, late June 1862, White, White, p. 98.

[11] Probably near Richmond, mid-July 1862, ibid., p. 99.

hardships, exert our utmost strength, and put our trust in God, who has so far been very gracious to us, we may hope after a while to taste the most blessed fruits from these present distresses."[12]

When the news reached Lexington of the battle of Gaines' Mill and the gallant part the college company had played in the charge of the Stonewall Brigade, Hugh became greatly excited and declared: "All the money in the world could not compensate me for the pain I feel at not being with them. But if they conquer, this will moderate my sorrow." He immediately set out for Richmond and caught up with his company after the battle of Malvern Hill (July 1, 1862). On July 3 he wrote his father,

The fighting was desperate, and the [Yankee] escape [to Harrison's Landing] was very wonderful. . . . Their army must be greatly weakened and demoralized. Many of the prisoners represent their soldiers as broken-spirited, rebellious, and ready to desert. . . . The truth is, their soldiers are not actuated by the spirit which animates ours. They can make a grand show, blow the trumpets, and bluster about their flag, but are quick to choose between defeat and death. Considering what they have at stake, the former is far better of the two. But it is not with us. Our earthly all is at stake.[13]

Jackson's command soon moved nearer Richmond, and the Stonewall Brigade bivouacked on the farm of one of Hugh's uncles in Hanover County, the ancestral home of the Whites. Hugh spent several days there, visiting and also attending one Sunday a service at the Second Presbyterian Church in Richmond, whose pastor was the Rev. Dr. Moses Hoge. An

[12] *Ibid.*
[13] Below Richmond, *ibid.*, p. 101.

interesting incident happened to General Jackson on this occasion, Hugh reported: "General Jackson was present, and immediately after the benediction, all eyes were turned upon him. The General seemed uneasy, really appeared confused, pushed for the door, and vanished almost in an instant. I could but smile to see him fairly conquered and made to run."

Unlike most of the Valley soldiers Hugh was favorably impressed with the area around Richmond. There was no famine abroad in the streets; neither was disease as prevalent as he had expected; and though the brigade was camped on the south side of the Chickahominy River, the air was as pure as that of the Valley.[14]

Here Hugh received from his aunt, Mrs. Hutchinson, "a token of remembrance" in the form of money which he prized highly as a renewed evidence of her affection for him. But he did not want her to think that the war had impoverished him. That was impossible, because he had nothing before the war—neither houses, land, nor money to bother about. His present worry, he wryly added, was his friends, who were always terrified for their personal safety and property. If it were not for them he would be as free from apprehension as "the wild Indian who calls all the hills his own."

Turning from badinage to more serious matters, Hugh told his aunt that, while he had been optimistic and perhaps over-confident in regard to the prospects of the Confederacy, he had to confess that the recent successes of the enemy in the western theater of the war had somewhat disturbed him. Still he was not disheartened; reminding her of the old adage that it is "much better to provide for the future than to grieve over the past," Hugh thought these reverses might be a bless-

[14] Same, Glenwood, July 14, 1862, *ibid.*, pp. 101–2. For the same incident see Henry Kyd Douglas, *I Rode with Stonewall* (Chapel Hill, 1940), p. 119.

ing in the long run if they destroyed Southern overconfidence and led Southerners "to gird afresh the weapons of war."[15]

Another matter to which Hugh was giving serious thought was the question of resuming preparation for the ministry. As to his own plans, he would gladly continue in the army until the struggle was over if it were not for the critical shortage of ministers, lamenting, "If the pulpits are vacant, everything is lost. I must therefore, if possible, return to the Seminary in the fall. I will remain [in the army] however, until that time, and if the skies are brighter and I am alive, I will resume my course of preparation for the ministry. In this work I desire to live and die."[16]

Hugh had previously told his ministerial brother Henry that his desire to devote his entire time to the ministry was primarily a result of disappointment in his efforts to spread the gospel through the army. Although his father had thought the army "a glorious field" in this respect, Hugh had not found it so. He even had doubts whether his influence for good had been felt in his own company, although he did tell his aunt he had not observed any misconduct in it, nor had he ever seen any intoxication. All constantly read the Bible and several would perhaps make a profession of religion if the opportunity were offered. But he could not say as much of the general deportment of the army as a whole. What he had seen while visiting friends in other units during the lull after the Seven Days' Battle, had confirmed and strengthened his belief in the doctrine of "total depravity."[17] On another occasion, as he commented on a rumor concerning peace which

[15] Near Richmond, early July 1862, White, *White*, p. 103. On May 30, 1862, the Federals reached Corinth, Tenn., and took possession of the town; in a few weeks Memphis was occupied.

[16] *Ibid.*

[17] Hugh to Henry, Lexington, late June 1862, *ibid.*, p. 99; Hugh to aunt, near Richmond, mid-June 1862, *ibid.*, p. 103.

was going the rounds of the army, Hugh hopefully wrote that if peace should smile on the Confederacy, he could then complete "the cherished plan" of his life "to preach the gospel," one which had been interrupted by the war, and join his father, two brothers, and a cousin, all ministers, in the "same good work."[18]

The visits of Captain White in and around Richmond were of short duration. On July 13, 1862, Jackson was ordered by General Lee to proceed with his divisions to Gordonsville to meet the thrust of another Federal army advancing from Manassas to Gordonsville, an important link in the line of communications between the Valley of Virginia and Richmond. This army, composed of the troops of Frémont, Banks, and McDowell, was commanded by General John Pope. Jackson encountered the vanguard of Pope's troops at Cedar Mountain, south of Culpeper, on August 9, 1862, and defeated it.[19]

En route to Cedar Mountain, Hugh took time to congratulate his sister, Mrs. Harriet McCrum, on the birth of another daughter. It was indeed a pleasure to turn his thoughts away from the scenes of "bloodshed and destruction to the quiet pursuits and joys of the home circle." He wrote that he hoped to see her soon and romp with the little ones of her household. The letter quickly returned to the subject of war, however. Hugh insisted that it must be carried to the enemy's doorstep:

If invasion is feasible, we ought to try it, that the burden of the war may be laid upon the homes of our enemies, to teach them how sore a thing it is when it comes to our own doors. If we re-

[18] Hugh to Henry, near Richmond, early July 1862, *ibid.*, p. 100.

[19] Vandiver, *Stonewall*, ch. xiv. Jackson's troops left their encampment around Richmond on July 16, 1862. Gen. Charles S. Winder of the Stonewall Brigade was killed at Cedar Mountain and Col. W. S. H. Baylor of the Fifth Virginia succeeded him.

main idle after our victories, it only requires a short time for the Yankees to recover from their defeat and panic. They are well nigh frightened to death for a while, but if we leave them in possession of all their cities and their homes, they feel secure, and soon create a new excitement in favor of war, and push the poor Dutch and Irish to fill their broken ranks. If the men refuse to volunteer, they can be forced [into the service], and we may soon expect to see another immense army gathering around us. But they have been thoroughly whipped at Richmond; their effort is seen to be foolish by their own people; and without doubt we shall be ultimately free.[20]

Of the battle of Cedar Mountain, in which the college company suffered no casualties, Captain Hugh White modestly stated: "We have met the boastful Pope, and whipped him thoroughly and this, I trust, will discourage the Yankees more, and fill our hearts with more lively hope and confidence in God." One circumstance of the battle particularly impressed Hugh. As he paused on a hillside during the battle and looked down in the valley below, the scene reminded him of a picture-book battle: "As we, on the left moved forward and gained the top of a ridge before us, we could see the line of battle extending around to the extreme right, all along which the smoke rolled up in great clouds, and the fire from both sides flashed fiercely at each other."[21]

Meanwhile General Lee, informed that General McClellan was transferring his army from Harrison's Landing to Fredericksburg for the purpose of uniting it with Pope's army, set out with General James Longstreet's divisions to reinforce Jackson on the Rapidan River. Then followed the Second Manassas campaign, which terminated in the battle of Second Manassas on August 29 and 30, 1862.[22]

[20] Madison County, Va., June 23, 1862, White, *White*, p. 110.
[21] Hugh to father, Gordonsville, Aug. 13, 1862, *ibid.*, p. 113.
[22] Vandiver, *Stonewall*, pp. 345–71.

On Sunday, August 24, 1862, as Jackson's troops rested on the south side of the Rappahannock River preparatory to their daring raid on Pope's rear communications, Hugh White penned what proved to be his last letter to his father: "All are as merry in camp as if the enemy was a thousand miles away. It is wonderful how indifferent men can become to the most horrible scenes. . . . This has been very little like the Sabbath. With spirits saddened by hunger and fretted by the constant roar of artillery, we have been kept in an uncomfortable frame of mind." The busy preparations for moving on the next day, such as seeing that the company cooked three days' rations and attending to other routine chores, had deprived Hugh of any real enjoyment of the Sabbath, and it was with difficulty that he had prevented these duties from driving all devotion from his heart. Yet he hoped to find time to attend the afternoon brigade services to be conducted by the Rev. Joseph C. Stiles.

Writing as if in foreknowledge that he would not survive the impending battle, Hugh said: "I ought now more than ever to seek strength, my happiness, my all, in God. How could I live without Him? With Him no storm can disturb my peace, no danger can come nigh, no harm can befall which will not do me good." He was confident that God would crown their efforts with victory and enable them to crush "the infamous [Pope]." With such leaders like Lincoln, Halleck, his chief of staff, and Pope, the enemy could never triumph over the Confederate leaders who were "as distinguished for their piety as they [were] for their bravery and skill." Significantly Hugh sent in the letter one hundred dollars as a donation to the Confederate States Bible Society and the committee for the publication of religious tracts and books for the soldiers. The final words in the letter of this dutiful son who always had lived in the shadow of his father's approval were: "You are constantly in my mind and firmly engraved upon my heart."[23]

The Stonewall Brigade suffered severe losses in the first day's encounter at Second Manassas, and one of its casualties was the attractive and promising Willie C. Preston, son of Jackson's friend, J. T. L. Preston of Lexington. Shortly before the battle the eighteen-year-old lad, who had been a student at both Washington College and V.M.I., arrived at Jackson's headquarters to enlist in the Liberty Hall Volunteers. At Jackson's invitation he remained there before joining the college company, eating and sleeping with the members of the staff. All became much attached to the young fellow "whose manners were so gentle, kindly, and different, and his beardless, blue-eyed, boyish face so manly and handsome," Dr. Hunter McGuire, Jackson's medical director, afterward related. Willie reported to the company just before the battle and was shot in its closing moments. That night, as Jackson and Dr. McGuire sat around the campfire waiting for Jim Lewis, Jackson's cook, to make some coffee, Dr. McGuire remarked that Willie Preston had been mortally wounded. The news stunned both Jackson and "the faithful, big-hearted" Jim, who, McGuire said,

rolled on the ground groaning, in his agony of grief, but the General's face was a study. The muscles in his face were twitching convulsively, and his eyes were all aglow. He gripped me by the

[23] Banks of the Rappahannock, Aug. 24, 1862, White, *White,* pp. 114–16. General Pope was particularly hated; in July 18, 1862, he had issued a series of orders dealing with the Southern noncombatants living in the area of his army. One of these stated that all male citizens of Virginia within the Federal lines would be tendered the oath of allegiance to the U.S. government. Those taking and subsequently violating it would be shot. Those refusing to take it would be banished beyond the Federal lines and, if they returned, would be treated as spies. The order was anathema to Southerners (Chambers, *Jackson,* II, 92).

shoulder till it hurt me and turned and walked off into the woods alone. He soon came back, however, and I continued my report of the wounded and dead.[24]

"This has been a day of weeping and woe to this household. . . . My heart is wrung with grief to think his sweet face, his genial smile, his sympathetic heart are gone. My heart aches with weeping," Willie's devoted stepmother, Margaret Junkin Preston, noted in her diary. "Alas! what sorrow reigns over the land! . . . It is like the death of the first born in Egypt. Who thinks or cares for victory," was her lamentation as she recorded the names of other stricken families in Lexington.[25]

At the close of the first day's battle at Second Manassas on August 29, Colonel W. H. S. Baylor, acting commander of the Stonewall Brigade, sent for Captain White and proposed that a prayer meeting be held that night, saying:

I know the men are very much wearied out by the battle of today, and that they need all the rest they can get to fit them for the impending struggle of tomorrow; but I cannot consent that we shall seek repose until we have had a brief season of prayer, to thank God for the victory of today, and to beseech His continued protection and blessing during this terrible conflict.

The proposal was promptly and joyfully accepted by Captain White, who, with Chaplain A. C. Hopkins of the Second Virginia, conducted the meeting with many of his comrades in attendance.

[24] Hunter McGuire, *Stonewall Jackson, Address at the Dedication of the Jackson Memorial Hall, Virginia Military Institute, June 23, 1897* (Richmond, 1897), p. 19. The next morning, before Willie Preston died, he gave a message to Capt. Hugh White to be delivered to Willie's father, but this message was never delivered because Captain White himself was killed a few hours later (*Central Presbyterian* in White, *White*, p. 118). Jackson later wrote Colonel Preston that he had planned to make Willie a member of his staff (Allan, *Preston*, pp. 147–48).

[25] Allan, *Preston*, p. 147.

The sanguinary encounter was resumed the next day. Colonel Baylor, with the issue of the battle hanging in the balance, seized the flag of the Thirty-third Virginia Regiment, rushed forward at the head of the brigade, and was mortally wounded in the midst of the foe. Captain White quickly grabbed the colors, and waved them in advance of his company; as he moved forward to the front with sword and hat in one hand, calling upon his boys to follow him, he caught an enemy bullet and died instantly. He was the only captain of the Liberty Hall Volunteers who was killed in battle, and his body was buried on the battlefield.[26]

His death was mourned by both friends and comrades. The Lexington poetess, Margaret Junkin Preston, wrote Hugh's mother: "You are honored to have reared such a son for immortality," and the Lexington *Gazette* described him as a young man "of strong mind, thoroughly cultivated—a manly character—a pure and generous heart—firm and daring courage, all of which made him worthy to be the leader of our College boys."[27] To General Jackson, Hugh was the ideal Christian soldier. They had both been members of the same church in Lexington and colaborers in the same Sunday school. Writing to Dr. R. L. Dabney, Jackson said that Hugh's Christian labors

were not confined to times of peace. In the army he adorned the doctrines of Christ, his Savior. When testaments or other religious works were to be distributed, I found him ready for work. Though his loss must be mourned, yet it is gratifying to know he left us a bright example and that he fell, sword in hand cheering on his men, and leading them to victory in repelling the last attack of the enemy upon that bloody field.

[26] A. K. McClure, "General Lee's Army," in *The Annals of the War* (Philadelphia, 1879), p. 198; White, *White*, p. 117.
[27] Margaret Junkin Preston to Mrs. W. S. White, White, *White*, p. 119; *Gazette*, Sept. 11, 1862.

To Hugh's father General Jackson said,

The death of your noble son and my esteemed friend, Hugh, must have been a severe blow to you, yet we have the sweet assurance that, whilst we mourn his loss to the country, to the church, and to ourselves, all has been gained for him.[28]

One of Hugh's fellow students at the Theological Seminary, James Power Smith, later of Jackson's staff, wrote in the *Central Presbyterian:*

Dear, dear Hugh, the purest, the truest, the best of all. . . . What a blessed ministry did we anticipate in his! How full of promise, of usefulness were his amiable, attractive qualities, his accurate and increasing attainments, and his quiet, yet earnest, active piety.

Lieutenant Givens B. Strickler, Hugh's successor as captain of the college company, extolled at length Hugh's qualities as a man and officer and exclaimed, "How rare are such characters!"[29]

Although the Army of Northern Virginia had been fighting and marching continuously from June 26 to the end of August 1862, immediately after Second Manassas General Lee decided to invade the North without giving his men any rest. So the army was set in motion on September 4, and the Stonewall Brigade, which was part of Jackson's old division, crossed the Potomac the next day and bivouacked the next night in Maryland. The brigade was "in excellent order and high spirits," one of its regimental commanders wrote. At Sharpsburg, Maryland, near Antietam Creek, an indecisive

[28] To Dr. R. L. Dabney, White, *White,* p. 119; to Dr. W. S. White, quoted in Chambers, *Jackson,* II, 457.

[29] J. P. Smith to the editor of the *Central Presbyterian,* quoted in White, *White,* p. 123; Lieut. G. B. Strickler to J. J. White, *ibid.,* p. 121. Lieut. Strickler was Hugh White's successor as captain of the Liberty Hall Volunteers. At the end of the battle of Second Manassas on Aug. 30, the Fourth Virginia mustered less than 100 men.

battle was fought on September 17, 1862. Lee's opponent
was his old antagonist, George B. McClellan. After this encounter Lee's army recrossed the Potomac and went into
camp in the lower Shenandoah Valley to rest and regain its
strength after the strenuous campaign in Maryland. Again,
on December 13, 1862, Lee encountered the Federal army
at Fredericksburg under the leadership of General Ambrose
E. Burnside, whose attacks upon the Confederate position on
the hills west of the town were easily repulsed with frightful
losses.[30]

In the hard fighting during the summer and fall of 1862
the ranks of the company of Liberty Hall Volunteers had been
reduced by casualties to such an extent that not enough men
remained to perform guard duties at Jackson's headquarters. After Sharpsburg this position was taken over by the
First Virginia Battalion, known as the "Irish Battalion."[31]

Following the Fredericksburg battle the Confederate
army went into winter quarters on the right bank of the Rappahannock River, and the college company, as part of the
Stonewall Brigade, was stationed near Jackson's headquarters
at Moss Neck, the baronial home of the Corbin family.[32]

In a religious revival which swept through the Army of
Northern Virginia in the early spring of 1863, at least two
members of the college company, Ted Barclay and Nathan
Lackey, made an open confession of faith. Ted had indi-

[30] Vandiver, *Stonewall*, chs. xvi–xvii. In the battle of Sharpsburg, the college company's losses were slight, only three being wounded. One of them
was Corp. S. R. Moore, who was struck on the brow with a musket ball
which passed out back of the ear. In a semiconscious condition he was
placed, about sundown of the day of the battle, in a wagon and taken eventually to the home of the Bedingers at Sheperdstown. He remained there
until he was taken by his father to Lexington (Moore, *Cannoneer*, p. 175;
War of Rebellion . . . Official Records of the Union and Confederate Armies,
ser. I, vol. XIX, pt. i, pp. 1010–13).

[31] Strickler, "Volunteers," p. 116.

[32] Bean, *Pendleton*, p. 88.

cated a growing interest in religion in the summer of 1862, but it was not until April 1863 that he publicly expressed a desire to affiliate with a church. This request was transmitted by the Rev. L. C. Vass, brigade chaplain, to the Session of the Lexington Presbyterian Church, and Ted was admitted *in absentia* to its "communion."[33]

The battle of Chancellorsville was fought May 1–5, 1863, in a densely wooded area known as the Wilderness, fifteen miles west of Fredericksburg. On May 2 Lee sent the bulk of Jackson's Second Corps around the Federal center and right of General Joseph Hooker's Army of the Potomac. In the late afternoon of that day Jackson struck its unprotected right flank, threw it into confusion, and drove it down the turnpike to within several hundred yards of Chancellorsville —a mid-nineteenth century version of a modern blitzkrieg.

It was during a lull in the fighting around nine o'clock in the evening that Jackson was wounded. The struggle was renewed at daybreak of the following day by General J. E. B. Stuart, who was placed temporarily in command of Jackson's corps, and the battle continued with fury until dusk. The Federals were forced back from their position at Chancellorsville and required to anchor their flanks on the Rappahannock. On the night of May 5 they withdrew across the river, returning to their old camps on its left bank.[34]

The events of May 2 and 3, 1863, were described by Ted Barclay to his homefolk:

[33] "A minute of the Session of the Lexington Presbyterian Church during the Civil War" (Rockbridge *County News,* Dec. 2, 1915). Nathan Lackey was not an alumnus of Washington College.

[34] Vandiver, *Stonewall,* ch. XIX; Earl Schenck Miers, *Robert E. Lee: A Great Life in Brief* (New York, 1956), ch. ix. General Longstreet, with two of his divisions, was not in the Chancellorsville campaign, having been previously dispatched to Southside Virginia to collect supplies for the Army of Northern Virginia.

General Jackson commenced [on May 2] a flank movement to [the Federal] right through a dense pine forest, Gen. Stuart clearing the road as we advanced. After three or four hours we found our division a mile in the rear of the enemies' line which extended across the plank road. . . . We advanced down the plank road, our line being three or four miles in length; presently the sharp rattle of the musket told plainly that the pickets had commenced the engagement, which was to be the greatest defeat the Federal army ever had and which was to cost us so many valuable lives. We came out of the woods, which had been concealing our movements, into an open field expecting every moment to engage the enemy, but they were so much taken by surprise that our pickets had driven their whole line. . . . We continued driving their rear until nine o'clock at night, having crossed one line of breastworks which the enemy had hastily thrown up. After we got in their rear, lying down behind their breastworks, we intended waiting until morning to renew the fight but the enemy thinking to retrieve himself made a night attack which they partially succeeded in capturing one of our batteries, but soon we were in line again and recaptured our battery together with quite a number of prisoners. Twas in this fight that Gen. Jackson lost his arm. . . .

The next morning every one knew that the most terrible battle of the war must begin. We marched slowly down the road, all the time under fire of several batteries of the enemy. We at first went on the left of the plank road, thinking that the main body of the enemy were posted there but soon we found out from the pressure on our right that it was the enemy's strongest point so we had to cross the road covered by the enemy's cannon, [and] here many a noble Southron fell to rise no more, among them Gen. Paxton who was shot through the heart from which he died shortly afterwards. A piece of shell struck my knap sack, but was too spent to hurt me. We went about a quarter of a mile to the left and took position behind the front line of the enemy's breastwork from which they had just before been driven. As soon as we were in line, our guns primed and bayonets fixed, Gen. Stuart, he being in command of the Corps, Gens. Jackson and Hill both wounded, called out for the Old Stonewall [Brigade] to follow. We went over the breastworks with a yell which was answered by a shower of leaden hail. Feeling that perhaps at that time prayers were going up at home for our protection I became almost unconscious of danger though men were falling fast and thick around me. We halted and commenced firing at the enemy about one hundred yards distant, we stood and fired until almost every man was killed or wounded; the force of the enemy being so much greater than ours. Major Terry, commanding our regiment, gave the order to fall back, but I was totally unconscious of what was going on and tried to rally the men, when Major Terry came up to me and ordered me to fall back as nearly all his regiment were killed or wounded.[35]

To the Liberty Hall Volunteers the greatest loss in the Stonewall Brigade was their leader, General Elisha Franklin Paxton, who was known personally to many of them. Scion of an old Rockbridge family, Frank Paxton as he was known, was an alumnus of Washington College and later of Yale College. He had studied law at the University of Virginia and, after having practiced law for a time at Lexington, gave it up on the advice of his physician and retired to an estate near Lexington. A steadfast Democrat of the state rights school and an immediate secessionist in the winter of 1860–61, Paxton offended certain local Unionists by his vehement advocacy of secession—among them the Rev. Dr. George

[35] To his sister, Hamilton's Crossing, May 8, 1861, Barclay Letters. A. P. Hill was a divisional commander in Jackson's Second Corps. Maj. William Terry of Wytheville, Va., was the regimental commander of the Fourth Virginia. Hospital Steward John Apperson noted in his diary of May 3, 1863, regarding the fighting on the morning of May 3: "The Stonewall Brigade covered itself in glory while its chieftain Jackson is suffering in the hearing of the guns. . . . The loss in the 4th Regt is almost appalling—went into the battle with 365 and lost 163. . . . The brigade charged the enemy's work 3 times before it was successful. Genl Paxton was killed; he was a brave man. ("Diary," May 3, 1863). The college company lost 3 killed and 16 wounded, having entered the battle with 28 men (Strickler, "Volunteers," p. 117; see Robertson, Stonewall Brigade, ch. xv, for Chancellorsville).

Junkin, father of General Jackson's first wife. During a heated discussion of secession in the Franklin Literary Society, a semipublic forum of those days for the discussion of current public issues, Jackson took umbrage at Paxton's remarks to Dr. Junkin. An estrangement between Jackson and Paxton resulted, and on the eve of the Civil War they were not speaking. In the maelstrom of war, however, this was soon forgotten, and their original friendly feelings were restored with greater warmth than ever. Paxton was among the first volunteers to leave Lexington for the front; the Rockbridge Rifles, of which he was an officer, departed on April 24, 1861, for Harper's Ferry. This unit was soon assigned to the Twenty-seventh Virginia Infantry, Stonewall Brigade.

From First Manassas, where Paxton's courageous conduct attracted Jackson's attention, to Chancellorsville, Paxton participated in every encounter in which the Stonewall Brigade fought. Though he had been promoted to major of the regiment in October 1861, he failed to be chosen in the popular election of field officers the following May. He then accepted a place on Jackson's staff with the rank of major. In November 1862 Jackson made him a brigadier general and placed him in command of the Stonewall Brigade, an act which some of the regimental officers resented.[36]

Although the Stonewall Brigade was with Jackson on the flanking movement of May 2, 1863, it was not in the fighting during the late afternoon and early evening of the day, for it had been previously ordered by Jackson to protect the rear of his column. After the fall of Jackson great confusion followed among the Confederate troops, and the Stonewall Bri-

[36] W. G. Bean, "A House Divided: The Civil War Letters of a Virginia Family," *Virginia Magazine of History and Biography*, LIX (Oct. 1951), 403–4. For the disaffection in the brigade, see *ibid.*, p. 404–5. At that time there was a vacancy in the command of the Stonewall Brigade.

gade was up nearly all night marching and countermarching on the turnpike.

Jackson's wounding depressed Paxton, and a few hours before he himself was shot, he told a member of his staff, Captain Henry Kyd Douglas, that he did not expect to survive the impending battle. At the crack of dawn the next day, May 3 (Sunday), the brigade was placed in line of battle not far from the enemy's position, and as it prepared to move forward, Douglas saw Paxton

sitting near a fence, in rear of his line, with his back against a tree, reading the Bible. He received me cheerfully. I had been with him but a few minutes when the order came for his brigade to move. He put the Bible in his breast-pocket, and directing me to take the left of the brigade, he moved off to the right of the brigade. I never saw him again.

Paxton was immediately shot and died almost instantly. On the evening of May 3 at the field hospital near the Wilderness Tavern when Jackson heard of Paxton's death, he "turned his face to the wall and wept." In the Jackson Memorial Cemetery at Lexington, Virginia, a simple tombstone bears the inscription:

> GENERAL E. F. PAXTON,
> Died at Chancellorsville, May 3, 1863,
> AGED 35 YEARS.
> "It is well with thee."[37]

Ted Barclay wrote that Hooker, "finding his plans all foiled and rations getting scarce, determined to recross the River and claim a great victory and try another 'On to Richmond' [movement] by a safer route at a more favorable time. So ends

[37] Henry K. Douglas to J. G. Paxton, Hagerstown, Md., Feb. 18, 1893, in John Gallatin Paxton, *Memoir and Memorials of Elisha Franklin Paxton, Brigadier-General, C.S.A.* (n.p., pref. dated 1905), pp. 103–4, 114.

the fifth book in the 'On to Richmond' and the end of another Yankee General."[38]

A few days later Ted drew a picture for his sister of the horrors of the battlefield over which the Stonewall Brigade passed in returning to its old camp site, renamed Camp Paxton in memory of its fallen chieftain:

Our own dead had been buried and the wounded removed but the Yankee dead and wounded lay thickly over the field. Many had not yet had their wounds dressed and lay groaning on the wet grounds praying every passer by to change their position or give them a drink of water and now as the excitement of the battle was over our men did all in their power to alleviate their suffering, thinking not of them as enemies who had come to subjugate us but as suffering mortals. Their dead lay thick over the grounds, some seemed as though they had died without a struggle without a visible wound but the small minie ball had done its work of death; others could hardly be recognized as human beings, mangled and torn by solid shot, shell, and grape, and these showed how awful had been their suffering, with teeth clinched and hands deeply buried in the earth, they seemed to have suffered agonies before death relieved them; and the poor horses were not spared, here laid some literally torn to pieces, others with feet shot off endeavoring in vain to get up. Our men humanely shot them as they would never get over their wounds.[39]

On May 10, 1863, General Jackson died at Guiney Station, south of Fredericksburg, where he had been removed from the army hospital in the Wilderness after the amputation of

[38] To his sister, Hamilton's Crossing, May 12, 1863, Barclay Letters. "On to Richmond" was the slogan, first used by Horace Greeley, editor of the New York *Tribune,* which influenced Gen. Irvin McDowell reluctantly to order an advance into Virginia. The battle of First Manassas followed. Hooker was the fifth general to try to capture Richmond, his predecessors having been McDowell, McClellan, Pope, and Burnside. Hooker was soon replaced, as Ted had predicted, as commander of the Army of the Potomac by Gen. George G. Meade.

[39] Camp Paxton, May 12, 1863, Barclay Letters.

his arm. Ted Barclay, who had been reared in the Calvinist tradition, believed that the General's death was God's way of rebuking the Southern people for having made him an idol. While the army mourned his death and a deep gloom had descended, yet there was no feeling of despair. Ted was convinced that God, if He wished to do so, could raise up "many a Jackson" and deliver the South from the power of the enemy.[40]

"Oh, What a blow this is! what a loss—how disheartening!" John Apperson, former hospital steward of the college company's regiment, recorded in his diary upon hearing of Jackson's death. "God gave him to us and He has taken him from us and we should trust to [Him] to raise [up] another in his stead. His death will cause the [Southern] nation to mourn, for no man of the war has so entirely won the affection of the people as Jackson." The next day (May 11) Apperson, who was stationed at the hospital at Guiney Station, went to the depot where the funeral party was to leave for Richmond. As the train moved off he mused, "The old Brigade has stood by the old hero since the beginning of the war and fought bravely."[41]

Subsequent to Jackson's death, and in part as a consequence of it, the Army of Northern Virginia was reorganized into three corps. The Stonewall Brigade remained in the Second Corps under new brigade and divisional commanders, Generals James A. Walker and Edward ("Allegheny") Johnson. Commenting upon Johnson, Ted said he was "a good general and brave man but one of the wickedest men [he] had ever heard of." Another member of the Stonewall Brigade, "Correspondent" of the *Rockingham Register*, described Walker as "an accomplished gentleman and gallant officer. He has fight in his eyes, and I doubt not he will fill the

[40] *Ibid.*
[41] "Diary," May 10, 11, 1863.

position with credit to himself." This writer also pointed out that four of the five former brigade commanders had been killed in battle, but he hoped General Walker would be fortunate enough to pass safely through the war until peace would return to "their bleeding country."[42]

Camp Paxton, located near Hamilton's Crossing, was situated in a dense forest with pure, sparkling water close by which made it a desirable location for the Stonewall Brigade. The morale of the brigade was high despite its heavy losses at Chancellorsville, a member of the brigade boasted, adding: "Whenever Mr. Joe Hooker wishes to test its merit as a fighting unit he will find the Stonewall Brigade did not die with its original commander [Jackson] and that it is anxious to prove it can fight as well since his death as before it."[43]

One of the principal grievances of the men in Lee's army was the extortion practiced by the sutlers. In the Stonewall Brigade the cost of the paper used in writing a letter was forty cents; a plug of tobacco one dollar and forty cents; a quart of peanuts one dollar—and all of this out of a private's monthly pay of eleven dollars. One of the sutlers had notified the men that henceforth he would not sell any item for less than a dollar. "These land sharks come among us with their goods, and as they are necessary, we have to buy them and

[42] Ted to sister, Camp Paxton, May 26, 1863, Barclay Letters; "Correspondent," in Rockingham *Register*, May 29, 1863; Douglas Southall Freeman, *Lee's Lieutenants* (New York, 1942–44), vol. II, ch. XXVII. General Johnson was called "Allegheny" because he had commanded troops in the Allegheny Mountains in the early days of the war. Under the new corps organization of the Army of Northern Virginia, the First Corps remained under Gen. James Longstreet, the Second was entrusted to Gen. R. S. Ewell, and the Third to Gen. A. P. Hill. Ewell and Hill had been divisional commanders in Jackson's Second Corps. James A. Walker, while a cadet at V.M.I., had challenged Jackson to a duel and was subsequently dismissed. In 1861 he formed a company, the Pulaski Guards, Stonewall Brigade, and soon was advanced from captain to colonel (William Couper, *One Hundred Years at V.M.I.* [Richmond, 1939], III, 179).

[43] "Correspondent" in Rockingham *Register*, June 12, 1863.

pay the enormous prices or do without," the "Correspondent" complained.[44]

About this time Ted Barclay wrote about clothes, the condition of the army, and religion:

> As you have been asking a good many questions about my clothes I will set you at rest on that point. I have worn out the suit, pants, coat, and socks, but as I was getting tolerably ragged, and the brigade secured a supply of English clothes, so I was one of needy ones I am rigged out in a splendid suit of blue, and I bought socks; my shirts are in very good condition yet and as I have to play turtle here (carry my earthly effects on my back) I do not wish to tote more. I had my boots mended and they will do for some time yet, but you may send my others down, but do not hurry and take any kind of article. I wish my boots to be soft and not too heavy, as heavy boots are apt to blister the feet in warm weather.
>
> ... General Longstreet has arrived here with his troops and our army is in much better condition than before the fight. I expect that we will make a forward movement soon, certainly there was never a more favorable time than the present, the enemy weakened by both battle and the expiration of the time of the nine months men.
>
> Mr. Junkin arrived here a day or so ago; he is staying with our company and preaches every day. There is great interest taken in the meetings, and many joined the church. Has my certificate of membership arrived in Lexington yet?[45]

In the meantime, while Lee's army was marking time on the Rappahannock following the battle of Chancellorsville, he was preparing for another spring at the enemy's throat, and on enemy soil.

[44] *Ibid.*

[45] To his sister, Camp Paxton, June 1, 1863, Barclay Letters. The Rev. William J. Junkin was the son of Dr. George Junkin. He was pastor of a Presbyterian church in Rockbridge County.

Six

"DIRTY, RAGGED AND BAREFOOTED"

IN early June 1863, the Army of Northern Virginia abandoned its camps on the Rappahannock and began its second northward trek. As the Second Corps marched by way of Culpeper toward the Blue Ridge, the veterans of Jackson's old command, wrote Sergeant Charles A. Rollins of the Stonewall Brigade, began to sniff the familiar pine-laden atmosphere of the mountains and to wonder whether they were returning "to our beautiful Virginia Valley, so fraught with the glorious memories of the past." When it was evident that the lower Valley was the army's destination, shouts of joy went up from the Stonewall Brigade, which was leading the vanguard of Ewell's corps. As it passed through the villages, it was hailed with cheers by the people who flocked in from the countryside. All kinds of dainties were dispensed by the hands of "pretty pink-cheeked mountain maidens." When the brigade had gained the crest of the mountain, its enthusiasm knew no bounds:

The laurel was in bloom and its cream-pink laden boughs bent down on the banks of the road as if to crown us returning victors to the scenes of our earlier conquests. The men at the head of the column, animated by a common impulse, rushed to the banks of the road, broke off clusters of the beautiful blossoms and stuck the stems in the muzzles of their guns. The rest of the column caught the contagion and as the brigade wound its way down the serpentine road it gave the deceptive appearance of columns of bouquets moving in opposite directions.

As each regiment of the brigade entered Front Royal, the scene of one of Jackson's victories in the Valley campaign of 1862, its colonel would wheel in his saddle and give the command, "Attention," followed by "Close order, march." Then the Stonewall Brigade band would strike up some martial air and the men would strut through the town with the precision acquired by long practice. "The glance from the eyes of the lovely girls crowding the sidewalks caused our hearts to go 'pit-a-pat,'" Sergeant Rollins of the Stonewall Brigade remembered.

From Front Royal the Second Corps marched directly to Winchester, which was occupied by the Federal troops of General Robert Milroy. After the defeat and the capture of the bulk of his army, the Stonewall Brigade thought it would make a triumphant entry into the town, but found itself denied this privilege. Its disappointment turned to chagrin when later General Jubal A. Early's division of the Second Corps came marching past the brigade arrayed in "new fancy shirts and hats, eating, and smoking cigars," plunder which the Federals and their well-stocked sutlers had abandoned at Winchester.[1]

[1] Charles A. Rollins, "On the road to Gettysburg," in the Pittsburgh *Chronicle Telegraph,* copied in the Lexington *Gazette,* Aug. 2, 1888; hereafter cited as Rollins, "Gettysburg," Lexington *Gazette.* This was a series of

As they resumed the march down the Valley after the capture of Winchester, the Stonewall Brigade was on ground which aroused memories of the first days of the war. At Shepherdstown the men were issued more substantial and varied rations than they had been accustomed to, canned goods, candies, cigars, and a desiccated soup of vegetables pressed into plugs like tobacco. The latter was prepared by being placed in hot water. Fording the Potomac at Shepherdstown, the men were forced to strip almost naked, but they were compensated by a "refreshing and no doubt a much needed bath." The contrast between the fertile fields, ripening grain, and the peace and contentment in Maryland with the scenes which they had left behind in war-ridden Virginia was very evident. The men of the brigade, most of whom were from the Valley, were reminded of the beautiful Shenandoah Valley before it was scarred by war.[2]

Ted Barclay gave an account of the "meanderings" of the Second Corps (of which the college company was part) from the Rappahannock River to Winchester and of the capture of Winchester:

We left camp [on the Rappahannock] on the 5th of June and marched by Spottsylvania C[ourt] H[ouse] to within a few miles of Orange C[ourt] H[ouse], turned off, came to Rapidan, forded the river to Culpeper C[ourt] H[ouse], thence to Sperryville,

---

articles published by Rollins. While stationed at Winchester, Milroy had taken possession of a fine, handsomely furnished residence and had brought on his wife and daughters to occupy it. The "rebel" girls often intimated to them that Jackson would swoop down upon the town some day and gobble up the whole "shebang." To this, the general's daughters were reported to have replied: "Just let Stonewall Jackson come, pa'll show them who's a general." When Milroy fled leaving behind him his artillery, the bulk of his troops, and his family, "the naughty rebel" maidens taunted them, "Where is your pa general now" (*ibid.*)?

[2] *Ibid.*

thence towards Warrenton, turned off the Warrenton road near Washington, the county seat of Rappahannock [County], crossed the Blue Ridge, then down the Shenandoah Valley to near Winchester, here we found the beast Milroy in a post near the town, strongly fortified.

Gen. Ewell thinking the place too strong to storm without loss of a great many lives sent our division, Gen. Johnson's, to the rear of Winchester, Gen. Early's down the main turnpike, and Gen. Rodes' to Martinsburg. We spent the day getting into our positions. About dark we opened on them with our artillery. I think it was the most beautiful sight I ever witnessed. We soon drove Milroy from his outer works to his main post, when we stopped shelling, and awaiting morning, to develop him. About daybreak we found out that he was endeavoring to cut through our lines in the rear towards Harpers Ferry. Gen. Johnson had his lines completed and ready for action nor had we long to wait as Milroy knew that success depended upon the vigor of his attack. The 4th La. and 3rd Va. brigades met the first assault, the enemy greatly outnumbering them drove them back a short distance, when Gen. Johnson galloping along the line told them the Stonewall [Brigade] was coming to their support and they soon rallied and in turn drove the enemy, our brigade firing only a few shots. The enemy seeing the hopelessness of getting through determined to surrender. . . . Gen. Milroy with the cavalry escaped, owing to an opening in our lines. . . .

I think we have a very good successor to Gen. Jackson.[3]

By leisurely marches up the Cumberland Valley, General Ewell with two of his divisions reached Carlisle, Pennsylvania, on June 27, 1863. Twenty-five years later Sergeant Rollins grew nostalgic in writing about this valley:

Ah! that holiday march up that rich valley, teeming with

[3] To his sister, near Sharpsburg, June 9, 1863, Barclay Letters. Jubal A. Early and R. E. Rodes were divisional commanders in Ewell's Second Corps. General Johnson commanded the other division in this corps.

plenty. Why, we felt as happy and content as the nabobs at summer resorts. We had even become accustomed to the scowls that
so disfigured what would otherwise have been handsome faces of
the girls, who flourished their tiny U.S. flags in our face and
wished us all the bad luck imaginable. But we took it good-na-
turedly. In the towns, especially, we saw many ex-soldiers [North-
ern], probably soldiers in citizens clothes; they could not hide
their martial bearing, and as we would sing pointedly to them,

"A'in't you glad you got out of the Wilderness, got out of the
Wilderness," they would give themselves away. Some would
laugh outright, others looked at us with a quizzical smile, as if asking, "How did you know I was at Chancellorsville?" While others
would give an appealing glance that almost voiced, "Don't give us
away, boys!"[4]

In the three-day encounters at Gettysburg, July 1–3, 1863,
Johnson's division of Ewell's corps was not engaged until the
late afternoon of July 2, when three of his brigades stormed
Culp's Hill and gained a foothold on the slope of this strategic
position. The Stonewall Brigade did not take part in this action, but during the night it joined the other brigades and
participated in the attempt the next morning (July 3) to capture the crest of the hill. Johnson repeatedly hurled his four
brigades against powerful Federal breastworks, but each attack was repulsed and a counterattack by the enemy forced
most of the Confederates to retreat to their former position
at the base of Culp's Hill.[5]

[4] "Gettysburg," Lexington *Gazette*, Aug. 2, 1888.
[5] In the first day's encounter at Gettysburg only A. P. Hill's corps, and
Rodes' and Early's divisions of Ewell's corps were engaged. Johnson's division of Ewell's corps was composed of four brigades commanded by Gens.
George Steuart, Francis T. Nicholls, John M. Jones, and J. A. Walker.
Walker's brigade was the Stonewall Brigade. On the afternoon of July 2,
while the other three brigades of Johnson's division were assaulting Culp's
Hill, the Stonewall Brigade was assigned the "degrading business" of pro-
tecting the left flanks of the attacking troops, "playing cavalry" as the boys

In the fighting on Culp's Hill the Fourth Virginia advanced from boulder to boulder upon the Federal breastworks until the men were almost on the top of the crest. But finding it impossible to advance any further and realizing that any attempt to retreat meant almost certain death, most of the regiment surrendered. In the college company one was killed, five wounded, and sixteen were captured, including Captain Strickler. As John McKee was pulled over the breastworks by a burly Federal, the captor said, "Gim-me-your hand, Johnny Reb; you've give' us the bulliest fight of the war." Lieutenant J. H. B. Jones managed to escape, and as he darted down the slope of the hill he lost his sword. Three bullets passed through his clothes in his flight, and the rock behind which he finally took refuge was peppered by gunfire.[6]

General Lee withdrew from Gettysburg on July 4 and retired to Virginia. He crossed the Potomac at Williamsport,

---

called it. While in this position, the Stonewall Brigade was subjected to savage artillery fire and the men suspected Johnson was exposing them to the enemy fire in order to draw it from Steuart's brigade which was advancing up Culp's Hill. Sergeant Rollins stated that Johnson was unpopular with the men of the Stonewall Brigade, who referred to him as "Brute" Johnson ("Gettysburg," Lexington *Gazette*, Sept. 27, 1888). For an excellent account of Johnson's division at Gettysburg on July 2, 3, 1863, see Clifford Dowdey, *Death of a Nation: The Story of Lee and His Men at Gettysburg* (New York, 1958), pp. 259–60.

[6] Moore, *Cannoneer*, pp. 193–94. After his capture Capt. Strickler was taken to Johnson's Island near Sandusky, Ohio. After the war he had a distinguished career in the Southern Presbyterian Church, serving for many years as pastor of the Central Presbyterian Church at Atlanta and closing his career as a professor at the Union Theological Seminary at Richmond. He was also rector of the Board of Trustees of Washington and Lee University. He died in 1913. Probably his interest in the ministry was first aroused at Johnson's Island (Henry Richard McFayden, "Confederates Studied to Preach," *Presbyterian Survey* [Richmond, Va.], July 1961). After Gettysburg, Lieut. J. H. B. Jones assumed command of the college company.

Maryland, and continued up the Shenandoah Valley to Martinsburg; when General Meade advanced to Warrenton, Lee crossed the Blue Ridge and took up a position near Culpeper. Meade then occupied the right bank of the Rappahannock River. In these positions the two armies remained inactive for several weeks.[7]

During the retreat from Gettysburg, Ted wrote his sister about the fighting on Culp's Hill:

Since I last wrote we have pulled through trying scenes. Through all of which, by the mercy of God, I have been spared whilst others have been cut down. In the third of the series [on July 3] of battles around Gettysburg our little band of boys were all killed, wounded, and taken prisoners, except Lieut. [J. H. B.] Jones, [David] Whitmore, and myself. Truly I feel thankful that I am spared. Our regiment has only 66 men left and the whole division suffered proportionally through the folly of our hard fighting Johnson. He has none of the qualities of a general but expects to do everything by fighting. Three or four times did he throw our gallant band against powerful breastworks, and Yankees without number each time mowing them down.

. . . I escaped by being in the rear of the regiment to prevent men going off the field unnecessarily. I had a very disagreeable position as I was exposed to the [enemy's] fire and could not fire myself, a position I do not like at all.

I will not venture an opinion on the battle as you can judge from our papers. What the result of it was—we were not whipped though we suffered heavily. The first two days fighting was entirely in our favor. How unfortunate it was we attempted to drive them from an impregnable position. We are now lying near Hagerstown, Md. Whether Lee intends going across the river [back to Virginia] I cannot tell, but if we do have to fight again we will have a fair field and I fear not the result.

[7] Douglas Southall Freeman, *Robert E. Lee: A Biography* (New York, 1934), III, ch. x; hereafter cited as Freeman, *Lee*.

. . . My dear sister, how differently I feel now exposed to death and danger with God as a protector, I care not what may be the privations and dangers knowing that God can bring me through them all.[8]

A few days later at Hagerstown, Ted described his destitution:

Our army has been in line of battle here for two days awaiting an attack from General Meade who does not seem disposed to hurry himself about it. . . . We are strongly entrenched, our line reaching from above Williamsport around by Hagerstown and joining the river again below Williamsport. General Ewell holds the left, General Hill the center, and General Longstreet the right.

I do not think that General Lee will stay here long. He is waiting for the river to fall but he will give the enemy a fight if they desire it. The army is in fine spirits, but dirty, ragged and bare footed. I have had on my clothes nearly a month, my pants are nearly worn out, you may make up two under shirts, two pairs of drawers, three pairs of socks, a pair of pants and a jacket if you think you can make it to fit; if not I think I can have one made here; do not make the clothes too large, make them up and keep them on hand until we get back to Virginia. The army is in such a bad condition as far as clothes are concerned and our means of transportation are so limited and provisions so far to haul that we are compelled to recross the river.

I feel lonesome sometimes with the few of us who are left. . . . Lieuts. Samuel W. Lyle and James W. Spohr who were not in the fight have joined us, so that there are now five, Lyle, Jones, Whitmore, Spohr, and myself. The rest I suppose are captured. I wish that when you send the clothes you would send me a small Bible if you can get one. My Testament got wet and is torn all to pieces. I have to borrow one when I want it.[9]

[8] Near Hagerstown, July 8, 1863, Barclay Letters.
[9] Same, Hagerstown, July 13, 1863, *ibid.*

Back on the soil of Virginia at Camp Stephens near Winchester, the Stonewall Brigade's first camp site in the summer of 1861, Ted recounted his blessings since that time:

We left Hagerstown on the night of the 13th, marched all night, forded the Potomac up to our arms, and to one o'clock today [July 14] when we got to this place, which you will recognize as the first camp we ever had when we came into [the] service. But, oh, how different [is] the camp of [18]63 compared to that of [18]61, then we had seventy-three men [in the company] whereas today only three of those seventy-three answer the roll call. Where are others? Many faces come up to my view who now lie slumbering beneath the sod awaiting the sound of the "last trumpet" to awaken them to give an account of the deeds done in the body. Among them the form of the noble [Edward A.] Mitchell. His prospects were as bright, his hopes as high as those of any of us. In a few weeks he laid down his life a sacrifice to his country's cause. Why have I been spared those two years of toil and danger whilst many promised to be bright and shining lights have been cut down?

I thank God I was not cut off in my sins but spared until by the mercy of God, I was brought from darkness into light. Now whatever awaits me, whether death upon the bloody battlefield or permitted to breath my last with kind friends around to attend to every want, I feel that I have a bright future before me. I would like to die amidst my friends, but if God has so willed it that I should lie upon the field with nothing to mark the spot where the soldier lies, I feel that when the cold waters of death are rippling around my feet I can, trusting to the merits of a redeeming Saviour, launch my bark upon its dark unknown surface and at last anchor in the harbor of heaven. But I trust I may be permitted to spend yet many a happy day in the Old Stone Cottage in peace and safety.

Now that we are in Virginia, I expect that we will camp here a week or so, and if Mr. Middleton will come down send me the things that I wrote for [in his last letter] and also a box of eatables if possible.[10]

In his next letter, Ted showed impatience at not having received any response to his request for clothes:

I have been waiting for a long time for a letter from home. . . . I suppose that you thought that I had been taken prisoner with the rest of the company and consequently would not waste a sheet of paper nor allow your highly interesting epistles to be lost.

This morning [July 20] Johnson's Division moved down (to Martinsburg) to destroy the Baltimore and Ohio R. R. which will take a day or two and then we will move back to [Camp Stephens] where I think we will rest until Lee gets his army shod and clothed.

I still have on my only shirt or rather a piece of shirt. Have had it on for over a month and there is no prospect of getting one shortly from the Quartermasters Dept., so I shall have to wait until I can get clothes from home. I have written two letters for clothes but as they have perhaps miscarried, I will try again. I want a complete rigging out except a hat. I also wrote for a box [of food] but I suppose there are not enough of men [in the company] to justify Mr. Middleton coming down. . . . But if it is possible send my clothes as quick as possible.

I heard an excellent sermon from Mr. Lacy on "Be ye not deceived, God is not mocked. . . ." There is still a great deal of religious feeling in the army. Oh, that this army was a bunch of Christian men, then we might indeed expect peace, no longer

[10] Same, Camp Stephens, July 14, 1863, *ibid.* Edward A. Mitchell of Columbus, Ga., was one of the students who participated in the flag episodes at Washington College in the spring of 1861. He died shortly after the battle of First Manassas. The Stone Cottage was the Barclay home about one-half mile west of Lexington; it is still standing. Mr. Middleton was a citizen of Lexington who often visited the camps carrying boxes to the soldiers from their parents.

then would we be punished by the fall of our cities and the repulse of our armies.

We have heard nothing from our boys captured at Gettysburg; hope they will soon be exchanged. It is quite lonesome with those [five] that are here.[11]

While the Army of Northern Virginia was moving across the mountains, Ted wrote his sister that his situation was desperate, for he was now not only ragged but "lousy" as well:

We are again on the tramp; we left the vicinity of Martinsburg on [July] 21st, after one of the hardest days of work [tearing up the B. & O. R. R.] I ever did.

We marched near Winchester, the next day from Winchester to Front Royal, a march of twenty-five or thirty miles, stood picket most of the night and today [July 24] marched to this place, 13 miles from Luray. Where we are bound I cannot tell but think we will go to Culpeper C[ourt] H[ouse].

If it is in the range of human exertion I wish you would send me the clothing, you cannot imagine my condition. I have no seat in my pants, the legs are worn out, have had but one pair of socks which are worn out completely, my shirt is literally rotted off me, but I was so fortunate as to get a white shirt and a pair of drawers, which both are now so lousy that I can scarcely bear them. This evening I caught between 50 or 100 on my shirt and drawers. Excuse plain speaking but it is certainly *not an exaggerated* state of affairs.

I would not bother you so often if I could possibly stand it or there was any chance of getting them here. I offered to give fifty

[11] To his sister, Martinsburg, July 20, 1863, *ibid.* In the winter of 1862–63, at the suggestion of General Jackson, the Rev. Beverly Tucker Lacy, eminent Presbyterian divine of Virginia, agreed to accept the position of unofficial chaplain of Jackson's Second Corps. Mr. Lacy at once organized an association of the chaplains of the Second Corps at the Round Oak Baptist Church in Caroline County, Va., located near Jackson's headquarters at Moss Neck. Lacy continued after Jackson's death as chaplain of the Second Corps.

dollars today for underclothes but neither money nor love can get them. I know this letter is rather complaining, but as it is the first one of that stamp and considering the desperate state of affairs I hope you will excuse it.[12]

Encamped near Orange Court House, Ted commented on the religious interest in the Stonewall Brigade:

Yesterday heard a sermon from the Rev. Mr. McNear of Monroe [County, now W. Va.], who is at present acting chaplain for our regiment, a very good sermon but rather too much on the Methodist order. In the evening attended a meeting of the Christian Association which meetings are very pleasant and instructive. After dark I attended the usual prayer meeting which is held every evening. The religious interest has somewhat abated since our march commenced, dangers which have been passed through seem to harden the hearts of men. A day or so ago I saw a game of cards going on, the first I have seen since [the battle of Gettysburg], and before [it] you could seldom hear an oath, now it grates on your ears at every turn. Still there is a great deal of interest in the Brigade. Yesterday it was stated that one of the Cols. in the Brigade was greatly interested and several line officers. We have two excellent chaplains in the Brigade, the Rev. Mr. Vass of the 27th [Virginia] and Rev. Mr. Hopkins of 2nd [Virginia]. I wish we had Wm. Junkin for ours, [for] he had a great deal of influence in the regiment [and] the men liked him very much. I wish often that he was back.

This morning I took off the only suit I have and had it washed and . . . now I feel clean, a feeling I have been stranger to for a long time, but [since] the suit is white it soon becomes dirty and we seldom have a chance to wash, so I suppose I will be dirty until winter puts an end to marching, as an active campaign seems to be the order of the day. I expect the next trial of arms will be on the banks of the Rapidan, it will be the bloodiest con-

[12] Same, Camp Stonewall Brigade, July 24, 1863, *ibid.*

flict of the war, [as] this army thinks they have the Gettysburg spot to wipe out. Send down my clothes by the first safe opportunity. I am going out this afternoon to gather some blackberries to make me a pie. We have been living on them since we came across the Blue Ridge.[13]

At last, in early August 1863, Jim Humbles, a free Negro of Lexington, arrived in camp with a box of clothes for Ted; he also told his mother of the offer of an "easy" position which he had received:

How thankful I was to get them no one knows but one who has been without clothes as I have. After dinner I took soap and went to the creek, took a good wash and put on my clothes, every article of which fits to suit the taste of the most fastidious. But how sorry I am that you were so much troubled to get them sent.

I am afraid from all accounts that I hear that Elihu [Ted's brother] is leading quite a reckless life. I pray God to turn him from the error of his way. I wish you all would write and tell me everything that concerns the family in any thing. You may think that such things are not interesting to me but since I have changed my course in life everything is interesting. I don't feel as I used to, I trust that I have now learned to view life in a different light, not intended to be spent in a gay and reckless manner but for higher and nobler purposes.

[13] Same, Aug. 3, 1863, *ibid.* For the wartime ministerial work of the Rev. L. C. Vass, see the Rev. J. William Jones, *Christ in Camp* (Richmond, 1888), pp. 514–24; for the Rev. A. C. Hopkins' wartime activities, see *ibid.*, pp. 465–78. After the war Mr. Hopkins was a well-known figure in Presbyterian circles in Virginia and West Virginia, serving a church at Charleston, W. Va., for many years. In May 1863, after the battle of Chancellorsville, a Christian Association was formed in the Stonewall Brigade for the promotion of "vital godliness" in the brigade. Among the college boys who joined were Captain Strickler, Ted Barclay, and Horace Paxton. See W. Harrison Daniel, "The Christian Association: A Religious Society in the Army of Northern Virginia," *Virginia Magazine of History and Biography*, LIX (Jan. 1961), 92–100.

... I have no doubt that the position would be a very pleasant as well as a profitable one and also suit me very well, but my sense of duty cannot let me leave the field for any easy position in such a time as this. I have no doubt far abler bodied ones are occupying those positions than myself but I trust that I may be able to stand the service this summer and fall, in which time I hope our cause, by the help of God, will be gloriously triumphant and we may all be permitted to return to our homes in peace and safety. God can shelter us in the storm of battle as well as at home.[14]

Two weeks later, from the camp near Orange Court House, Ted wrote that the depletions in the army were rapidly being filled with new recruits and that the men were in "fine spirits":

The Army has become rested and now we perform all the duties of a regular camp, drill, police, guard, etc. We have all the comforts of a regular army. Boxes are beginning to come from camp quite frequently from Staunton, as it is only a half day's ride on the cars from Staunton and we are camped near the railroad. We can get corn by paying $1.00 per dozen, but corn without tomatoes soon become stale; you see that even a soldier, and a rebel one at that, has his nice notions [and] we get to be quite gentlemen when we have been in camp sometime. We seem to have forgotten that we were glad to get "shorts" and raw bacon only a few weeks ago, but so it is always with man, never contented. I suppose if I were at home I would be discontented too but neverthe-

[14] To his mother, Camp Stonewall Brigade, Aug. 5, 1863, Barclay Letters. Jim Humbles was a free Negro who was often employed by parents of Rockbridge County to carry boxes to their sons in camp. After the war Humbles operated a confectionery establishment in Lexington. Elihu Barclay later served in the First Virginia Cavalry, losing a hand in battle. Whether the position offered Ted was a civilian or a military one is not clear. The offer apparently came from Ted's cousin, John Paxton, because Ted added a postscript to his letter, "Tell Cousin John I am very much obliged to him but feel compelled to decline the offer." At that time the Army of Northern Virginia was still in the vicinity of Orange Court House.

less I would like to try it again for a while. I think I would be
contented until the tomatoes were gone.[15]

In the next letter Ted told about an unusual brigade review:

Our army is now in fine condition and enjoying themselves as
much as soldiers can. General Ewell reviewed our brigade yesterday. We had quite a number of Orange and Madison [counties]
beauties to grace the field. After the review we were requested
to give them a rebel charge; we formed in line about 200 yards in
front and down the hill from them and charged up toward the
crowd of ladies, officers and [their Negro servants], the only priv-
ileged persons in the army, with a rebel yell . . . and as we came
on such a getting over the fence [in the rear by the Negroes]
you never saw. The ladies be it said stood their ground firmly,
never flinching and I think they wished the gallants of the Brigade
to capture them. As for my part I had a splendid [beauty] in view
[to capture] but she threw such a shower of smiles etc, as compelled me to retire. After the charge the Gens. and Cols. went off
to supper whilst we returned to camp to our *beef* and *bread* as
well satisfied as they.

Today the soldiers determined to have a sham review, so they
appointed their Gens. and Cols. from the ugliest men in the brigade (of course I would not come in under that score) fixed
themselves up in Shanghai twinings—provided themselves with
mules and such specimens of the horse flesh as you saw last winter and altogether it was quite a complete affair.

I have been playing the nurse for a day or so; my bed fellow,
George Chapin, has been quite sick but is now recovering from a
spell brought on by imprudent eating.[16]

The months of August and September 1863 passed without any major engagement between Lee's and Meade's ar-

[15] Same, Aug. 17, 1863, *ibid.*
[16] Same, Sept. 1, 1863, *ibid.* George Chapin was the son of the clerk of the
court, Rockbridge County.

mies. Early in September, General Longstreet with two of his divisions was detached from the Army of Northern Virginia and sent west to join General Braxton Bragg in an effort to destroy the Federal army of General Rosecrans near Chattanooga. Thus weakened, Lee evacuated Culpeper and retired to the south bank of the Rapidan River. On September 18 and 19, 1863, the combined forces of Longstreet and Bragg inflicted a disastrous defeat upon Rosecrans at Chickamauga, Georgia.[17]

Ted wrote in late September about a wedding in the family, fraternization between Southern and Northern soldiers, and cheering news from the West:

So I suppose it is a foregone conclusion that I am to have a M.D. for an uncle. Tell Aunt Phoebe Paxton if she can possibly put off the day until December I will endeavor to get a furlough and come home to witness the union of two such splendid specimens of the "Homus Genus." By all means if she cannot put off the day save me some of the peach pie and honey. . . .

I have opportunities here of sending letters through the line as the pickets are very friendly. We exchange papers, talk on the state of affairs, trade tobacco for coffee, etc. I will write to Sallie [Paxton of Paris, Ky., Ted's cousin] and send on through [the picket line] and if you wish to write enclose it in one to me and I will put it through despite orders. Tell Pax[ton, Ted's young brother] to stay young as long as possible and not to desire to leave home for he cannot better his condition. I speak from bitter experience. Oh, how pleasant home would be to me now, but it is better to think of these things as little as possible as I have devoted myself to the cause of the Confederacy, I will have to consider this my home.

The news is cheering from General Bragg. I hope he will have the skill to follow up his successes and it will result in the entire annihilation of Rosecrantz [sic] army, quite blood thirsty you

[17] Freeman, *Lee*, ch. x.

will perhaps think [me], but I really think that it would be for the good of mankind, if the whole Yankee race could be swept from the face of the earth.[18]

So panic-stricken was Rosecrans after his defeat at Chickamauga, that Meade, under orders from Washington, immediately sent two of his army corps to his relief. Lee, realizing that Meade was now incapable of offensive action, saw an opportunity to maneuver and place his army between Meade and Washington. Accordingly, on October 8 Hill's and Ewell's corps crossed the Rappahannock with the objective of turning Meade's right flank. Meade, however, had been informed of the movement and fell back along the Orange and Alexandria Railroad toward Centreville. Lee pursued Meade, and on October 14 Hill's corps came into contact with the rear of Meade's retreating army. In the engagement that followed at Bristoe Station, a portion of Hill's corps was badly mauled by the Federals.[19]

While the Stonewall Brigade rested at Warrenton on October 13, Ted described the movement of Ewell's corps in this maneuver:

We left our camp on the Rapidan very unexpectedly on the 8th. marched to Orange C. H. thence across to Rapidan, thence to Madison C. H., thence to Culpeper, thence here. As yet have had no general engagement but continued skirmishing as the enemy seem disposed not to give us a fight, but as Lee is pressing them

[18] To his sister, Camp Stonewall Brigade, Sept. 29, 1863. Barclay Letters. Phoebe Paxton, sister of Ted's mother, was married to Dr. John Wilson McClung of Rockbridge County. Sallie Paxton was the daughter of William B. Paxton, brother of Ted's mother. At that time, with the Federal army on the left bank of the Rapidan River and the Confederate on its right bank, fraternization between the soldiers was a common occurrence. After the battle of Chickamauga the inept Bragg failed to follow up his victory.

[19] Freeman, *Lee*, ch. x.

very hard I suppose will have a fight on the old plains of Manassas. The Yankee army is very much weakened. We have so far captured over a thousand prisoners and [General] Stuart is still bringing them in by small lots. The enemy have burnt a great quantity of stores and destroyed the bridges over the railroad. We are now on their left flank and [General] Hill is endeavoring to get in their rear but is somewhat behind time. They, the Yankees, may succeed in reaching their entrenchments around Centreville, if not I think they will get such a thrashing as will learn them a lesson for some time to come.

You may think that I am boasting too much, but though we may outnumber them I do not trust in our own strength, but in the arm of our omnipotent and righteous God.

I suppose I will lose another box if you sent it by Chapin as he has not yet come up but I will be willing to lose anything to accomplish the thrashing of the Yankees. If we do get into a fight depend upon your brother to do his duty though death be the consequence. And what if I do fall? I trust I am prepared, and what a cause to fall in, fighting for everything that we hold dear— But God can protect amidst the storm of war as well as elsewhere.[20]

On October 27, 1863, as the Stonewall Brigade rested in its camp after the Bristoe Station campaign, it was called out to witness the execution of a deserter from one of its regiments, the Second Virginia. Private Jacob Fitzmeyer described the execution as "awful":

Our brigade was the only one that witnessed it. . . . When the hour of his execution had arrived we were marched out and

[20] To his sister, Warrenton, Oct. 13, 1863, Barclay Letters. George Chapin was on furlough in Lexington, having been called home by his father's death. Later Chapin arrived with Ted's "overcoat, shirt, and the remnant of my box." But since he had been delayed on the road, he had opened the box and eaten the turkey and other "things," thinking they would spoil. However, the butter, a few sweet potatoes, the bottle of sorghum, the pickle, and cheese were saved (same, Camp Stonewall Brigade, Brandy Station, Oct. 27, 1863, *ibid.*).

formed into a hollow square and then the prisoner was marched in with the drums in front of him beating the Dead March and then next followed the men that were to shoot him. He was then taken to the stake, sat on his coffin with his hands tied fast to the back of the stake and blindfolded. The ten men that [were to shoot] him were marched five steps in front of him and after that was done, the preacher knelt in prayer with him and the [prisoner] was then shot. His father and mother were present and as soon as he was shot his body was put on a wagon and taken home. This was a very hard thing for his parents to see their son murdered in such a way.[21]

After the reverse at Bristoe Station, General Lee realized the impossibility of subsisting the army north of the Rappahannock River and in early November again withdrew it to the south bank. A few days later a minor disaster followed. Upon his retirement Lee had left a bridgehead at Rappahannock Station on the north bank of the Rappahannock, and on the night of November 7 General Meade surprised and captured this *tête-de-pont*, inflicting considerable losses upon its defenders. Following this debacle, Lee recrossed the Rapidan to its south side and put his troops in the old quarters which they had occupied before the Bristoe Station campaign.[22]

"We have just returned to our old camp," Ted wrote his sister on November 15, 1863, but he did not think the fighting was over for the winter; instead he anticipated stirring times there as soon as Meade seemed disposed to advance. Thanking his sister for a box of food which had come, he added, "I am afraid you deny yourselves some comforts to supply me. You make apologies in your letter for the contents of

[21] Same, Oct. 27, 1863; Jacob Fitzmeyer to father, Brandy Station, Oct. 29, 1863 (letter in the possession of Mr. William Fitzmeyer of Mt. Jackson, Va., who graciously allowed me to use it).

[22] Freeman, *Lee*, ch. xi.

the box but they certainly need none. If the home folks could only see how we enjoy them, I think they would be amply repaid for their trouble."[23]

In late November the apparent quiet which had settled along the Rapidan River was interrupted, as Ted had expected, by an enemy foray across the river. Meade crossed the river at Germanna Ford and headed south into the Wilderness, hoping to turn Lee's right flank. Lee, apprised by General Stuart of this maneuver, rapidly confronted Meade with his entire army behind entrenchments at Mine Run.[24] Ted described the preparations made by General Lee to meet this movement:

We were ordered from camp to the line of battle, along the banks of the Rapidan and commenced throwing up a line of works to connect with the Chancellorsville line. We worked two days and have details working today. We now have a line from Liberty Mills in Madison [County] to Fredericksburg, so we are prepared to meet the valiant Yank at any point in Northern Virginia.[25]

A few days later, November 25, Ted said they were ready for Meade's attack:

I have just finished a hard day's work, throwing up cannon pits and feel somewhat tired. . . . Meade is evidently determined to try another "On to Richmond" but we are prepared for them and they will meet with such a defeat as they have never had before as God will not prosper such a cause as theirs. Our army is in a fine condition and much stronger than most people suppose.

[23] Camp Stonewall Brigade, Nov. 15, 1863, Barclay Letters.
[24] Freeman, *Lee's Lieutenants*, III, 271–80. At that time Lee had with him only two corps, Ewell's and Hill's. Two divisions of Longstreet's corps were still in East Tennessee.
[25] To his sister, Camp Stonewall Brigade, Nov. 19, 1863, Barclay Letters.

I expect that before the close of this week or the first of next will witness another battle on the banks of the Rapidan. So much for war news. There seems to be a marrying fever in the [Stonewall] Brigade at present. I suppose there would be no chance for an humble private [like myself] but as I have no intentions there I need not care.[26]

A minor encounter which occurred at Mine Run on November 27 between Johnson's division (Ewell's corps), and a Federal corps disrupted Meade's plan and convinced him of the folly of attacking Lee. Meade then quietly decamped to the north bank of the Rapidan River, and Lee's troops returned to their positions south of the river. The Mine Run campaign ended military operations in Virginia for 1863, and both armies went into winter quarters.[27]

In the engagement at Mine Run Private Ted Barclay won a spot promotion to a lieutenancy. An order had previously been promulgated in the Army of Northern Virginia that a commission would be granted to any private or noncommissioned officer who should perform an act of gallantry in battle. Privates Barclay and George Chapin, tired of carrying muskets and cartridge boxes, had determined to be either "distinguished or extinguished" in the next engagement. At Mine Run, Barclay seized the colors of the Fourth Virginia after the color bearer had been shot down and, accompanied by Chapin, advanced in the face of a withering fire. Chapin was "extinguished," but Barclay continued forward, planted the flag in the no man's land between the opposing lines, and calmly walked back to the Confederate line. For this act of daring courage Ted was cited officially by Colonel Wil-

[26] Same, Nov. 25, 1863, *ibid.*
[27] Freeman, Lee, ch. xi.

liam Terry of the Fourth Virginia for gallantry and subsequently received the coveted lieutenancy.[28]

In his description of the engagement Ted, not disposed "to blow [his] own horn," modestly said:

As we are again in our old camp and the Yankee gone I suppose I can give you an account of our campaign. Yesterday week we marched down towards Germanna Ford and were about forming our line on the left of General Hill, when firing commenced in our rear. General Johnson supposing it to be Yankee cavalry sent out the 2nd. Virginia as skirmishers to hold them in check but they soon found out that instead of cavalry it was the third army corps commanded by General French, so our division about faced, formed our line and advanced. We drove their line of skirmishers back upon their line of battle when the firing commenced in earnest on the Yankee side. As yet our line had fired very little. At this time our color bearer was shot through both legs and the colors fell to the ground, I threw down my gun and took the colors, the line was reformed and with a rebel yell we dashed forward, but were met with such a terrible fire that we were compelled to halt, formed our line along a fence and held our ground until dark when we withdrew, being under fire about four hours. I was complimented on the field by General Walker's Adjutant General and General Walker also took my name, so you see I have endeavored to do my duty. Major Terry also since our return to camp has complimented me very highly. I now have a very honorable place though by some considered dangerous but I think that one place is as dangerous as another for God has appointed our day and we are perfectly safe until that day comes. Whether I will continue to hold it I cannot say as the colors do not properly belong to our company. But enough about myself for fear you think I am disposed too much to blow my own horn, a thing above all things I

[28] Moore, *Cannoneer*, p. 210. George Chapin was buried in the Lexington Cemetery, now the Stonewall Jackson Memorial Cemetery, and as long as Ted lived he always placed a wreath on Chapin's grave on Memorial Day.

despise. The next day we formed our line on General Hill's left and threw up a line of works (by the way, we, the army of Northern Virginia have become quite a good set of dirt diggers, but I do not think there is any disgrace in using all lawful means to preserve our lives, for enough gallant spirits have already fallen in this carnal war).

What a noble fellow was George Chapin, how that family have suffered. But whom God loveth he chasteneth. He intends only their gold to refine, their dross to consume.

We lay quiet in our works expecting the Yanks to advance, but they were not disposed to do so and on Tuesday night withdrew across the Rapidan; we then moved up to our old camp and now all is apparently quiet. Some think that the campaign is not yet over but unless they do something shortly the weather will declare an armistice.

How much I miss my bedfellow, George Chapin. You have no idea what an attachment grows between two soldiers, who are constantly together. What a noble fellow he was. A gentleman and a soldier, I wish I could add a professed Christian, but can we not still hope, as doubtless he was the object of many an earnest prayer and his life was such a moral one, though I do not place any confidence in morality, still his life was so free from any gross sin that I still have hopes that he now rests in Heaven. May God comfort the afflicted mother, sisters and brother.

I was so unfortunate as to lose my knapsack and now am using his clothes, but I may be able to draw clothes from the Q.M. They ought to furnish me and must. The shirts I get here are white and get dirty very quick, but I have already gotten too much from home and will depend in the future on the Confederacy. . . .

Oh! how much more enjoyment I have now; for my part I cannot see how a wicked man can be a good soldier.[29]

A few days after Christmas, Ted wrote about a Christmas dinner and rumors of a marrying "mania" at Lexington:

[29] To his sister, Camp Stonewall Brigade, Dec. 5, 1863, Barclay Letters.

I feel tonight like taking off gloves and pitching in to give you a regular down scolding. Two weeks have gone by and still no letter from home. I would let you know that I am still on "terra firma" and as glad as ever to receive one of your sunny epistles, for they are indeed as a ray of sunshine in these dark and troublesome times. How eagerly we all look for the mails and how happy to get letters none but a soldier can tell. But I will reprieve you for a few days but must insist that you make up for lost time by writing longer letters. I want no more half sheets. We are at last in winter quarters. I have been very busy for two days building me a hut; will try to finish tomorrow and then I will feel more at home. We have all been looking for Mr. Middleton for some days, but hear that the canal is broken so have in some measure given him out until the rainy season is past for it has been raining here incessantly for two or three days and suppose that you are visited with a similar blessing. How did you spend your Christmas? I was on picket on the Rapidan, had Confed. bacon and bread for breakfast, and bread and bacon for dinner, and for supper nothing. Hope you fared more sumptuously. Some of our officers disgraced themselves by getting drunk. Why is it (the birthday of our Lord and Saviour) should be especially set apart to be thus desecrated? Certainly it should be a day of rejoicing to us. But that it should be thus spent, how disgraceful and sinful.

I have heard that Miss Kate Compton is married and that to Lieut. Smith of V.M.I. Is it true? Marrying seems to have gotten to be quite a mania with the Lexington ladies. I wonder if Miss Barclay will not soon be off. I expect it would be a good idea for me to employ an agent to act for me before the crop is all sent to market. Will you consent to act for me? If so do not pick an inferior article. [Instead] I would prefer to wait for the next season, [as] I understand that there is a good show for the growing crop.

I expect Watson Woods will have to come into service again as I see Congress is after the substitute gents with a sharp pole.[30]

[30] Same, Dec. 29, 1863, *ibid.* Apparently Watson Woods, one of the original members of the company of Liberty Hall Volunteers, had subsequently hired a substitute.

In the winter of 1863–64, after the guns had been silenced along the Rapidan River, Ewell's corps guarded its fords eastward from Orange Court House to the western edge of the Wilderness, and the Stonewall Brigade was camped in the vicinity of Mt. Pisgah Church, near Raccoon Ford, five miles northeast of Orange Court House.

Seven

CAPTURE AT
THE BLOODY ANGLE

IN LATE January 1864, Ted Barclay, after having spent several days at home on a furlough, returned to the brigade winter quarters near Orange Court House. In a facetious mood Ted told of "the troubles, trials, and tribulations" of the journey:

> After getting to the city [Lexington], I rolled aboard the coach and four with nine large persons inside, so you may imagine I was somewhat mashed, though, as subsequent events will prove, managed to keep the "breff" in my body. After walking and riding in turns we managed to get to the far famed Cedar Grove. By the way I should have mentioned that one of the nine illustrious persons inside the stage was Miss Snodgrass herself who sat opposite me. Here, viz. Cedar Grove, I determined to make an advance so I cautiously threw out my skirmishers and introduced myself, she did likewise, so we were soon tete-a-tete. All went on admirably until within a short distance of Brownsburg, when the

stage went into a rut and Miss Snodgrass into my lap. Fearing that she might suffer damage by a too sudden rebound, what was more natural [for me] than to lay hold [of her]. But the stage having righted itself and the fair tiny lady being all right side up with care, we moved on harmoniously to Middlebrook where Miss Snodgrass got out at the head of the town and in taking out her trunk the boot of the stage was not well fastened, so when we started at a swift trot through the town, out pops my box on the ground and Mrs. Barclay's dried apples were soon walking all around the town. After getting to the hotel at Middlebrook gathering up the remnants of my box and nailing it up again we were soon all right and arrived at Staunton without further horrors where I had to sleep on the floor.

The next morning got on train and arrived safely at Orange and thence to camp.[1]

Ted quieted his mother's fears about the temptations of army life:

Do you think that I could for one moment think of returning to the beggarly elements of this world after enjoying the sweets of this Christian life? . . . Oh, do not believe for one moment that I could be induced to forsake the cause of Christ; it is the only thing that shed any light on this dark cloud of war, the only thing that smooths my rugged pathway. The life of a Christian must be dear to any one, but how doubly dear it is to a soldier. How sweet it is to feel that I am a Christian when all is dark and gloomy around me. The light that emanates from the cross of Christ drives away this gloom and makes my heart so light and happy.

. . . I have just had another manifestation of His mercy towards me in being safely spared through the battle of the other day,

[1] To his family, Camp Stonewall Brigade, Jan. 26, 1864, Barclay Letters. Ted was traveling on the stage coach on the Lexington-Staunton Plank Road which passed by Cedar Grove, a stopping place on the road. Brownsburg and Middlebrook were villages on the road.

though it was not a severe fight, it requires only one ball to end our lives, and when many a one passed harmlessly by that is the time to feel how sweet it is to be a Christian. When the balls are flying thick around you and dealing death all around, to commit yourself into His care is [comforting], knowing that He has power to [render powerless] the missiles of death. . . .

Excuse this scratch. I believe I am getting more careless about my writing every day but I console myself by saying that all great men wrote badly.[2]

In a letter written on February 22, 1864, Ted paid his respects to conscripts and the Confederate Congress; he was optimistic that "the beginning of the end can now be seen . . . [and] that peace, honorable and lasting, shall smile sweetly upon us:"

What does Mr. Patton do in regard to the substitute act and how does he manage to keep out? We received our first installment of conscripts yesterday and I thought at the time as the regiment were whooping and making all sorts of fun over them that some of them would feel cheap if they should find some kinfolk among the number so I kept mute as a mice and pictured to myself McTanner walking along in the crowd. Poor men I pity them, they seem to think that the army is the last place in the world to have to come to and cannot reconcile the idea that this is to be their home until we shall have achieved our independence. . . . Patriotism is at considerable discount with them and only equals Confederate Shuck [money]. By the way I expect our Shuck will considerably improve owing to the recent legislature of our Congress. All honor to our noble Congress who tax everything and put everybody into the army but themselves. But I suppose they think that the Confederacy is about played out in that thing which they call talent and do not think that it would

[2] To his mother, Camp Stonewall Brigade, Feb. 10, 1864, *ibid.* The battle referred to was only a minor skirmish at Morton's Ford on the Rapidan River (Freeman, *Lee's Lieutenants,* III, 333–34).

be advisable to expose themselves to the bullets of the Yanks which slay without fear, favor or affection. But I think he would be a fool indeed who would not be able, if he had the power, to devise means for his own safety. But the recent acts of Congress seem to meet with general favor and even the ever-fault-finding [Richmond] Examiner seems to be for once half pleased. I am glad to see the tone of the people is becoming more courageous and more worthy of Southerners battling for freedom and all that men hold dear. But look at our noble army voluntarily reenlisting for the war, none are found who shirk from their duty. On the other hand look at the Yankees offering enormous bounties and getting so few soldiers at that. Is not our cause brighter than it has ever been? God seems to be smiling upon us. We can never be conquered, I trust in God, and our own brave legions. I think that the beginning of the end can now be seen and before the snows of next winter, peace, honorable and lasting shall smile sweetly upon us. God grant that my hopes may not be wrong. But it is the general opinion in the army. Col. Terry said today he firmly believed that we would have peace before July [1864].

We have been having quite an interesting series of meetings lately and they still progress. They are conducted by Rev. Mr. Baker of Staunton, who is very plain but I think a good man. I hope they may be attended with good results. We have also had some interesting meetings of our [Christian] association since my return. Expect to have the Rev. Dr. Hoge to address us in a week or so.[3]

[3] To his sister, Camp Stonewall Brigade, Barclay Letters. In January 1864, the Confederate Congress abolished the system of substitutes in regard to conscription (A. B. Moore, *Conscription and Conflict in the Confederacy* [New York, 1924], p. 44). Confederate paper money had rapidly depreciated by January 1864 and inflation was rampant, the dollar being equal to four and one-half cents in gold. But on Feb. 17, 1864, Congress, to reduce the volume of paper money in circulation, passed a law requiring the people to exchange their paper money for long-time bonds (Clement Eaton, *A History of the Southern Confederacy* [New York, 1954], p. 238). The Richmond *Examiner* was an anti-Davis paper. The Rev. Dr. Moses Hoge, pastor of the Second Presbyterian Church at Richmond, Va., was a roving chaplain in the Army of Northern Virginia.

In his next letter Ted explained why the soldiers welcomed snow and mud, described a snow battle, and related some chitchat about routine life in camp:

We start on picket again day after tomorrow and as it has been raining and snowing for a day or so a walk of ten miles through the slush will not be very pleasant. The snow fell here to the depth of eight or ten inches, but the rains have swept it all off, and the mud is now as deep as the snow was, but we soldiers do not grumble at mud as it will retard military movements as long as it lasts. You see we are as big cowards as ever. This thing of soldiers being anxious to engage the enemy, or as our papers term it "spoiling for a fight" is all a fudge, we are never anxious, but when it comes all will do their duty. The day after the snow fell our division challenged [Rodes's] for a snowball, which was accepted by them, and they, headed by their officers drove us off the field capturing our colors, but we could not let it stand thus so sending for Gen. Walker, we formed again, and drove them through their camps recovering our colors and several of their officers. The only thing that happened to mar the pleasure of the day was an accident to Gen. Doles who was knocked off his horse by a piece of mud which I suppose was rolled in a snowball.

I suppose my letters are very uninteresting as we have nothing but our own comforts and trials to relate and confined to our little sphere, we have no news and know not what is engaging the attention of others who have free access to the world. A soldier is a little government by himself, has his own household duties to attend to, such as cooking, washing, mending, &c &c. I think the ladies should consider themselves fortunate who get an old infantry rebel for a husband; he could appreciate all the little curses which she would be subjected to in the management of household affairs.[4]

[4] Same, March 2, 1864, Barclay Letters. Gen. Robert E. Rodes, a Virginian and a graduate of V.M.I., was later killed at the battle of Winchester on Sept. 19, 1864. Gen. George Doles of Georgia commanded a brigade in Rodes's Division. John Garibaldi, a member of the Twenty-seventh Vir-

No sooner had Ted returned to camp after the tour on the picket line had been completed, than the Stonewall Brigade was alerted to cook two days' rations and be prepared to move any moment. A Federal cavalry raid, commanded by General Judson Kilpatrick, had crossed the Rapidan and was headed for Richmond. The order, however, was soon countermanded and the brigade remained in its quarters.[5] Writing to his sister about this raid, Ted assured her that the brigade had no fear of being overrun by a set of "demonized" Yankee cavalry. In fact, Ted wryly commented, the soldiers feared "our own as much as we do those of the Yanks." He further wrote:

By the way we have some of Dunns Battalion of cavalry assigned to our regiments as conscripts. [I] suppose they were caught stealing or straying through the country. Hope they may make better soldiers in the Stonewall Brigade, having us veterans as examples, then they did in the Batt[alion].

I expect there will be some change in the army shortly, as Gen. Longstreet has arrived here with his staff. Gen Ewell will resign because he cannot stand field service and that Gen. Longstreet will take his place. I hope it may be so. Never had much confidence in Gen. Ewell. Has Mr. Wallace ever taken charge of the farm? A great number are getting details from the army to farms. Has Mr. Patton gone into service or is he exempt?[6]

ginia, Stonewall Brigade, wrote that the snowball fight was "all nice except for General Doles" (Garibaldi to wife, Camp Stonewall Brigade, Feb. 22, 1864, Garibaldi Letters, Preston Library, V.M.I.).

[5] Same, March 9, 1864, Barclay Letters. Foiled in his attempt to capture Richmond, Kilpatrick joined the Federal Army on the Peninsula under Gen. Benjamin F. Butler. This raid is sometimes referred to as the "Dahlgren Raid." Col. Ulric Dahlgren was killed in the raid (Virgil C. Jones, *Eight Hours before Richmond* [New York, 1957]).

[6] Ted to sister, March 12, 1864, Barclay Letters. General Longstreet with his corps, having spent the winter of 1863–64 in East Tennessee, had returned to Lee's Army. General Ewell, plagued with the loss of a leg in the

On the first spring day of 1864 Ted wrote a long letter on the impending campaign, hoping that it would result in "a free, happy and independent people":

There is some stir in the army expecting an advance of the enemy. Doubtless they will shortly make a move as we have had delightful weather for some time and the roads consequently are in splendid condition. It is reported that Grant will assume command of the Army of the Potomac and direct operations against the heart of the rebellion [Richmond]. They seem to be bringing all their available forces and sparing no means or money to capture that desideratum of Yankee hopes. Inflamed by the frenzy of despair at the prospect of their fast failing cause and knowing that they must do something to quiet discontent at home, they will doubtless spare nothing to be successful in the coming campaign. But we are elated at the prospect of a speedy deliverance from Yankee rule and tyranny. Our army is in fine condition and daily increasing in strength. We doubtless will have a hard campaign and many noble and gallant spirits must fall but what is that in view of the tremendous issues at stake.

Never for one moment must we allow the thought of submission to Yankee rule enter our minds, in view of the difficulties to be encountered for. He who would be free must himself strike the blow. I trust that there is not one so recreant to his sense of duty as now in our hour of trial to desert that glorious banner covered all over with the names of battles which will render the Confederate States of America immortal as long as the world will stand. And I trust, as our army who have to stand the hardships of the war is thus determined and consecrated to the cause, that those at home will cheerfully bear the little inconveniences which must necessarily result from such a state of affairs and at least speak

---

summer of 1862, had been in bad health for some time and had been hospitalized at Charlottesville for weeks. He was not, however, relieved of his corps command until midsummer of 1864, Gen. Jubal A. Early succeeding him.

words of encouragement to the soldiers and not endeavor to shake their confidence in the cause of religious and civil liberty.

I think that all will work out harmoniously and after a few more trials we shall be a free, happy and independent people.

Whilst our temporal affairs are thus bright and prosperous how is it with our spiritual lives. Do we continue to grow in the Grace of God, are we found continually pressing forward to the work of our high calling—I trust we are. We had the sacrament of the Lords Supper administered on last Sunday in our Brigade. I think it is delightful to have these points for renewed consecration of ourselves to the Lord. Oh how devoted we should be. Every drop of blood in our veins should thank the Lord for this salvation, for He shed His blood for us. We have also had some delightful meetings of our Association. My duties of President expired at the last meeting and Captain Wilson was elected for the next three months. I have seen a notice of the memoirs of Captain [Hugh] White in the Central Presbyterian. Hope it will soon get to the army for the life of such a Christian must be of benefit to those who read it.[7]

At his mother's request, Ted next wrote about food and clothes—about which there was no serious complaint—and religion, and also about the prospect of a renewal of exchange of prisoners:

I suppose Rockbridge is having a slight taste of the war now, as you have so many gallant cavalrymen with you, but I do not expect you will have the pleasure of entertaining them long as Mr. Grant seems disposed to try his fortune on this side of the Rapidan as soon as the weather will permit. But he will not be able to advance for a week or two at any rate as the roads are in a horrible condition at present and from the looks of the sky will be worse before better.

[7] Same, March 21, 1864, *ibid.* In 1864, the Rev. Dr. W. S. White had published a memoir of his son, Capt. Hugh White.

As Mother wants me to say everything about myself I will do the best I can, but it is a rather dry subject to write upon. I am very pleasantly situated in a mess of ten, with one of the number, [W. E.] Day, as cook. We eat twice a day, corn bread, sugar and coffee, with a moderate allowance of an animal familiarly known as hog which constitutes breakfast, which we have at eight o'clock A.M., take a smoke or more as circumstances will permit, lounge around, read whatever I can get hold of, indulge in edifying and interesting conversations with my chums. By this time Day cries "dinner," we assemble in the kitchen, a room 6 by 8, and you may know that this is some crowding but by all turning at the same time and the same way, each manages to get to the oven, take a piece of "dodger" dip it in a little grease and water mixed, take a piece of the aforementioned gentleman (I mean hog not one of the mess) about as big as your two fingers, eat, take a drink of water and retire from the kitchen at about two P.M., smoke along until about four when the mail comes, read the papers and letters if fortunate to get any. Make comments on the news and express our opinions quite freely about the blood and thunder editorials in the Richmond papers, smoke again and go to bed. Program next day ditto, interspersed with the amusement of carrying wood on our shoulders. As to clothing—very well supplied, pants have a little hole in seat, but I expect to draw a pair in a short time; in the mean time I will have them patched. Have had my boots half soled and so my wardrobe is all right. My toe has gotten comparatively well, my health generally was never better, my appetite too good to suit the limited supply.

But I suppose you have gotten tired of this nonsense, and indeed is there not something of more importance than the health of the body, that which concerns the health of the mortal soul? Am I so sure of having neglected no means of preserving that whilst all things are so convenient around me for my growth in grace? There is nothing here to distract the attention, no excitement, the monotony of camp either serves to call our attention to better things or as men having nothing else to do go to the card table as they say to pass the time. Have I as one of Gods soldiers upon earth kept my courage and aims efficient? Will I be able to stand the review of souls on the last day? I feel that I have not done my whole duty to myself and my fellowmen. May God enable me to lead a more consistent and upright life.

I have read the life of Capt. White and Memoirs of Randolph Fairfax in the last week. Oh, that we all would live such pure and unapproachable lives. I received the copy of the life of Capt. White sent by Aunt Phoebe, but had read it before that copy was sent me. Please return my thanks to her for this.

We are all gladened by the prospect of a speedy exchange, if we can get those who are now prisoners we will have quite a spectable company.

How does the Spring campaign work under the leadership of Mr. Wallace? Raise us lots of bread and meat as that is all we are afraid of now. For if grub runs out we will have to cry "hold enough." And I expect to make a requisition on your smoke house occasionally, whenever opportunity presents.[8]

Almost a year after the death of General Jackson, Ted gave an account of a lecture on his life and character:

I heard an elegant sermon from Mr. [Beverly Tucker] Lacy on the text—"Let me fall now into the hand of the Lord." Chron. XXI-13. His style of preaching is just suited to camp and his sermons

[8] Same, April 6, 1864, *ibid.* In the winter of 1863–64, because of the shortage of forage for the army horses, General Lee had sent units of his cavalry to Rockbridge County, where forage and grazing could be obtained. Randolph Fairfax of Alexandria, Va., a graduate of the University of Virginia, was a member of the Rockbridge Artillery. A very promising soldier, he was killed at the battle of Fredericksburg on Dec. 13, 1862. The father subsequently published a memoir of his son. Until 1863, a system of exchange known as the "cartel" had been in force between North and South whereby prisoners of war were paroled until they could be exchanged. But in 1863 General Grant suspended the cartel on the ground that the Confederates had violated it. Since the exchange favored the Confederates more than the Federals, they endeavored to have the cartel revived. Mr. Wallace was the manager of the Barclay farm.

are generally attended with good results. Yesterday evening he delivered his "Eulogy on Gen. Jackson" by the request of our Association, and I suppose that there were 3000 persons present, but his address was so good that not one person left the ground until he had finished. It was the most attentive audience I ever saw. And how beautifully and touchingly he held up to our view the character of our dearly-loved General as worthy of imitation, especially as Christians. He just reviewed his early life, his difficulties in acquiring an education, his private life at West Point, his success in his studies, his first experience as a soldier in the Mexican war; next as a private man in the capacity of professor at V.M.I. and member of the church and teacher in the colored Sabbath school in Lexington. Then the great part he had taken in his great struggle for political and religious freedom. He spoke of his private feelings in regard to the war as expressed by him to himself—Mr. Lacy. He followed him all through his campaigns down to the bloody and dearly bought field of Chancellorsville. He spoke of the revival in the army in "62" [1862] and said that he had often noticed Gen. Jackson night, after night before retiring, humbly kneeling and imploring the help of God, when he was alone in his tent and knew not that any one could see him, but his form was reflected through the tent by the light of his candle. He spoke of him as father and husband. His death bed he described so beautifully. Closing his address he spoke of Gen. Paxton's body being brought to the hospital where Gen. Jackson lay wounded. He [Lacy] said "As I left the suffering couch of the lamented Jackson, and gazed upon the noble features of the gallant Paxton, cold and still in death with a calm smile resting upon his face and still the stern decision of a Roman so forcibly shown in his face, I thought it was indeed a double bought field."

I think that the address will certainly be productive of good, as he several times appealed to the old brigade in language which was calculated to move the hardest heart.[9]

After some badinage, on April 17 Ted told his sister the kind of chaplains the army needed:

[9] Same, April 8, 1864, *ibid.*

I received your letter of the 9th. a day or so ago, but as I had a severe spell of ennui, or spring fever, I have delayed writing, and I suppose if I wish any more "pretty paper" I had better hurry up, but I believe I like the old blue [paper] the best, of which I think you have an inexhaustible supply. You see that you are not the only one who has pretty paper, but yours didn't have pretty cross lines like mine has. I think that I will write across to satisfy Mother's fancy of full sheets. I want you to stop taunting me about my pretty weather [when] on picket. It seems to afford you some satisfaction, you cold hearted creature. Of course I enjoy it.

I am glad to hear that there were two young misses in Lexington whose brains were not completely carried away with a review of the gallant and meritorious V.M.I.'s by a real live Gen. I see Lexingtonians are as big Mummies as ever, when any body new comes to town, it is always Mr. this and Mr. that but they will get bit some of these days. Missouri acquaintance, Ah!! Beware of the dashing cavalier maybe he is more dashing than you ever think.

I'd like to know when you ever saw a cavalryman who was ever injured by hardships as you are pleased to term them. Don't believe the reports about starvation; as you say it is all newspaper twaddle. By the way that is a funny word, but a very expressive one, where did you come across it?

We have all sent off our extra baggage and are now prepared to move along rapidly as we have only one blanket and change of clothing. I kept my overcoat, didn't like to trust it to Richmond. Will send it home by Mr. Middleton if he comes down, that is if he will bring me anything in the shape of grub in exchange for it. I have all my baggage hauled so will have an easy time this summer. I suppose you have almost despaired of my commission. It has gone to Richmond to Jefferson Davis, but the old man has so much of the same sort of trash to attend to that it takes a long time to get around but it will get around after while. In the meantime I am getting all the benefits of it, anyway I am called Lieut. as big as any body, if I can't sign myself an officer. You'll direct letters to Lieut. Barclay after while. Don't take all I have said as good earnest or you would think your brother has turned mummie. I care very little about the honors of the office, but it is the privileges I have; on that account I prize it.

I heard an excellent sermon today from Mr. Hopkins. He is such a good nice man. I think he is one of the most pleasant men I ever saw. Anyone coming into camp would not imagine that the gay young man enjoying with such zest in a game of ball or pitching quoits or playing marbles was a Chaplain. But these are the kind of men that we want for Chaplains, not stiff unsociable men but men who will mingle with the soldiers in all their amusements. All of the men like Mr. Hopkins and Mr. See on that account and they always have good congregations. I have a great notion to cross out this letter but fear that you would not be able to read it and it would be such a pity to not be able to read this, it is such an elegant production. This is a pretty way to spend Sunday evening writing this nonsense but I feel in a good humor so I hope that you will not blame me.[10]

On the eve of the Wilderness campaign Ted was confident of victory:

I am surprised at you placing any credence in the rumors of the movements of the army, as I have so often told you not to believe these idle rumors. Why, the Richmond [papers] actually had us in line of battle and heavy skirmishes going on several days ago whereas there was not a hostile gun fired yet.

I have not yet seen Mr. Middleton but he is in camp. Some of his boxes were brought down this evening, the rest will be down tomorrow. My last box was just given out so this one comes in very acceptable time. But I fear that things are becoming almost as scarce at home as in camp though I know that you would willingly share the last morsel with me; still I do not wish you to send me boxes if it costs any inconvenience at all. We always get enough to sustain life at any rate and it would not be a relish to

[10] Same, 1864, *ibid*. Ted's remark about the cavalry was a standing joke in the infantry.

me if I thought you were depriving yourselves of anything for me. A soldiers life surely is rough but it is by no means as hard as generally represented to be. We have a great many friendships of which homefolk are deprived, for instance you cannot get around one oven in a sociable way and eat your meals; neither are your ears charmed with the rattle of the fife and drum &c &c. A soldier is after all not so much to be pitied as you would suppose. Elihu [Ted's brother] is still with us, I do not know when he will leave, hope he may be induced to stay as I think it would be of immense good to him.

I have read the Richmond papers of today and see that Gen. Burnside has abandoned his idea of advancing on Richmond by the south side and has joined Gen. Grant on the Rapidan. If this be true we will in all probability have a fight here either this or next week as Grant will endeavor to fall upon Lee before he has time to consolidate his troops. But I think we are prepared. Our army is certainly in fine condition and we have a leader in which all have confidence. But more than this our cause we believe to be a just one and our God is certainly a just God, then why should we doubt. No, I think you may confidently expect a glorious issue in the impending campaign, a campaign between right and wrong, we are backed by an army of good and true men, the other by a bunch of lawless outcasts and mercenaries. True the struggle will be a bloody one but it is noble to die in so just a cause.

I would like to survive the conflict, I would like to see our land free from tyrants' grasp and established as one of the stars in the galaxy of nations, but if I am to fall God help me to say "Thy will be done." I must say that to me life is sweet and death has some terrors, but the love of Christ is able to remove all this, the grace of God is sufficient to dispel all clouds and I believe that I will be supported in the hour of death by His almighty arm whether I fall upon the bloody field or am permitted to die in peace at home. There is something awful in stepping off this world even with the hope and faith in the gospel. God increase our belief. I have just finished completing our company prayer meeting, for which purpose I laid aside my sheet. Oh, that I could conduct it in such a manner as to impress upon some of our numbers to leave the ranks of sin and fly to God. Some must certainly fall this summer. Oh, that all were prepared then we would have no doubt to fear the issue, their souls would be safe and it matters little what would become of this earthly tabernacle, for it is only the case which contains the immortal soul, that soul which is destined to spend an eternity of bliss or one of woe. May God impress it upon their minds, if we can do nothing more we can at least pray for them.

My own condition I believe is good. I believe that I have come to a saving knowledge of Christ Jesus. I hate sin though I commit it daily. But as it is bed time I will close.[11]

In February 1864, General U.S. Grant, fresh from a succession of victories in the West, was placed in command of the armies of the United States. Although General George Meade remained the titular head of the Army of the Potomac, General Grant actually took over its operations, and in early May he started on the road which would eventually take him to Appomattox. During the month of May there was either continuous fighting or maneuvering, and some of the bloodiest battles of the war occurred at the Wilderness, Spotsylvania, and Cold Harbor.

On the night of May 2, Grant set his army in motion, and by May 4 it was across the Rapidan and in the Wilderness. Although Lee did not discover until midnight of May 3 that Grant was moving by his right flank, he had previously alerted the corps commanders to hold their troops in readiness to march at a moment's notice. At noon on May 4 the Stonewall Brigade broke camp at Mt. Pisgah, turned south at Morton Hall, corps headquarters, to the Orange-Fredericks-

[11] Same, May 1, 1864, *ibid*. There was a feeling in the Army of Northern Virginia that the Federal Army was composed of riffraff and foreign mercenaries.

burg Turnpike, and bivouacked about dusk on the turnpike near Locust Grove Tavern on the western edge of the Wilderness.[12]

That morning Private James McCown of Rockbridge County, who had recently joined the Stonewall Brigade, buoyantly confided to his diary:

Every thing is in motion, winter quarters broken up. A short time ago everyone of the 100 huts had life in them. Now as I look back its streets are silent like a deserted village. We are on the march. The morning is bright and pleasant; all nature seems smiling on this spring morning. What a grand sight is the [Army of Northern Virginia] in motion. The whole brigade is all life—seems as though they are never to be conquered. General Walker is our Brigade Commander. How brave and gallant he looks as he rides at its head, and well he may be—to command the Stonewall Brigade is no small honor.[13]

Resuming the march eastward on May 5, Ewell's corps soon came into contact with Warren's Federal corps, and a savage battle ensued between them in the Wilderness—a region covered with a dense forest and an undergrowth so thick that it was difficult to see one hundred yards in any direction. Private McCown described his feelings as he readied himself for his first experience in battle:

[12] Lieut. J. L. Doyle, "The Campaign in May, 1864," MS, in Jed Hotchkiss Papers, Library of Congress; hereafter cited as Doyle, "May, 1864." The manuscript was written in 1867. Doyle was a member of the Thirty-third Virginia Infantry, Stonewall Brigade. While Ewell was moving eastward along the Turnpike on May 4, 1864, Gen. A. P. Hill was advancing in the same direction in a parallel road, the Orange-Fredericksburg Plank Road. General Longstreet's corps, encamped near Gordonsville, had orders to move on May 4 toward Fredericksburg.
[13] "Diary," May 4, 1864, Rockbridge *County News*, Feb. 12, 19, 1953 (hereafter cited as McCown, "Diary").

After forming in line there is an awful silence. He that a short time ago jested is now grave. Many are seen during this quiet to take out their Bibles and read and silently ask God to spare and shield them in the hour of battle. How awful is this inaction. Home flashes up the dear ones and thousands of thoughts crowd in on me. In this state of mind, our Captain Kurtz approaches [the four new recruits in the company] with a sad but determined face. . . . His words are kind but brave; tells us we will, in short time, be engaged in battle and as none has been under fire, he wanted us to stand up like men and do our duty. Our skirmish line is advanced. Now we are ordered to lie down. Oh, what moments of silence. All nature seems to expect some awful shock.

Just then there jumps from my front a rabbit. My attention is attracted to this strange appearance. I was on my feet and that moment our brave Captain was yelling, "Give it to them Company K." Amid this storm of lead and hail we stood until we were reported to be flanked by Hancock's [troops]. We then fell back. The Yankees see the advantages. Our line wavers. At this moment above the rattle, General Walker swinging to his stand in his saddle with head up and upraised hand. His voice is heard to rally the Stonewall Brigade, [shouting], "Remember your name." The colors advance in the face of a deadly fire from the Yankees. Still they float. . . . We advance and sweep everything before us. The day is over. Dead and dying lie around us. . . .

So closed this awful day, the first fighting I have ever done and the Lord has delivered me. All thanks to Him.[14]

During the night of May 6 General Grant headed south toward Spotsylvania Court House, hoping to interpose his army between Lee's troops and Richmond. But Lee had foreseen this move. He put his army in motion toward Spotsylvania Court House and, arriving there before Grant, entrenched his army behind breastworks.

On May 10 a bloody engagement took place at the salient,

[14] *Ibid.,* May 5, 1864. Gen. Winfield S. Hancock was a corps commander.

known as the Bloody Angle or the Mule Shoe, which was occupied by troops of Ewell's corps—Doles's brigade of Rodes's
division and all of Johnson's brigades. The Stonewall Brigade
occupied the western slope of the salient from its apex or toe
to the position held by Doles's troops. Johnson's other two
brigades were on the eastern slope of the salient. In mid-
afternoon of May 10 the Federals emerged from the woods
in front of Doles's Brigade, caught it unprepared to resist—
the men were sitting behind the salient with their guns
stacked—and captured several hundred of the brigade. But
when the Stonewall Brigade hit the enemy's flanks, they broke
and fled to the woods from which they had emerged.[15] On
May 11 Private McCown noted in his diary:

I went over the field of yesterday and it was an awful sight. The
dead and wounded lie thick. The field is covered with things left
by the Yankees and many of our boys supplied themselves with
blankets, boots, paper and envelopes. Late this evening General
Lee rode along the lines. The troops were wild with joy to see our
beloved General. He was mounted on Traveler, his gray horse.
. . . We are ordered to sleep on our arms. [My tent mates and]
myself lie down under one blanket, knowing what will be in the
morning; work of a bloody kind. This may be our last night together.[16]

The movements of the enemy during the night of May 11
were ominous to the Confederates in the salient. A scout who
had been sent into the enemy's line reported a large body of
troops massed in the woods in front of the salient, and the
jingling of canteens and the heavy tread of marching Federals were clearly audible. "As a matter of fact," Clifford

[15] Clifford Dowdey, *Lee's Last Campaign, The Story of Lee and His Men
against Grant, 1864* (Boston, 1960), ch. viii (hereafter cited as Dowdey,
Last Campaign).
[16] McCown, "Diary," May 11, 1864.

Dowdey has written, "the Federals did everything except send over a flag-of-truce messenger announcing their intentions." At midnight a rain began which continued throughout the night, turning the salient into a quagmire. The Stonewall Brigade, however, fared well with the Federal pup tents they had picked up in the Wilderness. Orders were given to the company officers of the Stonewall Brigade to be on the alert and to hold each traverse—cross lines within the salient—to the last.[17]

About dawn of May 12 firing was heard on the sectors on the eastern side of the salient, positions occupied by Johnson's other brigades, and soon some of the troops there broke and fled, followed by exultant Federals who came pouring into the salient. The fleeing Confederates, running to the rear, shouted to their comrades of the Stonewall Brigade that the salient had broken in two places and that the other brigades had been captured. In vain did the officers and men of the Stonewall Brigade endeavor to rally the fugitives. To the battle smoke was added a heavy fog which, in the absence of any breeze, hung low over the woods. "The scene was terrible," Lieutenant Doyle said as he described the greatest crisis which had ever confronted Jackson's old brigade:

The figures of men seem dimly through the smoke and fog seemed almost gigantic, while the woods were lighted by the flashing of the guns and the sparkling of the musketry. The din was tremendous and increasing every instant, men in crowds with bleeding limbs and pale, pain-stricken faces were hurrying to the rear and, mingled with these could be seen many unwounded who had escaped from the wreck of their commands.[18]

[17] Dowdey, *Last Campaign*, p. 200; Doyle, "May, 1864."
[18] "May, 1864."

Despite the demoralizing effect of seeing their divisional comrades fleeing, the men of the Stonewall Brigade held their position in the line. When the head of an enemy's column bore down from the toe of the salient upon the flank of the Fourth and Fifth Regiments of the brigade, "these stout souls," steadied by their officers, faced to the right, the direction from which the enemy attacked, and, soon joined by the other brigade regiments, repelled several Federal assaults. In this fierce fighting both General Walker and Colonel William Terry of the Fourth Virginia, senior regimental officer, were wounded and left the field. Although the brigade was without a leader it fought on until about six o'clock, when a new column of Federals, advancing from the front and rear, overpowered the Stonewall Brigade by sheer numbers and captured most of its officers and men. General Lee managed, however, to plug up the hole in the line, and the Federals were driven out of the salient and the earthworks retaken.[19]

On May 12, after his capture, Private McCown jotted down some of the details of the fighting in the Bloody Angle earlier that morning:

Last night four of us lay down under a pelting rain and slept soundly. Now we are separated. History will speak of this day at Spotsylvania Court House as one of the bloodiest and most terrible of battles. The enemy's loss is terrible in dead and wounded. Ours is slight, we being behind works. We were awake at an early hour by the yells of thousand [of Yankees] on our front and to the Brigade on our right. They charged line after line, one behind another, on they came. We were ordered to reserve our fire until [they were] near enough to tell on them. Then how warmly we gave it to them. Line after line recoiled before our withering fire. Another coming up, they recoiled and on they came. The Brigade on our right was broken, and we were exposed to a front and side

[19] *Ibid.*

line. It was terrific beyond any description. Captain Kurtz remarked to me during the hottest of the fighting, "This is the hottest place I was ever in." Every twig seemed cut down. We continued desperately not dreaming of [capture] until we were
completely surrounded by their overwhelming numbers. When I
surrendered I was beside Captain Kurtz and the flag of our regiment. The color bearer remarked they should not have our colors,
so he tore the [flag] off and stuffed it in his bosom—the work of
only a minute.[20]

The same fate also overtook the other brigades of Johnson's division, and Generals Edward Johnson and George
Steuart were both caught in the Yankee net. After the battle
of Spotsylvania Court House the Stonewall Brigade ceased
to exist as a separate organization; its survivors who escaped
capture (about two hundred) and the survivors of Johnson's
other brigades were later formed into one brigade under the
command of Colonel William Terry.[21]

All of the Liberty Hall Volunteers present in this battle ex-

[20] "Diary," 1864. One of McCown's tent mates was captured at the Bloody
Angle; the other two escaped.

[21] Gen. James A. Walker, "The Bloody Angle," *Southern Historical Society Papers*, XXI (1893), 229–38. Gen. George Steuart was a Marylander.
Among the casualties at the Spotsylvania Court House on May 12, 1864, was
Serg. Joseph T. Chester. A senior at Washington College, he was a member
of the original company of Volunteers, although he was not present at its
muster on the Court House Square in Lexington on June 8, 1861, having
been called home by his mother's sickness. He hastened back and joined
the company at Winchester and from then until his death he was present in
every engagement in which the Stonewall Brigade engaged, having passed
unscathed through all of them. He was buried in the trenches at Spotsylvania, and a year passed without any news about him until former Governor
Letcher, who knew this promising lad at Lexington, wrote his parents of his
death. It was one of the strange quirks of fate that Joseph T. Chester's first
cousin Charles Chester Yemen of Vermont—named for Joseph's father—was
fighting in a Federal brigade opposite the Stonewall Brigade at the "Bloody
Angle" of Spotsylvania Court House (Samuel Hall Chester, *Memories of
Four-Score Years: . . . An Autobiography* [Richmond, 1934], p. 45).

cept two privates and Lieutenant J. H. B. Jones, who had been in command of the company since Gettysburg, were either killed, wounded, or captured. Lieutenant Ted Barclay was among those captured. After the battle of Spotsylvania Court House, as after all engagements, new recruits were received, and at Appomattox, when the Liberty Hall Volunteers stacked arms for the last time, only eight members were present: Lieutenant Jones, Sergeant J. Fudge, and Privates A. A. McClung, T. M. Turner, H. Ott, E. (probably D.) Whitmore, S. P. Williams, and B. F. McNutt. Only Jones and Turner were members of the original company.[22]

The Confederate prisoners, including the Liberty Hall Volunteers, were herded together and hustled off to Fort Delaware. As they passed through the enemy's line, they met long columns of Federal troops and wagon trains hurrying to the front, and they were amazed at the overwhelming superiority of Northern manpower and equipment. They belonged to General Burnside's Ninth Corps which was camped nearby, the officers lounging and smoking in their tents within sound of musketry at Spotsylvania Court House and apparently unconcerned as to the outcome of the strug-

[22] Strickler, "Volunteers," p. 118; "Paroles of the Army of Northern Virginia . . . Surrendered at Appomattox Court House, Va., April 9, 1865" (*Southern Historical Papers* [Richmond, 1887], p. 90). Serg. J. Fudge was originally a member of the Smyth Blues, Company "D," Fourth Virginia, and apparently he transferred or was assigned, after the dissolution of the Stonewall Brigade at Spotsylvania Court House in May 1864 and the subsequent consolidation of its remnants into Terry's brigade, to the Liberty Hall Volunteers. Ted Barclay was in error when he said that "at Appomattox there were but five members of the company left to surrender, and only three of these were members of the original company—Lieutenant Jones . . . and Isaac Taylor . . . and Thomas M. Turner" (Barclay, "Volunteers," p. 135). Taylor was neither present at the surrender nor was he a member of the original company (see the roster of the company in the *Appendix*). It might be added that since Ted was not at Appomattox, he was perhaps relying upon what other members had erroneously stated.

gle. Here the prisoners saw the first Federal Negro troops, "standing, grinning and jabbering" along both sides of the road and looking "revengefully at these ragged heroes of the Confederacy." Many of them taunted the Confederates by saying that, if they had been their captors, the prisoners would not have lived "to tell the tale." In describing this episode later Lieutenant Doyle caustically said, "The Negroes' bloody-thirsty desires were happily [satiated] at the 'Crater' before Petersburg when these dusty heroes had abundant opportunity to 'flush their maiden swords.' "[23]

From May 17, 1864, to the summer of 1865, Ted Barclay was confined at Fort Delaware. Apparently he got in touch with his Kentucky relatives, William Paxton's family, shortly after his arrival, and they supplied his needs. Ted wrote his sister on June 7: "I am comfortably situated, have an abundance of bedding and will get clothes this week. I have heard from Cousin Sallie [Paxton] and Uncle William [Paxton], both of whom have kindly offered me assistance." In another letter of July 21, Ted said he had received from them "A box of clothing, also a box of provisions and money, so you can see I am not suffering from the want of anything that can be furnished me. All I want now is liberty and I hope there will be an exchange of prisoners and I will be permitted to return to the Old Dominion." The greatest privation, he added, was the lack of news of his family, especially of his two brothers, Elihu, who was in the cavalry, and Paxton, who, if drafted into the army, would be subjected to "all

[23] "May, 1864." In the summer of 1864, Grant, having failed to break Lee's lines at Petersburg, approved a project of tunneling under the Confederate lines and breaching them by an explosion. On July 30 at daybreak the mine was exploded, but in the desperate battle which followed the explosion the Confederates repulsed the Federal attack. The colored troops of Burnside's corps bore the brunt of the fighting, and their presence so enraged the Southerners that they displayed a frenzied fury in the encounter (ibid.).

the dangers of the field and the temptations of camp."[24] Ted's last letter, written on August 21, 1864, would indicate that he expected to be exchanged soon:

I received your letter dated the 17th of July a day or so ago and would have answered it immediately but as there was a prospect of going south myself I postponed it until it was decided who should go and as I am not among the fortunate ones I will now write.

I am greatly relieved at hearing of the welfare of you all. I feared it might be otherwise.

I have been very well supplied and am as comfortable as circumstances will permit. I requested Lieut. [J. L.] Doyle, who left here with the homeward bound prisoners to write to you all. He was in my mess while here.[25]

[24] June 7, July 21, 1864, Barclay Letters. Private McCown, who could not rely upon loving relatives for assistance, was not as fortunate as Ted Barclay. In his diary of May 21, 1864, he recorded: "This is my first day in my new home, the U.S.A. From what I am told [by home town boys who had been confined at Fort Delaware for months] I must expect harsh treatment and scanty rations. . . . My morning rations consisted of three crackers, ordinary size, square, and cup of coffee. Good enough for a sick man and he would likely grumble. Dinner—three strips of bacon, crackers, and a cup of soup (if such it could be called)" (McCown, "Diary," May 21, 1864). On May 29, McCown confided to his diary: "Here we are shut out from the world and starving on this Northern Bastile." Three days later he described the food situation as desperate: "Morning rations late and small in quantity. The prisoners, many of them are catching rats and are eating them. Those who eat them say they are as nice as squirrel. I see them cooked but can't quite go for the rats but many do so. They look nice enough. Oh, for one good square meal."

[25] Ted to sister, Fort Delaware, Barclay Letters. The fear he expressed in the letter about the welfare of his family was doubtless due to the news which had reached Fort Delaware of the occupation of Lexington, June 11–14, 1864, by Federal Gen. David Hunter's troops. Ted Barclay was not released from Fort Delaware until July 1865. Returning to Lexington, he was successively engaged in various enterprises: manager of the family estate, a participant in the movement to extend the Valley Railroad from Winchester to Lexington; coeditor of the Lexington *Gazette;* manager of the Lexington

194   THE LIBERTY HALL VOLUNTEERS

Among the visitors at Fort Delaware in the summer of 1864 was the Rev. Dr. George Junkin, former president of Washington College. Since his hasty exodus from Virginia in April 1861, he had lived quietly at Philadelphia, preaching occasionally, publishing a volume entitled *Political Heresies*, and ministering to the wounded and dying of the war. Immediately after the battle of Gettysburg, he hastened to the battlefield to conduct a service. Many Confederate prisoners were in the audience, among them the Liberty Hall Volunteers who had been captured in the battle. The scene between Dr. Junkin and the college boys which illustrated their mutual feelings was described by one who was present:

Dr. J[unkin] delivered a very pungent discourse; the services were of a very solemn character. After they were concluded, these college young men all remained to take their old preceptor by the hand. Among the number was a college chaplain; and it was most touching to see the aged man of God throw his arms around the young man's neck and weep, exclaiming, "I never thought *you* would be engaged in this work!"

As they gathered around him, apparently glad to meet him again, he took from his pocket the old classbook, and commenced to call the roll, and rehearsed the history of each member, showing how all had suffered more or less in consequence of their resistance to the best government which God had ever given to men.[26]

Manufacturing Company; and president of the Rockbridge Land Company. For many years he, like some of his forebears, was a member of the Board of Trustees of Washington and Lee University. He died in November 1915 (Rockbridge *County News*, Dec. 7, 1915).

[26] Martin L. Stower to George Junkin, Gettysburg, Pa., Dec. 28, 1863, in Junkin, *Junkin*, p. 550. Stower was a professor at Pennsylvania College, and the George Junkin to whom the letter was addressed was the son of Dr. George Junkin. He was a resident of Philadelphia, one of Dr. Junkin's sons who had remained in Pennsylvania when his father moved to Lexington in 1848. Dr. George Junkin died in Pennsylvania on May 20, 1868, and was

On June 1 and 2, 1864, Dr. Junkin put in an appearance at Fort Delaware. He had been sent there by the Publication Board of the Northern Presbyterian Church to distribute religious tracts to the prisoners and to preach to them. Private McCown, a prisoner, described the visit:

[June 11] visit of Rev. Dr. Junkin. He was distributing tracts which we were very glad to get, reading matter being so very scarce. He tells us Lexington is captured and V.M.I. burned by [General David] Hunter.

[June 12] Sunday. Dr. Junkin preached for us in the morning and evening to a large crowd of ragged Rebels. They wore nothing but their drawers and shirts and were barefooted. How strange all this must look to the doctor. He talked much of Lexington and how much he loved the people and of it being the resting place of his dead wife and daughter [Elinor, Stonewall Jackson's first wife]. He was much affected, spoke in feeling words of the Liberty Hall Volunteers, how he loved them and how already many had yielded up their young lives for the cause they thought right, while he believed it wrong.

He held in his hand a cane, saying, "This is a gift from Stonewall Jackson, my son-in-law. [Dr. Junkin's] appearance reminds me so much of home. How often have I sat and listened to him in the Presbyterian Church when all was peace.[27]

Of the total number of members of the company of Liberty Hall Volunteers, 181, more than half, 109, were recruits who were added to the original company at different times during the war. Some were conscripts, others volunteers, and undoubtedly many of them were from Rockbridge County;

---

buried in this state. In the 1930s his body was removed to Lexington and was reinterred in the Junkin plot in the Stonewall Jackson Memorial Cemetery. The college chaplain, referred to in the letter, is unknown. In fact, the *Washington College Catalogue* of 1860–61 does not list a college chaplain.

[27] "Diary," June 11, 1864.

they have Rockbridge County names. Only six of the recruits had been Washington College students, and it is impossible to ascertain the war records of most of the nonstudent recruits. It is interesting to note that Washington College furnished one student, Albert Ludwig, of the class of 1860–61, to the Northern army. He was the son of E. A. Ludwig, instructor of modern languages at Washington College. Young Ludwig was killed in the fighting around Petersburg in 1865.[28]

Although the Washington College students were outnumbered by the outsiders, they formed the hard core of the company, furnished its leadership, and gave it character. Of the eleven commissioned officers only one was not a student, and of the twenty-three noncommissioned officers eighteen were college boys.

Twenty-seven members of the company were killed in action or died from wounds received in battle, sixteen died from diseases, and seventy-two were wounded. Undoubtedly some of the sick and wounded of the original company were discharged for physical unfitness, but there is no record of these cases; on the other hand, the number of those, especially of the recruits, who recovered and returned to the company is unknown. Forty-eight, exclusive of the eight who surrendered at Appomattox, were captured and some saw further service after being exchanged. Others, such as Captain Henry Ruffner Morrison and Lieutenant John N. Lyle, transferred to other units after being exchanged. A few transferred directly from the company to other branches of the service.[29]

The largest number killed in any battle was seven at First

[28] For a roster of the company see the Appendix. This roster was taken from Strickler, "Volunteers," pp. 111–14.

[29] Compiled from the roster.

Manassas; the largest number wounded in any battle was sixteen at Chancellorsville; and the largest number captured in any battle was sixteen at Gettysburg. It was said that no punishment was ever inflicted on any member of the original company, either for disobedience to orders or for personal misconduct.[30]

[30] *Ibid.;* Barclay, "Volunteers," p. 135.

APPENDIX
AND
SELECTED BIBLIOGRAPHY

Appendix

ROSTER OF LIBERTY
HALL VOLUNTEERS

ROLL OF THE ORIGINAL COMPANY

The war record of the members of the original company was obtained from Washington and Lee University, *Historical Papers,* no. 6 (Lynchburg, Va., 1904), pp. 111–21, and "Register of Students, 1834–1866," at Washington and Lee University, MS.

COMMISSIONED AND
NONCOMMISSIONED OFFICERS

* Captain: J. J. White, resigned commission, Sept. 1861. See sketches in Ch. I, n. 29, Ch. II, n. 38.
* First Lieutenant: John Newton Lyle, captured at Kernstown. For additional information, see Ch. IV, n. 19.

* Student at Washington College before the war.

* Second Lieutenant: Joseph J. Sherrard, Hampshire County, Va., transferred to another branch of service.
* First Sergeant: William A. Anderson, Rockbridge County, Va., wounded at First Manassas. See sketch, Ch. II, n. 9.
* Second Sergeant: D. E. Ruff, Lexington, wounded at Second Manassas.
* Third Sergeant: E. A. Mitchell, Columbus, Ga., died in service, July 1861.
* Fourth Sergeant: Charles W. Bell, Rockbridge County, Va., killed at First Manassas.
* Fifth Sergeant: Charles F. Nelson, Augusta County, Va., killed at Kernstown.
* First Corporal: G. B. Strickler, Rockbridge County, Va., later first lieutenant and captain, wounded at First Manassas and Second Manassas, captured at Gettysburg, and imprisoned at Fort Johnson, Ohio, until 1865. For additional sketch see Ch. VI, n. 6.
* Second Corporal: Frances T. Brooke, Spotsylvania County, Va., transferred to Thirtieth Virginia Infantry.
* Third Corporal: William Paxton, Rockbridge County, Va., killed at First Manassas.
* Fourth Corporal: William T. Meade, Clarke County, Va., transferred to artillery.

PRIVATES

* J. P. Amole, Rockbridge County, Va., wounded at Chancellorsville and Mine Run and captured at Spotsylvania Court House.
* J. M. Anderson, died in the service.
J. Harry Arnold, Rockbridge County, Va.
* Jacob W. Arnold, Rockbridge County, Va., later fourth sergeant and transferred to another branch of the service.

* Student at Washington College before the war.

* A. Tedford Barclay, Rockbridge County, Va., later ensign for gallantry at Mine Run, wounded at the Wilderness, captured at Spotsylvania Court House, and imprisoned at Fort Delaware. For additional sketch see Ch. VII, n. 25.

* William J. Bell, Augusta County, Va., wounded at Kernstown.

John A. Bird.

* Benjamin A. Bradley, Rockbridge County, Va., killed at First Manassas.

* Andrew Brooks, Augusta County, Va., captured at Kernstown, exchanged, and killed at Chancellorsville.

* William Brooks, Augusta County, Va., died in the service.

* Joseph T. Chester, Mount Holly, Ark., third sergeant in the summer of 1861, killed at Spotsylvania Court House.

* G. K. Davidson, Rockbridge County, Va., later second corporal, captured at Kearneysville.

* Thomas J. Godwin, Botetourt County, Va., later third corporal, wounded at Chancellorsville and captured at Gettysburg.

Bronson B. Gwynn, Lexington, Va., wounded at First Manassas and Chancellorsville.

* Robert J. Hallett, Norfolk, Va., later captain and the assistant adjutant general.

S. A. Johnston, Rockbridge County, Va., later fourth sergeant, wounded at Kearneysville and the Wilderness.

* J. H. B. Jones, Rockbridge County, Va., wounded at the Wilderness, second lieutenant in command of the company at Appomattox.

* Harry E. Jordan, Richmond, Va., transferred to a North Carolina Regiment and died of wounds received in battle, June 1864.

Matthew S. Kahle, Lexington, Va.

* Student at Washington College before the war.

George W. Lackey, Rockbridge County, Va., later fourth corporal, wounded at Second Winchester, Sept. 1864.

H. R. Laird, Rockbridge County, Va., transferred to the First Virginia Cavalry, postwar student at Washington College.

C. M. Lam, wounded at Sharpsburg.

* John P. Lightner, Augusta County, Va., died in the service.

* Samuel H. Lightner, Pocahontas County, (W.) Va., theological student, wounded at First Manassas and died in service.

* N. B. Logan, Botetourt County, Va., killed at Petersburg.

* Samuel H. Lyle, Rockbridge County, Va., later first lieutenant after Kernstown, wounded at Chancellorsville and Mine Run and captured at Spotsylvania Court House.

* J. W. McCoughtery, Jefferson County, (W.) Va., killed at Second Manassas.

J. T. McKee, Rockbridge County, Va., later third corporal, captured at Kernstown, exchanged, and captured at Gettysburg.

* James S. Mackey, Rockbridge County, Va., wounded at the Wilderness and captured at Spotsylvania Court House.

* Everard Meade, Clarke County, Va., wounded at Second Manassas.

* J. Julius Moore, Rockbridge County, Va., later third sergeant, captured at Gettysburg.

* Samuel R. Moore, Rockbridge County, Va., later fourth sergeant, wounded at Sharpsburg.

* Henry Ruffner Morrison, Rockbridge County, Va., captured at Kernstown. For additional sketch see Ch. IV, n. 19.

* Henry H. Myers, Lexington, Va., later first corporal.

* Student at Washington College before the war.

* Cyrus F. Neel, Monroe County, (W.) Va., wounded at First Manassas and transferred to signal corps.
* W. B. Ott, Rockbridge County, Va., killed at First Manassas.
* Copeland R. Page, Lexington, Va., later third corporal.
* Alexander S. Paxton, Rockbridge County, Va., later second sergeant, wounded at Chancellorsville, Mine Run, and Petersburg.

Horace A. Paxton, Rockbridge County, Va., wounded at Kernstown and Chancellorsville and captured at the Wilderness.

* William L. Paxton, Rockbridge County, Va., third corporal, killed at First Manassas.

Alexander B. Ramsey, Augusta County, Va., wounded at Chancellorsville, Bealton Station, and the Wilderness and captured at Bell Grove, 1864. Postwar student at Washington College.

* Joseph S. Raymond, Greenbrier County, (W.) Va., promoted first sergeant after First Manassas, wounded at Kearneysville, captured at Gettysburg, exchanged, wounded at Bealton Station and Mine Run, captured at Spotsylvania Court House, exchanged, and captured at Bell Grove.

* Thomas W. Read, Rockbridge County, Va., died in the service, 1862.

J. T. Redwood.

* John W. Reiley, Jefferson County, (W.) Va., transferred to the Assistant Adjutant General Office.

W. E. Richardson, died in the service.

Thomas H. Roberts, wounded at Sharpsburg and captured at Spotsylvania Court House.

Thomas S. Rollins, captured at Spotsylvania Court House.

* Student at Washington College before the war.

* Cyrus D. Strickler, Staunton, Va., killed at First Manassas.
* James L. Suddarth, Lexington, Va., captured at Second Manassas.
* William J. Thompson, Rockbridge County, Va., died in the service, 1861.
* Thomas M. Turner, Goochland County, Va., captured at Gettysburg, exchanged, and surrendered at Appomattox.
* Calvin Utz, Botetourt County, Va., killed at First Manassas.
  John A. R. Varner, Lexington, Va., captured at Kernstown, exchanged, and captured at Gettysburg.
  John G. Watson.
* Hugh A. White, Lexington, Va., elected captain after Kernstown and killed at Second Manassas.
* Charles Williams, Botetourt County, Va.
  John T. Wilson, Rockbridge County, Va., wounded at Second Manassas.
* H. L. Wilson, Augusta County, Va., killed at First Manassas.
* William N. Wilson, Rockbridge County, Va.
* J. Watson Woods, Buckingham County, Va., captured at Kernstown.

RECRUITS

Information on the war record of the recruits is to be found in the Washington and Lee University, *Historical Papers*—no. 6, pp. 111–21. In addition to the roster, the names of those who were either killed, captured, or died in the service are given.

Alexander Adair, killed at Gettysburg.
R. B. Almond.

* Student at Washington College before the war.

* T. F. Amole, Rockbridge County, Va., wounded at Gettysburg and wounded and captured at Moncacy Creek.

John R. Anderson, died in the service.

Robert M. Anderson, killed at Petersburg.

A. S. Bacon.

George Baine.

George Bare.

H. A. Bartley, wounded at Chancellorsville and Bealton Station.

H. M. Benson, wounded at Chancellorsville.

Charles Brooks, wounded at Second Manassas.

Moffett Brooks, died in the service.

William L. Brown.

J. H. Bryan.

J. W. Buchanan.

T. N. Burke.

Abraham Bushong, captured at Petersburg.

R. Carr.

G. R. Cash.

George Chapin, Lexington, Va., wounded at Chancellorsville and killed at Mine Run.

Robert Clifton, died in the service.

G. A. E. Clyce.

J. H. Coffman, wounded at Belle Grove and captured at Petersburg.

J. M. Copper.

G. Crist.

James B. Culton, third lieutenant.

Samuel M. Day, killed at Chancellorsville.

W. E. Day, wounded at Spotsylvania Court House.

John Dunlap.

R. K. Dunlap, wounded at Second Manassas and Chancellorsville.

* Student at Washington College before the war.

Samuel M. Dunlap, captured at Gettysburg.

W. K. Echard.

John H. Ervine, captured at Petersburg.

James Gaylord.

* A. M. Glasgow, Rockbridge County, Va.

F. Gordon.

Thomas Green.

John Gross.

John E. Guy.

Worth O. Gwynn, Lexington, later first corporal, captured at Second Winchester May 1862, exchanged, and captured at Gettysburg.

A. H. Hall.

William Helmuth.

J. Hodge, captured at Petersburg.

P. G. Holt.

Gardiner P. Hutton.

P. C. Irvine.

J. Jackson.

* William M. Johnson, Rockbridge County, Va., captured at Spotsylvania Court House.

R. J. Johnson.

J. T. Lackey.

M. F. Lackey.

Nathan A. Lackey, killed at Chancellorsville.

W. H. Lackey, captured at Gettysburg.

M. H. Lam, wounded at Petersburg.

M. F. Larew, died in the service.

Edward Lewis.

A. T. Link, wounded and captured at Second Winchester, Sept. 1864.

William Lunsford.

* Student at Washington College before the war.

R. McCalpin.

William A. McCleland, captured at Spotsylvania Court House.

A. A. McClung, surrendered at Appomattox.

Charles B. McClung.

J. W. McCraw.

J. C. McCray.

William T. McCurdy.

Joseph McFadden.

Benjamin F. McNutt, surrendered at Appomattox.

John W. Miley, wounded at the Wilderness and died from wounds.

J. F. Moore, captured at Gettysburg.

John P. Moore, wounded at Chancellorsville and Spotsylvania Court House and killed at Petersburg.

W. Dorman Moore, killed at Kearneysville.

William Moore.

* John D. Myers, Lexington, Va., transferred to First Virginia Cavalry.

Dennis O'Brien.

Henry Ott, surrendered at Appomattox.

W. L. Patterson, wounded and captured at Petersburg.

J. Mc. Paxton, wounded at Second Manassas, second corporal after Kearneysville, and wounded and captured at Gettysburg.

J. M. Pettigrew.

Samuel Pettigrew.

* William C. Preston, Lexington, Va., killed at Second Manassas.

D. L. Roadcap.

W. R. Rollins.

Lafayette Rowsey.

* Student at Washington College before the war.

D. H. Rozen.

Daniel Sheckle.

——Shelton, captured at Petersburg.

George W. Shields.

W. S. Smiley, captured at Gettysburg and died in the service.

A. Snyder.

D. Snyder.

James W. Spohr, wounded at Bell Grove.

William Steele, killed at Spotsylvania Court House.

* J. D. Sterrett, Rockbridge County, Va., transferred to the Fourth Virginia Infantry.

G. H. Stoner, killed at Petersburg.

W. Stoner.

Thomas Stratton.

I. M. Taylor, Rockbridge County, Va., captured at Gettysburg.

David Trevey.

John H. Welsh, wounded at Petersburg.

Thomas S. White.

David Whitmore, surrendered at Appomattox.

G. W. Whitmore, captured at Spotsylvania.

W. R. Wilbourn.

Samuel H. Wilhelm, died in the service.

S. P. Williams, surrendered at Appomattox.

J. Edgar Wilson, wounded at Petersburg.

Marion H. Withers, killed at Petersburg.

William A. Youell, killed at Petersburg.

Madison Zollman, killed at Petersburg.

* Student at Washington College before the war.

SELECTED BIBLIOGRAPHY

MANUSCRIPTS

Apperson, John Samuel. "Civil War Diary, 1861–1865." Virginia Historical Society, Richmond.

Barclay, A. T. ("Ted"). Letters. In the possession of Mr. Houston Barclay, Lexington, Va.

Doyle, J. L. "The Campaign of May, 1864." Jed Hotchkiss Papers, Library of Congress, Washington, D.C.

Garibaldi, John. Letters. Preston Library, Virginia Military Institute.

Langhorne, J. H. Letters. Virginia Historical Society, Richmond.

Lyle, John Newton. "Stonewall Jackson's Guard, The Washington College Company" McCormick Library, Washington and Lee University.

Maynard, George F., III. "The Stonewall Brigade." Senior Honors Thesis, Washington and Lee University, Lexington, Va., 1953.

212   THE LIBERTY HALL VOLUNTEERS

Morrison, Henry Ruffner. "Diary, 1862." In the possession of the author.

Shields, Harvey Gerard. "Rockbridge County, Virginia, and the Civil War." Senior Honors Thesis, Washington and Lee University, Lexington, Va., 1960.

Strickler, Givens B. "Liberty Hall Volunteers." Address delivered July 14, 1910, at the reunion of the survivors in the Robert E. Lee Memorial Chapel, Washington and Lee University. William A. Anderson Papers, Alderman Library, University of Virginia.

White, J. J. Letters. Southern Historical Collection, University of North Carolina, Chapel Hill.

BOOKS AND ARTICLES

Anderson, Ellen Glasgow, "The Wounding and Hospital Care of William A. Anderson," *Virginia Magazine of History and Biography*, vol. LXII (Oct. 1954).

Allan, Elizabeth Preston. *Life and Letters of Margaret Junkin Preston*. New York, 1903.

Allan, William. *History of the Campaign of Gen. T. J. (Stonewall) Jackson in the Shenandoah Valley: from November 4, 1861 to June 17, 1862. With full maps of the region and battlefields by Jed Hotchkiss*. Philadelphia, 1880.

Barclay, A. T. ("Ted"). "The Liberty Hall Volunteers from Lexington to Manassas," in Washington and Lee University, *Historical Papers* no. 6 (Lynchburg, Va., 1904) pp. 123–36.

Bean, W. G. *Stonewall's Man: Sandie Pendleton*. Chapel Hill, 1959.

Bean, W. G. "A House Divided: The Civil War Letters of a Virginia Family," Virginia Magazine of History and Biography, vol. LIX (Oct. 1951).

Casler, John. *Four Years in the Stonewall Brigade.* New York, 1893.

Chambers, Lenoir. *Stonewall Jackson.* 2 vols. New York, 1959.

Chester, Samuel Hall. *Memories of Four-score Years: . . . An Autobiography.* Richmond, 1934.

Couper, William. *One Hundred Years at V.M.I.* 4 vols. Richmond, 1939.

Daniel, W. Harrison. "The Christian Association: A Religious Society in the Army of Northern Virginia," *Virginia Magazine of History and Biography,* vol. LXIX (Jan. 1961).

Dowdey, Clifford. *Death of a Nation: The Story of Lee and His Men at Gettysburg.* New York, 1958.

Dowdey, Clifford. *Lee's Last Campaign: The Story of Lee and His Men against Grant.* Boston, 1960.

Dufour, Charles L. *Gentle Tiger: The Gallant Life of Roberdeau Wheat.* Baton Rouge, 1957.

Eaton, Clement. *A History of the Southern Confederacy.* New York, 1954.

Eby, Cecil. *Porte Crayon: The Life and Letters of David Hunter Strother.* Chapel Hill, 1960.

Freeman, Douglas Southall. *Robert E. Lee: A Biography.* 4 vols. New York, 1934.

Freeman, Douglas Southall. *Lee's Lieutenants.* 3 vols. New York, 1942–44.

Goode, Lizzie Redwood. "Wartime Scenes on Pennsylvania Avenue," *Confederate Veteran,* vol. XXXI (Oct. 1923).

Henderson, G .F. R. *Stonewall Jackson and the Civil War.* American ed. New York, 1937.

Johnson, Thomas C. *Life and Letters of Dr. Robert Lewis Dabney.* Richmond, 1903.

Jones, J. H. B. "Liberty Hall Volunteers at First Manassas," Rockbridge *County News,* Feb. 2, 1911.

Jones, J. W. *Christ in Camp; or Religion in Lee's Army.* Richmond, 1888.

Jones, V. C. *Eight Hours before Richmond.* New York, 1957.

Junkin, George. "Exodus of Dr. Junkin," *Presbyterian Standard,* May 17, 1861, in David X. Junkin, *The Reverend George Junkin, D. D., LL.D., A Historical Biography.* Philadelphia, 1871.

McClure, A. K. *Annals of the War.* Philadelphia, 1879.

McCown, James L. "Diary," Rockbridge *County News,* Feb. 12, 19, 1953.

McFadyen, Henry Richard. "Confederates Studied to Preach," *Presbyterian Survey* (Richmond) vol. LI (1961).

McGuire, Hunter. *Stonewall Jackson: Address at the Dedication of the Jackson Memorial Hall, Virginia Military Institute, June 23, 1897.* Richmond, 1897.

Miers, Earl Schenck. *Robert E. Lee: A Great Life in Brief.* New York, 1956.

Moore, A. B. *Conscription and Conflict in the Confederacy.* New York, 1924.

Moore, Edward A. *The Story of a Cannoneer under Stonewall Jackson.* New York, 1907.

Paxton, John Gallatin. *Memoir and Memorials of Elisha Franklin Paxton, General, C.S.A.* N.p., pref. 1905.

Robertson, James I. *The Stonewall Brigade.* Baton Rouge, 1963.

Rollins, Charles A. "On the Road to Gettysburg," Pittsburgh (Pa.) *Chronicle Telegraph,* reprinted in Lexington *Gazette,* July 26, Aug. 2, Aug. 16, Sept. 27, 1888.

Strickler, Givens B. "Liberty Hall Volunteers," Washington and Lee University, *Historical Papers* no. 6 (Lynchburg, Va., 1904), pp. 111–22.

Strother, David Hunter. *A Virginia Yankee in the Civil War: The Diaries of David Hunter Strother.* Edited by Cecil Eby. Chapel Hill, 1961.

Vandiver, Frank. *Mighty Stonewall*. New York, 1957.

Walker, James A. "The Bloody Angle," *Southern Historical Papers,* vol. XXI (1893).

White, W. S. *Sketches of the life of Captain Hugh A. White of the Stonewall Brigade.* Columbia, S.C., 1864.

White, W. S. *Rev. William S. White, D.D., and His Times, 1800–1873: An Autobiography.* Ed. by his son, Rev. H. M. White, D.D. Richmond, 1893.

INDEX

INDEX

[All places mentioned are located in Virginia unless otherwise indicated.]

Albemarle Co., 113

Allen, James W., 53

American Revolution, 9, 14, 21

Anderson, William A., 11; biographical data, 43n

Apperson, John S., 89n, 118n, 138n, 142

Appomattox Court House, 184, 191, 196

Army of Northern Virginia, 9n, 22, 134, 135, 136n, 142–45 *passim,* 155, 160, 167, 175n, 184n, 185

Army of the Potomac, 136, 141n, 176, 184; *see also* United States Ninth Corps

Army of the Shenandoah, 21, 25

Ashby, Turner, 102, 103

Ashland, 123

Augusta Co., 24n, 102, 105

Baker, Rev., 173

Baltimore and Ohio RR, 154, 155

Banks, N. P., 18, 19, 81, 99, 101, 104, 108, 109, 117, 118, 128

Barclay, Miss, 168

Barclay, Alexander Tedford: about the ladies, 91; his wardrobe, 92, 93, 114, 116, 144, 146, 147, 152, 154, 155, 156, 157, 166; problems about reenlistment, 93, 94, 114; religion, 112, 135, 152, 156, 157, 166, 172, 178; on brigade review, 159; promotion, 165; confident of victory, 173, 181, 182; capture of, 191

Barclay, Elihu, 157, 158n, 183, 192

Barclay, John, 110

Barclay, Paxton, 160, 192

219

Barton, Mrs. David, 25
Bartow, Francis, 40
Bath, W.Va., 83, 84
Baylor, W. S. H., 22, 24, 79n, 83, 101, 132, 133
Beauregard, P. G. T., 37, 39
Bedinger family, 135n
Bee, Bernard E., 40, 41
Bell, William J., 105, 106
Benjamin, Judah P., 71, 88, 89n
Berkeley Springs, W.Va., 83, 84n
Bird, Mr., 103
Black, Pete, 53n, 66, 119n
Blackburn's Ford, 39
Bloody Angle, see Spotsylvania Court House
Boyd, Belle, 77n
Bragg, Braxton, 160, 161n
Brent, Ned, 23
Bristoe Station, 161, 162, 163
Brownsburg, 170, 171n
Brown's Gap, 118, 119, 120
Bull Run, 39, 40, 41
Burnside, Ambrose E., 135, 141n, 183, 191, 192n
Butler, B. F., 175n

Cabell, Dr. James L., 58, 59
Camp Harman, 48, 49n, 53, 54, 58, 61n
Camp Maggot, 48
Camp Paxton, 141, 143
Camp Stephens, 23n, 27, 31, 32, 33, 34, 78, 153, 154n
Carlisle, Pa., 148
Caroline Co., 155n
Cedar Grove, 170, 171n
Cedar Mountain, battle of, 79n, 128n, 129
Central Presbyterian, 56, 134n, 177
Centreville, 47, 48, 65, 66, 70n, 98, 161, 162

Chancellorsville, 136n, 139, 144, 149, 180, 197
Chapin, George, 159n, 162n, 165, 166n, 167
Charlottesville, 113
Charlottesville Classical School, 24n
Chesapeake and Ohio Canal, 76
Chester, Joseph T., 64n, 71n, 72n; killed at Spotsylvania Court House, 190n
Chickahominy River, 119, 126
Chickamauga, Ga., 160, 161n
Christian Association, 156, 157n, 173, 177, 180
Cockran, Mr., 15, 16n
Cold Harbor, 184
College Boys, see Liberty Hall Volunteers
College Company, see Liberty Hall Volunteers
Colored Sunday School, viii, 133, 180
Compton, Kate, 168
Confederate Congress, 172, 173n
Confederate money, 92, 173n
Confederate States Bible Society, 130
Conscripts, 172, 175
Corbin family, 135
"Correspondent," see Rockingham Register
Crater, battle of, 193n
Cross Keys, 118
Culpeper, 145, 147, 155, 160, 161
Culp's Hill, 149n, 150n, 151
Cumberland Valley, 148

Dabney, Rev. Dr. Robert L., 56, 57n, 58n, 122
Dalgren, Ulric, 175n
Dam (No. 5), 75–77
Davis, Dr. J. Staige, 58, 59

Davis, Jefferson, 28, 112n, 181
Day, W. E., 178
Dead March, 163
Deserter, execution of, 163
Doles, George, 174n, 187
Douglas, Henry Kyd, 140
Dowdey, Clifford, 188
Doyle, J. L., 185n, 188, 192, 193
Dunns Battalion of Cavalry, 175

Early, Jubal A., 146, 148n, 149n, 176n
Edmondson, J. K., 24
Ellsworth, Elmer, 46n
Evans, N. G., 40
Ewell, Richard S., 108, 109, 143n, 148n, 149n, 152, 159, 161, 163, 164, 165, 167, 168, 175n, 185, 187

Fairfax, Randolph L., 179n
Fairfax, Thomas Lord, 38
Fairfax Court House, 61, 64, 65
Falling Springs, 13
Falling Springs Presbyterian Church, 13
Falling Waters, 33, 34, 35
Federal Negro troops, 192
First Corps, Army of Northern Virginia, 143n
First Kentucky Regiment, 65
First Virginia Battalion, 135
First Virginia Infantry, 18
First West Virginia Cavalry (U.S.), 107
Fitzmeyer, Jacob, 162
Fort Alabama, 99
Fort Delaware, Del., 107, 192, 193n, 194
Fort Sumter, S.C., 4
Franklin, W.Va., 109, 113, 114
Franklin Literary Society, 139

Fredericksburg, 98, 103, 135, 136, 141, 164
Frémont, John C., 108, 109, 117, 118, 119
French, W. H., 166
Frenchburg, W.Va., 87n
Front Royal, 101, 109, 114, 147
Fudge, J., 191n

Gaines Mill, 123, 124, 125
Garibaldi, John, 174n
Garnett, Richard B., 22, 69n, 81, 104n, 105
Garnett, Robert S., 15
Gelwicher, Mr., 80n
Germanna Ford, 164, 166
Gettysburg, Pa., 104n, 149n, 150, 151, 154, 155, 156, 157, 196
Goode, Lizzie Redwood, 46n
Gordonsville, 128, 185n
Graham, Rev. Dr. James R., 25n, 80, 91
Graham, Mrs. James R., 24, 25n
Graham, William, 9
Grant, U. S., 176, 177, 183, 184, 186, 192n
"Grayson Dare Devils," 26
Greeley, Horace, 141n
"Greenway Court," 38
Guiney Station, 141, 142
Gwynn, Bronson, 45–46

Hagerstown, Md., 151, 152, 153
Halleck, Henry H., 120
Hamilton's Crossing, 138n
Hampden-Sydney students, 16n
Hampshire Co., W.Va., 86
Hancock, Md., 83
Hancock, W. S., 186n
Hanover Co., 125
Harman, J. A., 49n

Harman, M. G., 15
Harman, W. H., 15, 16n
Harper, Kenton F., 53
Harper's Ferry, W.Va., 15, 16, 98, 117, 139, 148
Harris, Carter J., 55
Harrisonburg, 108, 109
Harrison's Landing, 123, 129
Hawkinstown, 101n, 102, 103, 110
Henry House, 40, 47
Hill, A. P., 137, 138n, 143n, 149n, 152, 161, 162, 164n, 166, 167, 185n
Hoge, Rev. Dr. Moses, 125, 173n
Hooker, Joseph, 136, 140, 141n, 143
Hopkins, Rev. A. C., 132, 156, 157n, 182
Humbles, Jim, 157, 158n
Hunter, David, 193n, 195
Hutchinson, Mrs., 126

"Irish Battalion," see First Virginia Battalion

Jackson, A. H., 79n
Jackson Brigade, see Stonewall Brigade
Jackson, Elinor Junkin (1st wife of T. J. Jackson), 79n, 139, 195
Jackson, Mary Anna (2nd wife of T. J. Jackson), 79, 80, 91
Jackson, Thomas J. ("Stonewall"): interest in volunteers, ix, 53, 54, 70; discipline of, 27; caricature of, 32; called "Stonewall," 41; praise of volunteers, 60; mentioned, viii, 8, 16, 21, 22, 25, 32, 33, 39, 40, 41, 45, 63, 69n, 70n, 73n, 75–83 passim, 87, 88, 91, 95, 98–106 passim, 108–12 passim, 114–26 passim, 128–37 passim, 139, 140, 141, 142, 146n, 148n, 155n, 179, 195
Johnson, Edward, 108, 109, 142, 143n, 148n, 149n, 150n, 151, 154, 165, 166, 187, 190
Johnson's Island, Ohio, 150n
Johnston, Joseph E., 18, 21, 28, 33, 34, 37, 47, 49, 68, 88, 98, 102, 103, 108
Jones, J. H. B., 150n, 151, 152, 191
Jones, J. M., 149n
Junkin, D. X., 8n
Junkin, Rev. Dr. George: views on secession, 4–6; resignation, 6–7; appearance at Fort Delaware, 194n, 195; mentioned, 8n, 79n, 139, 144n, 195
Junkin, George (son of Dr. Junkin), 194n
Junkin, George G., 8, 79n
Junkin, William J., 144n

Keizer, Mr., 15
Kelley, B. F., 81
Kent, Major, 25, 96n
Kernstown, 79n, 103, 106, 108, 110
Kilpatrick, Judson, 175n
Kurtz, Capt., 186, 190

Lackey, Nathan, 135, 136n
Lacy, Rev. Beverly Tucker, 154, 155n, 179, 180
Langhorn, J. H., 83n, 96n
Lee, Robert E., 119, 123, 128, 129, 134, 135, 136, 150, 151, 154, 159, 160, 161, 163, 165, 175n, 179, 184, 186, 187, 189; see also Robert E. Lee Memorial Chapel
Letcher, John, 8n, 10, 15, 68, 88
Letcher, S. H., 24
Lewis, Jim, 131

Lexington, viii, 7, 8, 10, 24, 25, 79n, 92, 124, 133, 138, 139, 140, 159, 167, 170, 180, 181, 193n, 194

Lexington *Gazette*, 9n, 10, 13, 17, 18, 133, 193n

Lexington Presbyterian Church, viii, 5, 11, 136, 195

"L.H.V.," *see* John N. Lyle

Liberty Hall Academy, 9, 14

Liberty Hall Volunteers: devotion to Jackson, ix, 3, 7, 32, 70, 89, 106, 107, 121, 142; origin of name, 9; officers of, 11; designated "Co. I, Fourth Virginia, Stonewall Brigade," 25; boyish appearance of, 26; recreation of, 29, 73, 74; camp life of, 31; at First Manassas, 41, 42; duties as headquarters guard, 63, 67, 79; called "Jackson's pet lambs," 83; indignation at Sec'y of War's treatment of Jackson, 88, 89; at Gettysburg, 150, 151; dissolution of, 191; character of original membership of, 196; casualties, 196; roster of, 201–206; mentioned, vii, viii, 9–20 *passim*, 24, 32, 37, 39, 45, 55, 56, 58n, 63, 64, 66, 67, 69, 70, 74, 80, 82, 85, 87, 91, 94, 98, 99, 100, 104, 110, 111, 114, 130, 133–96 *passim*, 168n, 195

Liberty Mills, 164

Lincoln, Abraham, 3, 4, 5, 7, 45n, 46n, 97, 117, 130

Locust Grove Tavern, 185

Logan, Lloyd, 91n

Logan, Miss., 91

Longstreet, James, 39, 104n, 129, 136, 143n, 144, 152, 160, 175n, 185n

Loring, W. W., 70, 81, 88, 89n

Louisiana Tigers, 65, 66n

Ludwig, Albert, 196

Ludwig, E. A., 196

Lyle, John N.: description of volunteers, 10; description of Jackson at First Manassas, 45; use of the Zouave drill manual, 63; captured at Kernstown, 107; mentioned, 6n, 11, 13, 14, 15, 17–21 *passim*, 25, 26, 31, 32, 33, 37, 38, 40, 43, 45, 47, 48, 53n, 57n, 60, 64, 66, 67, 73n, 77n–82 *passim*, 84, 85, 86, 89–101 *passim*, 106, 107, 108n, 110, 196

Lyle, Samuel W., 152

McClellan, George B., 47, 98, 101, 108, 119, 123, 135, 141n

McClung, A. A., 191

McClung, Dr. John W., 161n

McClung, Dr. Joseph, 90

McCown, James, 185, 187, 189, 190n, 193n

McCrum, Harriett, 128

McDowell, Irvin, 37, 40, 47, 108, 117, 141n

McDowell, 109, 113

McGuffey, W. H., 56, 57n

McGuire, Hunter, 131

McKee, John, 150

McNear, Rev., 156

McNutt, B. F., 191

Madison Co., 159, 161

Magill, Anne Tucker, 24

Malvern Hill, 125

Manassas, First, 40–42, 55, 63, 96, 139, 154n

Manassas, Second, 129, 131, 132, 134

Manassas Gap RR, 101

Manassas Junction, 17, 18, 37, 39, 40, 71, 72n, 104

Martinsburg, W.Va., 23n, 26, 30, 33, 76, 77n, 99, 100, 151, 155

Meade, George G., 141n, 151, 152, 159, 161, 163, 164, 165, 184
Mechum River Station, 109, 112, 113
Middlebrook, 171n
Middleton, Mr., 153, 154n, 168, 181, 182
Miller, Rev. Charles, 48
Miller, Rev. John, 13
Miller family, 80, 90
Millwood, 37, 38
Milroy, R. H., 109, 146n, 148
Mine Run, 164, 165
Mitchell, Edward, 52n, 153, 154n
Montgomery Co., 6n, 26n
Moore, Lewis T., 25, 79, 96n
Moore, Sam, 42
Morgan, W. H., 9
Morrison, Henry Ruffner, 59, 71, 78n, 85, 97n, 99, 100, 102, 103, 104, 105n, 106, 107, 108n, 110, 196
Morton Hall, 184
Moss Neck, 135, 155n
Mt. Jackson, 98, 101n, 102
Mt. Pisgah Church, 169, 184
Mt. Solon, 114

Nelson, Alexander L., 7, 9, 11n, 59
New Market, 109
Newtown, 19, 20, 103
New York Zouaves, 45, 46n, 63
Nicholls, Francis T., 149n

"Old Short-Grass," 54
Old Stone Cottage, 153, 154n
"O. P. H.," 80n
Orange and Alexandria RR, 161
Orange Co., 159, 161
Orange Court House, 147, 156, 169, 170, 171
Ott, H., 191

Patterson, Robert G., 26, 33, 37, 78
Patton, Mr., 172, 175
Paxton, Elisha Franklin: death at Chancellorsville, 138–40; mentioned, 22, 24, 58, 59, 137, 180
Paxton, Horace, 157n
Paxton, John, 158n
Paxton, Phoebe, 160, 161n, 192
Paxton, Sallie, 160, 161n, 192
Paxton, William, 161n, 192
Pendleton, Albert G., 78, 96n
Pendleton, Alexander ("Sandie"), 79n
Pendleton, William Nelson, 9n
Political Heresies, 194
Pope, John, 128, 129, 130, 131n, 141
Port Republic, 118
Potomac River, 6, 7, 33, 47, 74, 76, 83, 84, 98, 110, 134, 135, 150
Preston, Col. James F., 25, 26n, 30n, 42, 53, 71, 96n
Preston, John T. L., viii, 8, 69n, 70, 131, 132n
Preston, Margaret Junkin, 8, 132, 133
Preston, William Ballard, 26n
Preston, Willie C., 6, 131, 132n
Pughtown, 99
Pulaski Guards, 143n

Raccoon Ford, 169
Rapidan River, 129, 147, 161n, 164, 165, 169, 172n, 175, 177
Rappahannock River, 103, 130, 136, 144, 145, 147, 151, 163
Rappahannock Station, 163
Raymond, Joseph, 122
Reid, Samuel McDowell, 24n
Richmond, 17, 70, 98, 108, 109, 113, 141n, 142, 181, 182, 183
Richmond Examiner, 173n

Robert E. Lee Memorial Chapel, viii
Rockbridge Co., ix, 7, 9, 23, 60, 94,
    102, 113, 138, 144n, 177, 179,
    185, 195, 196
Rockbridge Rifles, 139
Rockfish Gap, 9
Rockingham *Register*, 142, 143n
Rodes, R. E., 148n, 149n, 174n, 187
Rollins, Charles A., 145, 146n, 148,
    150n
Rollins, Thomas S., 23
Romney, W.Va., campaign of, 19,
    76, 88, 89, 90, 92
Ronald, Charles A., 25, 78n, 110
Rosecrans, Gen. William S., 160, 161
Round Oak Baptist Church, 155n
Rouss, C. B., 80n

Scott, Winfield, 42, 43n
Second Corps, Army of Northern
    Virginia, 136, 142, 143n, 145–48
    passim, 149n, 161, 164n, 169, 185,
    187
Second Presbyterian Church
    (Richmond), 125, 173n
See, Rev., 182
Seven Days' Battle, 124, 127
Sharpsburg, Md., 134, 135n
Shenandoah River, 38, 101
Shenandoah Valley, *see* Valley of
    Virginia
Shepherdstown, W.Va., 135n, 147
Sherrard, Joseph R., 11, 25, 31, 60,
    78, 80
Shields, James, 101, 104, 118, 119
Smith, Lt., 168
Smith, E. Kirby, 41
Smith, Gustavus W., 64n, 65, 66, 70,
    71, 72n, 79
Smith, James Power, 134
Smyth Blues, 78, 191n
Snodgrass, Miss, 170, 171

Southern Confederacy, 3, 4, 21, 57,
    92, 126, 128
Southern Presbyterian Church, 57
Sperryville, 147
Spohr, James W., 152
Spotsylvania Court House, viii, 22,
    147, 184, 186, 187, 189, 190, 191
Staunton, 14–17 *passim*, 24n, 102,
    108, 113, 158, 171
Steuart, George, 149n, 150n, 190n
Stiles, Rev. Joseph C., 130
Stone Bridge, 40
Stonewall Brigade: Artillery,
    Rockbridge, 9, 21, 33, 179n;
    Infantry, Second Virginia, 21, 132,
    156, 162, Fourth Virginia, vii, 21,
    26, 39, 42, 67, 73n, 76, 79, 83n,
    96, 99, 105, 107, 113, 138n, 142,
    150, 165, 180, 189, 191n, Fifth
    Virginia, 16n, 21, 24, 33, 34, 79n,
    189, Twenty-seventh Virginia,
    21, 24, 139, 154n, 174n, Thirty-
    third Virginia, 21, 185n; social
    classes in, 21; brigade drill, 27;
    at Chancellorsville, 137, 138n;
    inflation in, 142, 143; capture of,
    190; mentioned, viii, 21, 22n, 26,
    37–40 *passim*, 139n, 141, 142,
    143n, 145–49 *passim*, 153, 154,
    159, 161, 162, 175, 184, 187–90n
    passim
Stonewall Jackson Memorial
    Cemetery, 140, 166n, 195n
Stower, Martin L., 194n
Strasburg, 18, 72, 98, 100–103
    passim, 108, 109
Strickler, G. B., 157n; biographical
    data, 150n; mentioned, vii, 11,
    59, 111, 134, 157n
Strother, David Hunter ("Porte
    Crayon"), 83, 84
Stuart, J. E. B., 33, 136, 138, 162,
    164

Sudley's Springs, 40
Swift Run Gap, 108, 109, 110, 112

Tarleton, Banastre, 9
Taylor, Isaac, 191n
Terry, William, 107, 138n, 166, 173, 189, 190
Third Corps, Army of Northern Virginia, 143n, 149n, 161, 164n
Third Tennessee Infantry, 18, 19
Thirty-first Virginia Infantry, 79n
Tucker, John Randolph, 24
Turner, T. M., 191n

Unger's Store, W.Va., 84, 86, 87
Union Theological Seminary (Presbyterian), 56, 150n
United States Ninth Corps, Army of the Potomac, 191
University (of Mississippi) Greys, viii
University of Virginia, 24n, 58, 59n, 113n, 138, 179n
Utterback, Penelope, 67

Valley Army, 81, 93, 99, 102, 103, 104, 113, 117, 118, 119
Valley of Virginia: description of, 3, 18, 71, 79, 145, 147; 1862 campaign, 109–19 passim, 146; mentioned, 25, 37, 39
Vass, Rev. L. C., 136, 156, 157n
Virginia Central RR, 15
Virginia House, 15
Virginia Military Institute, viii, 8, 10, 21, 131, 180, 181
Virginia Militia, 16n, 93n, 102, 110, 195
Virginia Secession Convention, 4, 7, 26n, 93

Wade, Mrs., 63
Wade, Capt. James M., 37
Walker, James A., 142, 143n, 149n, 166, 174, 185, 186, 189
Wallace, Mr., 175, 179n
Warren, G. K., 185
Warrenton, 148, 151, 160
Washington, George, 21
Washington, D.C., 46n, 47, 76, 98, 101, 108, 161
Washington and Lee University, vii, 150n, 193n
Washington College: flag episodes, 6–7; alumni of, 79; mentioned, viii, 4, 9–12 passim, 14, 22, 23, 24, 26n, 32, 54, 55, 56n, 58n, 60, 79n, 131, 136n, 138, 154n, 194, 195n
Washington Peace Conference, 4
Waynesboro, 16n
West Augusta, 22n
Weyer's Cave, 120, 122n, 123
Wheat, Roberdeau, 65, 66n
White, Henry, 124, 127
White, Hugh A.: at seminary, 11; decision to enlist, 11–12; reunion of college mates, 23; disturbed about religious conditions in army, 29, 34, 67; description of First Manassas, 44; questions returning to the seminary, 51, 94, 127; complains of military discipline, 62; religious work, 122, 133; captain, 110–11; last letter to father, 130, 133; mentioned, viii, 12, 22, 24, 43, 44, 61n, 68, 76, 83, 84, 105n, 106, 110, 112, 113n, 121, 122–30 passim, 132n, 133, 177n, 179
White, James J.: comment on brigade personnel, 21; on regimental officers, 25; on army life, 27, 34, 50, 51; thanks wife

for food, 28; domestic worries, 32, 33n; enraged at Yankee pilfering, 34; describes a fox race, 49; resignation, 54–61; biographical data, 24n; mentioned, ix, 11, 13, 15, 19, 22, 23, 26, 29, 30, 38, 42, 43, 46, 61n
White, Mary Reid, 24n, 32, 42, 48, 55, 58
White, Thomas, 111, 112
White, Rev. Dr. W. S., mentioned, viii, 11, 12, 48, 63n, 113n, 177n
Whitmore, David, 151, 152, 191
Wilderness, the, 136, 141, 149, 164, 169, 182, 184, 185, 187, 189
Wilderness Tavern, 140
Williams, Charles, 14
Williams, S. P., 191
Williamsport, Md., 6, 150, 152
Wilson, Capt., 177
Wilson, James, 122

Winchester: hospitality to Confederates, 24; abandonment by Johnston, 37–38; Jackson's return to, 99–101; his withdrawal from, 100; battle of 1862, 115–16; Confederate capture of, 147–48; mentioned, 6, 7, 18–23 passim, 25, 26, 34, 69, 70, 76–81 passim, 83, 86, 88–92 passim, 95, 98, 102, 103, 104, 106, 107, 110, 153, 155
Winder, Charles S., 104n, 128
Wise, Henry A., 15, 16n
Woods, John, 92
Woods, Watson, 51, 168n
Woodstock, 103
Wythe Greys, 107
Wytheville, 138n

Yale College, 138
Yancey, William L., 6
Yemen, Charles Chester, 190n

THE LIBERTY HALL VOLUNTEERS
was composed and printed by
Connecticut Printers, Inc.
Hartford, Connecticut.
Types used were Caledonia and Scotch.
Paper is Perkins and Squier
RR Antique Wove.
Binding is by the Russell-Rutter
Company, New York.
The book was designed by
John J. Walklet, Jr.